WOODWORKING SCHOOL

WOODWORKING SCHOOL

A project-by-project course for the creative woodworker

Peter Collenette

Project Collaboration
Len Woodard

GREENWICH HOUSE
Distributed by Crown Publishers, Inc.
New York

A *Quill* BOOK

This 1984 edition is published by Greenwich House,
a division of Arlington House Inc,
distributed by Crown Publishers, Inc.

ISBN 0-517-43900X

H G F E D C B A

Library of Congress Number 84-80696

This book was designed and produced by
Quill Publishing Limited
32 Kingly Court
London W1

Art director Nigel Osborne
Editorial director Christopher Fagg
Senior editor Liz Wilhide
Editor Sabina Goodchild
Designer Alex Arthur
Editorial assistant Michelle Newton
Art assistants Ellie King, Fraser Newman
Illustrator Ray Brown
Photographers John Heseltine, Jon Wyand

Filmset by QV Typesetting Ltd, London
Origination by Hong Kong Graphic Arts Service Centre Ltd, Hong Kong
Printed by Leefung Asco Printers Ltd, Hong Kong

AUTHOR'S ACKNOWLEDGMENTS
Very special thanks go to Len Woodard, in whose London
workshop our major projects were executed; he also made
important contributions to their design. His advice, hard
work and good humor were invaluable — as were the
help of his partner Phillip Owtram and their
assistant Em Vandekar.

The section on machinery owes much to the expertise, demonstrations and
hospitality of Nigel Voisey and Ashley Phillips at Woodmen in Bicester.

Quill would like to extend special thanks to: Jakki Dehn, Formica, Martin
Grierson, David G Jones at Erddig Joiner's Shop, Meyer International,
Peter Milne, Michael Reed.

CONTENTS

This book has two aims. Firstly, to provide a comprehensive guide to the materials and equipment used in fine cabinet-making; and secondly to outline useful working methods in terms of design, basic approach, skill and technique.

To demonstrate how all these may be brought into play, we have included a series of original projects which show in step-by-step detail how to make a variety of pieces of furniture.

A recurring theme in the book, however, is the importance of seeking and finding alternatives. Although the projects illustrate a great many specific points, they are primarily intended to start you thinking and doing for yourself and in your own way — exploring new solutions as well as applying traditional ones.

Each project was undertaken in very real workshop conditions, to a time-scale and on a budget. This meant using certain materials and techniques in preference to others: for example, all but one of the pieces were spray-finished. But we were simply fitting the job to the resources and the resources to the job — something you will need to do yourself.

The best woodworkers are adaptable at all times and innovative when necessary. By presenting the options available, we hope this book will help and inspire you to perfect the ways that work for you.

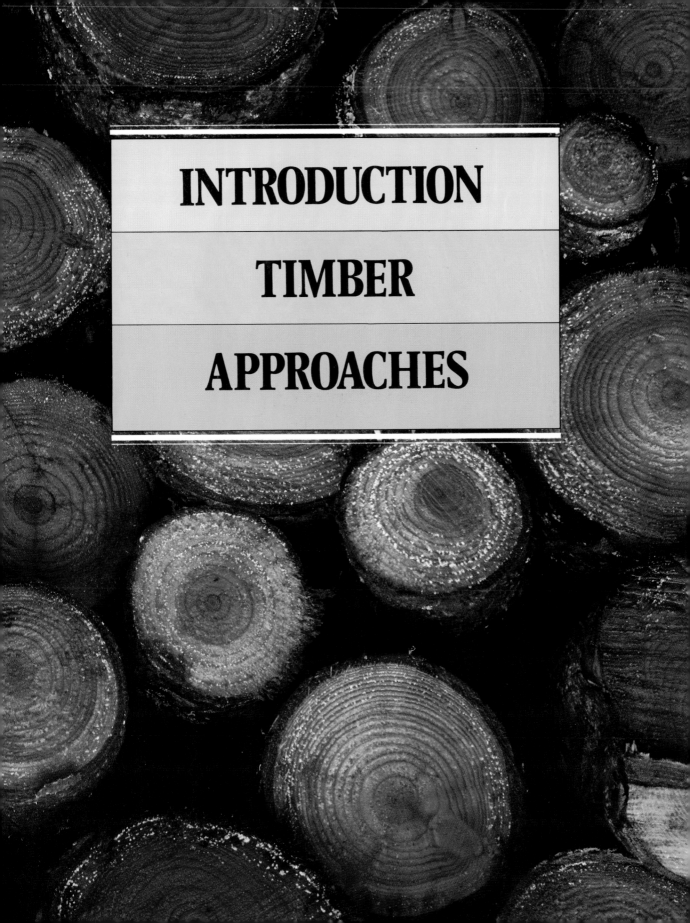

INTRODUCTION

TIMBER

APPROACHES

INTRODUCTION

Fine woodwork lies within everyone's reach. Everyone knows what a saw, a chisel, a plane looks like and at least roughly what they do; at some stage most people have tried working with wood. The same could never be said of metal, stone or clay.

Some go no further, however, and prefer not to mend a chair or put up a shelf unless it is absolutely necessary. Others learn just enough to tackle work at home to a certain standard. This book is for a third group: those who find they enjoy woodwork, and want to develop their skills.

'Enjoyment' is too mild a word for the intense pleasure of a job that is going really well. All woodworkers know it; it forms a powerful incentive to improve — although higher skills generate higher standards. Nevertheless, the difference between the beginning woodworker and the complete craftsman is, as a rule, only one of degree. The craftsman was once a beginner too, and the approach is no secret. You can, and indeed must, emulate it from the very outset. Three rules apply: know what you are doing; strive for real accuracy and keep your tools as sharp as you possibly can.

To know exactly what you are doing at all stages of a job does not demand hard-won manual skill, but is a matter of having thoroughly assessed the options. Know which timber is which, what each looks like, how each behaves and how much it costs. Know the types of boards on the market and the characteristics that distinguish one from another. Find out what your tools can and cannot do. Investigate any possible jointing techniques, all the different types of glue and their properties, fittings and finishes.

In other words, become very inquisitive. Nose around timber merchants and hardware stores, read books and magazines, and question both suppliers and woodworkers. Experiment with what you find intriguing. Only nowadays do people often seek to master the craft who have not had the advantage of serving an apprenticeship (probably still, after all, the best way to learn). They must grasp their knowledge wherever they can find it. And only the very well-informed woodworker knows how to do things cheaply and with the tools and skills he or she already has; how to make things that last; how to get precisely the right effects. The well-informed woodworker can always 'think around' a problem and come up with at least one way out. Teaching your hands to do what you want is another matter, but it need never cause despair. If you have acquired enough information you can usually think of a less demanding method, or a detail will conceal any doubtful work. There is absolutely nothing wrong with that — what matters are the results, and skill does take time to develop.

In the long term, however, it is important not to be limited by lack of manual skill. Here again, the key is no arcane faculty passed down to craftsmen by their forebears; it is simply accuracy. An accurate joint fits straight away, and stays together longer than a loose one. It also looks as if it fits, just as a straight edge looks straight. Do not underestimate the ability of the human eye (or hand) to detect variations.

Set yourself high standards. Remember that ⅛in (3mm) is twice as much as 1/16in (1.5mm), and four times as much as 1/32in (0.75mm). Measure, mark and cut with dead accuracy — ideally splitting the line you have marked, if it is in pencil. Aim to get every cut perfect, with no tolerance at all. You will not achieve that the first, second or third time you try, but you will improve much faster than people who allow themselves generous margins and forgive their own mistakes. By the same token, it pays to be meticulous in finishing, especially during preparation and rubbing-down. That way you have a sporting chance of professional results from a very early stage.

The more sophisticated machines do eliminate a great deal of hand work — but they certainly do not make accuracy any the less vital. Although they can cut very cleanly and very fast, time after time, this capacity is worthless unless the operation is carefully and conscientiously set up in the first place; otherwise your work will merely be quick and shoddy rather than slow and shoddy.

Clearly, knowledge and accuracy depend on practice. The more woodwork you do, the more accurate and capable you will become — and the more your enjoyment will increase. Putting in the hours will always be worthwhile.

It would be foolish to pretend that everything can ever go smoothly all the time. You will make any number of mistakes — some understandable, and some bizarre. You will cut pieces too short, drill holes in the wrong places, and find that components inexplicably fail to fit or to stay where they should. Occasionally the job may appear to assume a malevolent personality of its own.

Minimize problems by taking things at a steady pace. Although experienced people can work very fast, they never rush. Allow yourself sessions which are long enough for your concentration to build up. Double- and treble-check your measurements, no matter how sure of them you are, and heed the little voice which tells you to make quite sure you are fitting the hinges the right way round after all.

When you do something you would rather not have done, appraise the situation clearly. If you have to start again, do so without fuss and take in the lesson that the job is trying to teach you. If you can get away with making a repair or changing your plans instead, the exercise may be helpful. Be constructive in your thinking.

Razor-sharp tools, the third basic essential, may sound an obvious or unimportant requirement. They are neither. Many people have never used a really sharp chisel, plane or even saw, and do not realize what degree of sharpness can be achieved. Consequently they do not appreciate how much more accurately, cleanly and quickly sharp tools cut than blunt ones, or how they are generally safer because they require less force in use. Above all, they contribute enormously to the smoothness and hence the pleasure of work, adding a further incentive which is denied to those who plod on without them.

These three precepts are perennial, and accuracy and sharpness are permanent demands on the craftsman. But the first and overriding rule — to understand what you are doing — has changed its meaning over the centuries, because the number of options available in every sphere has increased so greatly. Today's woodworker inherits an immense, fascinating and still expanding body of knowledge, skill and design. Before considering the available alternatives, it is well worth tracing how this heritage has grown.

In medieval times woodworkers relied on a single basic material — local timber. In temperate western Europe, oak and similar hardwoods were used for buildings and furniture alike. The furniture was massive and simple, largely taking the form of tables, benches and chests. These were held together by heavy joints, wooden pegs or a combination of the two, just like buildings. Most tools were not so very different from the hand tools that we are using today: saws, chisels, wooden planes, auger drills.

The impulse for development came from three neighboring quarters. First, more complex requirements of usage produced cupboards, and cabinets with drawers, to name but two examples. Second, lusher tastes in ornament called for (and were nourished by) refinement and innovation in carving, inlay, marquetry and surface finishes. Third, international trade made foreign timbers available. These three factors have remained vital in the evolution of furniture ever since.

The sixteenth, seventeenth, eighteenth and early nineteenth centuries in England saw the replacement of oak, first by walnut and then by mahogany, as the most favored timber, plus countless developments in style and decoration. Constructional methods, however, underwent only one series of major changes. In Tudor times, frames enclosing unglued panels were already replacing solid slabs as the usual way of covering large areas. This was, and is, an excellent way of countering the natural shrinkage and swelling to which timber is subject as humidity varies. Soon afterwards, however, came the introduction of veneering — the gluing of thin sheets of wood as a surfacing over thicker pieces of different species. This greatly enlarged the vocabulary of design, for veneers often make the wisest use of costly exotic timbers whose wandering grain bestows beauty

Right *This early seventeenth-century armchair typifies the 'oak' period. Its heavy framing bears more than a slight resemblance to the joinery found in buildings. The back employs a frame-and-panel construction no different in principle from that used in wall paneling.*

Left *A framed chest of 1600, again in oak, displays European influence in carving — and especially in its inlay work: the technique came from abroad.*
Below *These are some of the highly decorative 'bandings' and 'stringings' obtainable today. They are normally glued down after veneering: the picture shows a special tool for making the necessary grooves.*

Left *George I walnut chest-of-drawers with bracket feet. Note the top and sides: by this period cabinet-makers were using large veneered slabs, in preference to the frame-and-panel method of construction employed on the chest.*

but also structural weakness. Fine veneers often need wide boards to display them, so widespread veneering paradoxically led to the reappearance of slab construction — in a much more advanced form than any the medieval artisans had devised.

Meanwhile, the constant progression of style took handmade furniture to what many still consider its zenith in the late Georgian and Regency periods. Many would say, too, that the ensuing Victorian era was a time of confusion and regression in terms of visual appeal. But it also saw the real onset of the technical progress which has brought machine tools and artificial timber-based boards. These are the two major features of modern furniture-making completely unknown in earlier times.

Certain other areas of woodwork, such as wheelwrighting, have all but died. Some have come into their own. Others have simply undergone their own parallel evolutions: the carpenter, for example, still builds houses, or at any rate installs structural timbers and basic fitments, while the joiner still makes doors, windows, staircases and other fitted items which require a workshop. Carvers carve. Woodturners make any object which requires a lathe: a restricted but, many would say, uniquely enjoyable form of work.

The furniture-maker or cabinet-maker — the terms usually mean the same — stands a little apart from them all, using his art to bring many different things into balance. On the one side lie

Right *Hand planes have evolved some very sophisticated variants, although nowadays the power router will perform many of their specialized functions. The best antique tools fetch very high prices, but secondhand suppliers are still well worth investigating.*

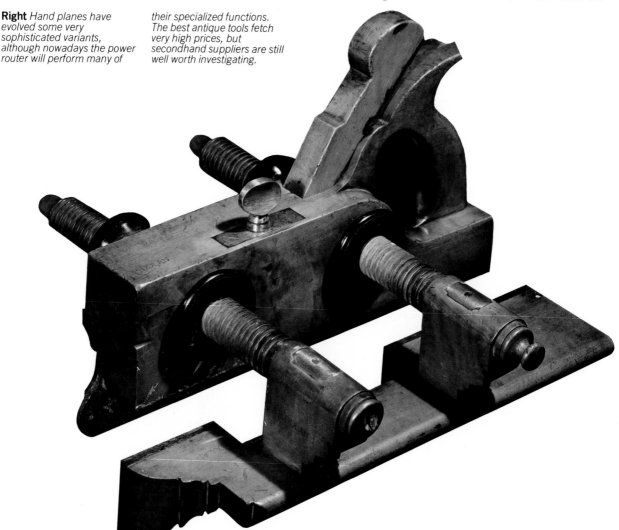

a very particular set of demands made by convenience and comfort, together with the indefinable yet inescapable requirements of visual and tactile beauty. On the other side are the tools and materials — solid timber, veneers, man-made boards, and to some extent metal, plastics and glass.

Harnessing all these factors to a common purpose is the task of design. It is important to realize that everything made is designed, whether consciously or not. From the very naming of a project — 'chair', 'desk' — to the final stages of finishing, a series of decisions are being made. The point is that each should be taken in full awareness of every alternative. Only thus will the best possible result emerge from the resources available to you.

That is one reason why much of this book consists of original designs which have been physically executed and taken through to the stage of finished items. Each project illustrates clearly how general principles can and must be used to solve very specific problems. But, by the same token, we do not claim that any of our designs represents an ideal: and you, for your part, should never let yourself be intimidated into thinking that a particular approach is the only one.

To be sure, rules and facts exist in woodwork as anywhere else. But everyone is perfectly free to interpret the rules and use the facts according to their own logic, quite possibly in entirely new ways. This, in turn, furnishes another good reason why woodwork is both easy and exciting.

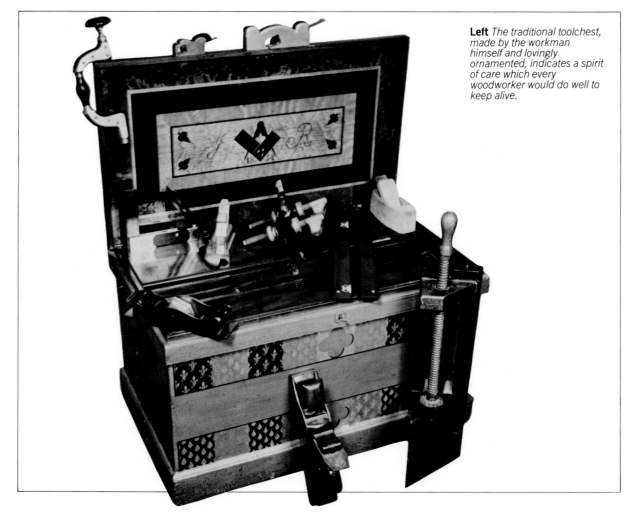

Left The traditional toolchest, made by the workman himself and lovingly ornamented, indicates a spirit of care which every woodworker would do well to keep alive.

Left *The chair (pages 178-185) achieves a familiar shape by structurally unusual means. Its drop-in seat (**below**) could be upholstered.*

Right *This writing table (pages 144-151) makes its effect through a slightly exaggerated shape and coloring. As with the backstands of the chair, a plain hardwood has been sprayed with opaque lacquer rather than exposed.*

Left *The desk-top cabinet (pages 90-99), in solid hardwoods throughout, is a miniature item requiring exceptional accuracy in its making.*

Below *The dining table (pages 114-128) attempts a decorative effect which is intense without being overwhelming.*

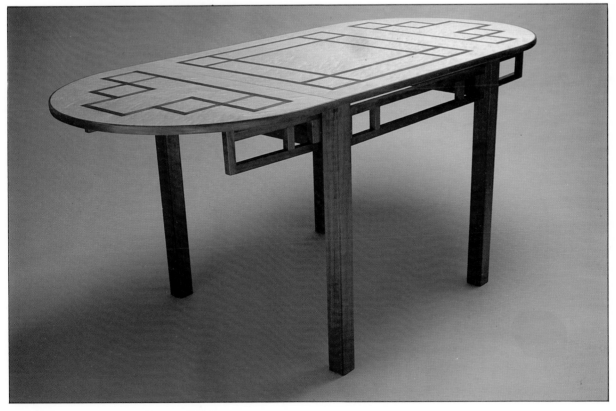

TIMBER

ondrously varied, wood is always revealing new faces, even to the most experienced woodworker. In this it is quite unlike most other common raw materials. No piece of wood is ever the same as another, even if both come from the same part of the same tree; and they may, in fact, easily come from different continents.

The study of timber is a wide-ranging botanical and physical science, which encompasses the investigation of how trees grow, how they interact with their surroundings (everything from Siberian forest to equatorial jungle), their internal structure, and the diseases and pests that attack them. Forestry — the business of growing the right trees at the right pace for the right amount of money — also involves the consideration of a very complicated series of factors, including land use, ecology, marketing, transport, timber quality and many others. The physical properties of timber itself are also studied–the precise strengths of different species in their various grades, the ways they respond to differing conditions, how easily they can be worked, and how readily they can be made into board materials.

Much of this information, although fascinating, is no use to the home furniture-maker, yet there are areas in which it is clearly important to gain expertise. Some of this knowledge will only come with familiarity; but a good deal can and should be acquired right at the beginning.

BASIC CHARACTERISTICS

The fibers and vessels of which wood is comprised run along the length of the tree, although not necessarily straight along. They constitute the grain — a word which is also used to refer to their direction and even to their texture.

The grain of a piece of timber indicates both the particular traits of the species and the conditions under which the tree grew. The moderately straight grain of oak, beech and maple still contains a fair amount of curling and twisting, which reflects the vagaries of the species' native temperate climates. Yew — typically rather gnarled — is notorious for 'wild' grain, a characteristic which leads to a high degree of wastage when cutting usable pieces. But some tropical and subtropical woods, such as jelutong and ramin, possess grain of a startling straightness and uniformity.

Growth of wood
1 Spiral grain is just one of the characteristics the woodworker may encounter in the timber he obtains.

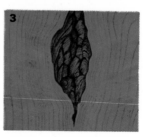

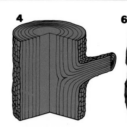

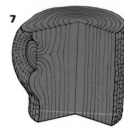

2 and **3** Pockets of bark are sometimes found right inside the tree when it is sawn open.

4 The growth of a branch distorts the grain.
5 If it dies and the stump is covered, a loose 'dead knot' results.
6 Mineral deposits, if substantial, are a hazard for cutting tools. Species in

which internal defects are common yield smaller usable pieces than others, and mean more wastage.
7 If a branch is cut off while alive, the new tissue encloses the stump more tightly.

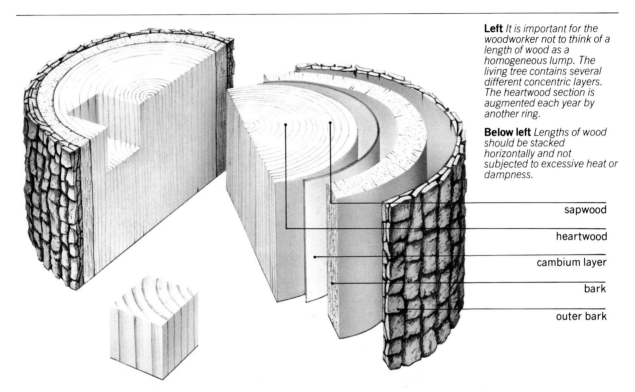

Left *It is important for the woodworker not to think of a length of wood as a homogeneous lump. The living tree contains several different concentric layers. The heartwood section is augmented each year by another ring.*

Below left *Lengths of wood should be stacked horizontally and not subjected to excessive heat or dampness.*

sapwood

heartwood

cambium layer

bark

outer bark

As a tree grows, new fibers and vessels are constantly added all round its outer surface, forming the familiar rings by whose number the tree's age can be assessed once it is felled. The wider each ring is, the more wood has been added each year: in other words, the faster the tree has grown in that period.

In softwoods, the rings can be distinguished clearly because each is made up of 'springwood' or 'earlywood' and 'summerwood' or 'latewood', the latter being denser and darker. Wide rings contain proportionately more springwood, which is why fast-grown softwoods are weaker than slow-grown ones.

Certain hardwoods ('diffuse-porous' as opposed to 'ring-porous') also have distinct spring- and summerwood. In this case, however, wider rings contain more summerwood, so that faster-grown trees are denser and stronger.

The outer rings of a tree form the 'sapwood', which channels essential chemicals up the trunk. The rest is 'heartwood', which no longer fulfills that function. Each year the innermost sapwood turns into heartwood as a newly grown ring augments the sapwood on the outside. In many species the sapwood is a different color from the heartwood, usually much lighter, and it is always easier prey to insects. For these reasons it is often discarded when the timber is used.

'Rays' radiate from the center at intervals along the tree's length. In some hardwoods, notably oak, they are quite visible and very distinctive.

These and other features of the wood, for example knots (the beginnings of branches), compose its 'figure': that is, the pattern — if any — on the surface of a cut piece. This can be strikingly beautiful, or inconspicuous and dull; it depends not only on the species and individual tree, particularly whether the grain is straight or not, but also on the way the timber has been cut.

Broadly speaking, there are two ways of cutting a log into boards. Plain- or flat-sawing simply involves a series of parallel cuts. With the exception of the cut through the middle (if any), these will be tangential: running, as it were, up the sides of the growth rings and cutting through them obliquely. This type of cutting usually reveals a fairly bold figure.

Converting a log
*Plain-sawing (**1**) is the simplest method of converting a log, but it gives each board a different orientation in relation to the rings. True quarter-sawing (**2**) produces more uniform and usually plainer timber which is less prone to distortion. **3** This is a common approximation.*

Quarter-sawing is based on radial cuts — or rather on cuts which are as nearly radial as speed and economy will allow. Such cuts cross the growth rings at right-angles, or roughly so, and therefore do not make a feature of them; so in general this procedure, which is rather more sophisticated than plain-sawing, paradoxically produces plainer timber of a more even texture. However, radial cuts run parallel to the rays and expose many of them; where the rays are prominent, as in oak, quarter-sawing is done especially because of the attractive figure they provide.

Below *The figure on a plain-sawn piece (tangential to the rings) differs from that on a quarter-sawn (radially cut) piece.*

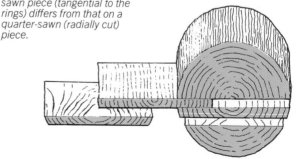

Left and **below** Today more than ever, timber comes from every part of the globe. Unfamiliar species are constantly appearing on the market, and many have characteristics which make them as useful as established favorites.

The more nearly timber is square in section — equal in width and thickness — the less these considerations apply. On a 3 x 2in (75 x 50mm) piece you can bring either a radially or a tangentially cut surface into view simply by turning the piece over.

It is crucial to develop an extremely sensitive feel for the ease or difficulty with which timber can be worked. In fact, you have no choice about this, because the matter will soon force itself on your attention whether you understand it or not! The exact orientation of the grain greatly affects the cutting actions of such tools as chisels, planes and routers. The further the grain is out of parallel to the face on which you are working, the more likely it is that you will have to turn the piece round or come at it from another angle if you are not to split or tear out the wood instead of cutting through it.

Even where the grain is fairly straight, one direction is often easier than the other, and produces a smoother finish — while certain cuts may prove almost impossible. This is particularly true of pieces whose grain is constantly changing direction. Interlocked grain, found in tropical species such as sapele, even consists of neighboring bands of grain going in opposite directions. This can make life very difficult too, and it sets a high premium on keeping planing tools razor sharp as well as finely set.

Above *Material and workmanship are (or should be) inseparable aspects of the same achievement.*
Below *These are the furniture moldings most commonly available from stock — usually in softwood or ramin.*

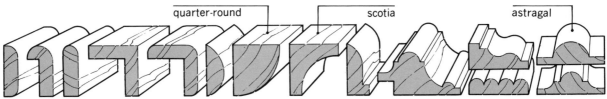

quarter-round   scotia   astragal

Clearly, the endgrain — the surface exposed by a cut at right-angles to the grain — is a special case. It is more difficult than other surfaces to get smooth, although it can be shaved with hand planes and chisels, again provided they are sharp. It also takes up moisture more easily, which makes it harder to glue and means that many finishes darken it a good deal more than the rest of the wood.

BUYING TIMBER

Only constant practice will develop a knowledge of what to expect from timber. Then you can act appropriately — whether at the design stage or while you are actually cutting and finishing.

Likewise, there is no formula for knowing one timber from another. Once again it comes down to familiarity. However, that develops surprisingly quickly if you apply yourself. If you see a wood you cannot identify, make a guess — and then, if possible, check whether you are right. Things are made easier by the fact that the number of really common timbers is relatively small: perhaps two dozen or so, out of something like 40,000 known species.

Different woods have very different textures. Oak has an open grain, coarse to the touch; sycamore has a close grain, which gives a smoother, denser surface. Brazilian mahogany lies somewhere in between. Softwoods could be described as close-grained, except that their

Left *Proper storage and seasoning help to ensure that timber will be easy to use. Getting to know suppliers and how they operate is essential for effective woodwork; without an appreciation of the species available and the sizes and conditions in which they are sold (not to mention their prices), it is difficult even to start planning a project.*

general softness adds another element.

Chemistry makes a further contribution by adding, for example, the oiliness of teak and afrormosia, and the pockets of sticky resin in certain softwoods — not to mention the delicious scent of sandalwood and cedar of Lebanon, and the peppery smell of keruing.

Color is another distinctive characteristic. Maple, birch, willow and sycamore are (in general) milky-white. Freshly-cut padauk is bright red. Ebony is very black (but macassar ebony is piebald). Parana pine has scarlet streaks; rosewood can be purple; satinwood is golden; zebrawood is striped. Some timbers fade, others darken. The variety is stunning, and extra-

ordinary contrasts can often be readily seen in a single board of, say, walnut. All pieces of a given species may not come up to the same standard; on the other hand, unpromising timber may turn out to yield a remarkable patch of color — or figure, or both.

Other considerations matter more to the architect than the furniture-maker. Weight is not usually crucial, density being important largely for its effect on the general appeal of the wood, plus the finish it will take. Hardness, however, is sometimes worth thinking about, since a very soft material such as western red cedar bears no comparison with, say, teak or ash when rough usage is likely. As for structural strength, sensible dimensions are the best insurance — although care is needed where the component must be small or shaped; if the margin looks tight, grain directions should be taken into account as well. Remember, too, that some woods are especially prone to splitting, while some (not necessarily the hardest) are tough. Lastly, durability — or the degree of natural resistance to decay and insect attack — is a vital consideration in outdoor items, but not otherwise.

The basic distinction between softwoods and hardwoods should also be understood. Much is made of the imprecision of these terms, but for all woodworking purposes, they are perfectly adequate.

Softwoods, with minor exceptions, come from evergreen trees with very thin, needle-like leaves. Largely, though not exclusively, they grow in the cool and the cold parts of the world, major producers being Scandinavia, the USSR and Canada. On the whole they are, in fact, softer than hardwoods –- although there are very soft hardwoods, such as balsa and obeche, and moderately hard softwoods, such as larch and yew.

Far fewer species of softwoods than of hardwoods are generally available, and they are more alike than the hardwoods are. None are strongly colored, though shades vary from pale brown and pinkish to nearly white. Hardwoods, by contrast, can vary spectacularly in texture and color. Quite apart from their physical differences, moreover, a number of species bear further connotations — either historical, or less easily defined — which have to do with the periods and places of their greatest use, and sometimes with their lands of origin. Trends in furniture design also play a part.

In addition to all these qualities and associations, timbers are sharply distinguished by availability, size and price.

Pinus sylvestris (redwood, red deal, yellow deal, Scots pine) and *picea abies* (whitewood, white deal, spruce, Norway spruce) are both softwoods. They differ from almost all other timbers in being marketed as 'dimension stock' — that is, already cut down to sectional sizes, which can be as small as ½ x ¾in (12 x 19mm). This eliminates much work on the user's part, and these timbers are the basic material of all carpentry and much joinery. In fact, the term 'softwood' often refers in practice to them alone. If you go into a DIY shop, builder's merchant or general timber merchant and ask for a

Far left *This cabinet by David Savage in yew (botanically a softwood), on its stand of padauk with a yew panel, displays some of the possibilities offered by contrasting woods.*
Above *A wedge is hammered into a log to prevent it from closing up and 'binding' as it goes through the bandsaw.*

particular size, without specifying any wood, you will almost certainly get one of these two.

While some countries now use, at least in theory, the metric system, the standard sizes to which most dimension stock is cut are the nearest metric equivalents of common imperial dimensions. Usual widths and thicknesses are drawn from 12, 16, 19, 22, 25, 32, 36, 38, 44, 50, 63, 75, 100, 125, 150, 175, 200, 225, 250 and 300mm. These correspond to ½, ⅝, ¾, ⅞, 1, 1¼, 1⅜, 1½, 1¾, 2, 2½, 3, 4, 5, 6, 7, 8, 9, 10 and 12in respectively.

Lengths go in increments of 300mm. Be careful here, because a foot equals 304.8mm. While 6ft is 1828.8mm, the metric 'equivalent' — what you will actually get, unless the supplier still sticks to the old ways — is only 1800mm. Ensure that the timber will be long enough for the job.

Minimum and maximum lengths vary, but only the smallest supplier will usually sell pieces under 6ft (1800mm) — except perhaps of exotic species.

Another point causes much understandable confusion in those who are unused to buying timber. Logs are sawn at the mill into particular widths and thicknesses: 2 x 4in (50 x 100mm), 1 x 3in (25 x 75mm) and so on (some being cut more accurate than others). This leaves a rough surface which is perfectly adequate for many purposes in carpentry — but not for furniture, or for any other indoor woodwork that is intended to be seen. Consequently, timber that has been planed smooth is also available. That comes in a very similar range of sizes: from as much as 9 x 2in (225 x 50mm) and 4 x 4in (100 x 100mm) or so downwards.

The point to watch is that these pieces are still described as being the same size as they were originally — before having had approximately 3/16in (5mm) planed off them each way. A piece of '25 x 50mm sawn' is that size. Once planed ('prepared', or 'PAR' for 'planed all round'), it will measure only about 20 x 45mm. This is its 'finished size'. But its 'nominal size' is still 25 x 50mm; that is what it is still called, or perhaps 'ex 25 x 50mm'.

This happens because it is easier to plane down from a sawn size than down to a finished size: no accuracy is needed. But as a result the supplier does not know exactly what the finished size will be. Indeed, it will vary between pieces planed in different batches from the same sawn size.

The trick is to allow for this decrease and unpredictability in size when you design. If you go out looking for planed timber, you will not find a piece exactly 25 x 50mm. To accommodate this discrepancy, plan in such a way that you can use a piece 20 x 45mm — or perhaps the next size up, say 32 x 50mm or 25 x 63mm, which will actually be about 27 x 45 or 20 x 58mm respectively. Sizes can always be adjusted further by planing at home.

The smaller sizes of planed timber, including nominal thicknesses below ½in (12mm), are often available in ramin — a pale, straight-grained hardwood — instead of softwood. Widths over about 9in (225mm) are available in parana pine, a softwood. *Pseudotsuga taxifolia* (Douglas fir) is another softwood sometimes available in standard sizes.

The everyday softwoods are subject to a grading system which refers largely to the straightness and evenness of the grain, especially with regard to the number of knots. For the buyer, this may mean a simple division between 'standard' or 'standard joinery' quality on the one hand, and 'joinery' or 'best joinery' quality on the other. But even those labels hint at the confusion of terminology which is endemic in the world of wood. Roughly corresponding to them are 'fifths' and 'unsorted' ('U/S'), the two strangely named grades used in the timber trade itself.

'Clear' is a word often used to describe knot-free timber — a fairly rare commodity in dimension softwoods, though there are many clear hardwoods. This is further complicated by the fact that the best timber of a particular grade from, say, a particular mill in Sweden may well be better than the worst examples of the next grade up from, say, a particular mill in Poland. Strangely enough, too, knotty redwood (sold as 'knotty pine') can fetch higher prices than clearer grades because people like the effect it gives.

The hardwood trade is different. Firstly, most hardwoods are much more expensive than the common softwoods. Secondly, although many builder's and general timber merchants keep a few hardwoods as dimension stock, sawn to size and perhaps planed (the commonest apart from ramin being certain types of mahogany, followed by oak, beech, and teak, together with teak's near-double afrormosia), in general the buying of hardwoods demands initiative. This is largely because the worldwide nature of the trade has made it impossible to maintain the consistency found in the softwood supplies of Europe, Scandinavia and Canada. The usual expectation is that the user will 'convert' hardwoods himself to the particular sizes needed — often from sawn 'waney-edge' boards; that is, ones with the outside shape of the tree still present down at least one edge. (These are also referred to as 'unedged' or 'U/E'.)

The metric system notwithstanding, hardwoods and all except dimension softwoods are commonly sold in cubic feet rather than by length and sectional size. One cubic foot ($1ft^3$ /$0.037m^3$) represents a volume of 1 x 1 x 1ft (300 x 300 x 300mm), or any other combination of dimensions whose product is the same. This is at least straightforward, but it demands careful calculation, and the pieces involved may be very substantial — entailing consequent wastage.

That is not to say that you cannot find hardwoods sawn square-edged ('S/E'), down to sizes close to those the furniture-maker normally uses. But, except in the case of those from thin trees, which only come in small sizes anyway, you may have to search hard — or pay more to have pieces cut down especially. Many hardwood merchants are simply unaccustomed to dealing with small buyers, and some are frankly unwilling. The few who specialize in amateur requirements, sometimes even by mail order, are well worth locating. Several deal in exotic woods whose names can be as entrancing as their colors and figures.

Hardwood grades, where used, are as bizarre as softwood grades. The top two are 'prime' and 'FAS', which stands for 'firsts and seconds'. Lower down come 'selects' and 'no. 1 common'. English hardwoods are often graded as 'first quality' (or prime), 'second quality' and 'merchantable'.

When buying timber, brief yourself thoroughly first. Know which species, sectional size, amount and general quality you want; decide whether the timber must be planed or whether sawn will do. If it matters, know what color and figure you would prefer. Visit a well-stocked supplier, ideally where the pieces can be examined before buying. Timber merchants who supply the building and DIY trades often make this possible by racking their stock; with more specialized firms it will be harder, if indeed it is allowed at all. Most of all, however, be flexible. Make sure you are equipped to consider, alternatives, rather than insisting that only one set of specifications will do. Especially for a single item of furniture, any number of practical obstacles may stand in your way.

Lastly, take a tape measure to enable you to identify sizes more easily and to check actual (as opposed to nominal) dimensions. Other useful equipment includes a block plane (to smooth small areas when you want to examine the grain) and a pocket calculator.

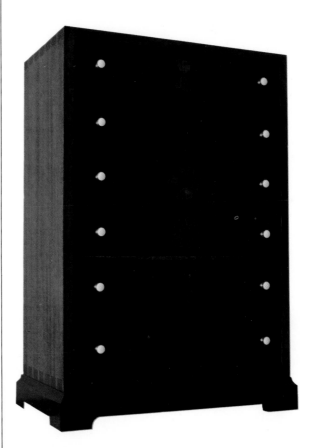

Above *David Savage designed and made this appealing chest-of-drawers in Honduras mahogany (the nearest species now available to the Spanish mahogany of days gone by). The poppy motif of red-stained sycamore is inlaid into the solid drawer-fronts.*

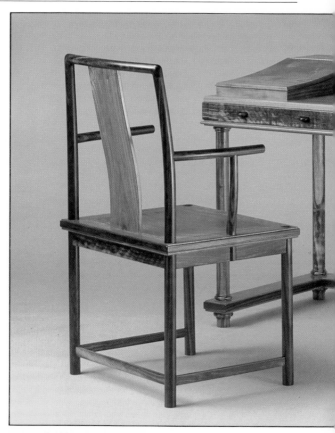

Left *Jakki Dehn used American black walnut for these music cabinets. The inlaid lines are in boxwood, the commonest wood for this purpose, while the squares are holly, mother-of-pearl and ivory. The varied materials suggest a musical arrangement.*

Left *and* **below** *Walnut was again the principal material for Martin Grierson's desk and Chinese-style chair — two further virtuoso pieces.* **Below left** *Making and fitting the curved lids for the desk's storage compartments demands a particularly high degree of skill.*

WOOD AND MOISTURE

It is essential to understand the relationship between wood and the moisture in the atmosphere. A growing tree contains a high proportion of water. In the extreme cases of certain softwoods, water accounts for as much as two-thirds of the tree's weight. This 'moisture content' (MC) is given as a percentage of the weight of the rest of the timber. If all the water were removed (which is impossible) the MC would be 0 percent. An MC of 25 percent means that other substances in the wood still weigh four times as much as the water. These softwoods, however, have an MC when 'green' — that is, immediately after felling — of 200 percent: the water weighs twice as much as the rest.

The moisture is contained in three ways. A little is 'constituent'; it forms part of the wood's chemical make-up, a state of affairs which cannot be changed. A further small proportion is 'bound' in the cell walls. But most of it is 'free': it simply lies in the spaces of the cells.

As a result, felling a tree initiates a series of unstoppable changes. Without the processes of life to give the tree's fabric a balance of its own, the timber starts to seek a new balance: this time with the surrounding air. The moisture begins to evaporate, and continues to do so until the wood reaches an 'equilibrium moisture content' (EMC) in relation to the atmosphere. That does not mean that it contains the same amount of moisture, per cubic inch or foot, as the air. The crucial factor is the air's 'vapor pressure' — found by an equation which involves both the pressure of the air and its humidity. In everyday terms it is the humidity that matters; temperature alone is not the determining factor.

The EMC of wood in the average heated room is about 10 percent: a piece of green timber whose MC is, say, 75 percent will dry out by 65 percent if left in such a location. If the timber is drier to start with, or the room is damp, the change will be less pronounced. Conversely, dry timber placed in a damp environment will always take up moisture.

These processes are inescapable; and, although they will stop if conditions dictate, and age may lessen their force, their potential never disappears — no matter how old the timber may be. What is more, finishing treatments can only slow them down, not prevent them altogether, because no finish is impermeable to water vapor. The pro-

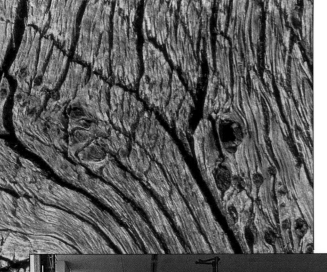

cesses must never be left out of account, for a number of very good reasons.

The main one is that, once the free moisture has all evaporated (usually when the MC descends to about 30 percent), the bound moisture in the cell walls begins to follow it and the wood consequently starts to shrink. The further the MC drops below this level, the greater the shrinkage; by the same token, a rise in the MC will cause the wood to swell.

Suppose a beech tree is felled and plain-sawn into wide boards which are dried to an MC of 19 percent (a procedure during which they shrink). If a 6in (150mm) wide piece from an outer board is then cut and dried further, by the time its MC has dropped to 12 percent, it will only be about 5½in (125mm) wide.

Loss of moisture from felled timber can induce all sorts of stresses, triggering splits and distortion as well as just shrinkage (far left). Wood, in fact, never ceases to be affected by the humidity of its surroundings. Ideally it should be left to condition until the last possible moment in the surroundings where it will be used — or at any rate worked (left).

'Moisture movement', as the process is often known, varies widely between species; some, such as parana pine, are notorious for it, and others such as iroko are relatively 'stable'. Moreover, drying which is too rapid — for example, in timber exposed to strong sunlight — will cause the moisture from the outer cells to evaporate faster than that from the inner cells can replace it, so that unwelcome stresses soon build up. Small cracks on the surface ('surface checks') are one immediate sign.

These stresses are aggravated by the fact that movement is far from uniform throughout the wood. Along the length of a piece, it is generally so small that you can safely ignore it. The movement between the center of the tree and its circumference — that is, radially — is frequently only about half as much as the movement at right-angles to the radius (tangentially, or around the rings). Because both movements take place at once, pulling in different directions with differing forces, timber changes not only its size, but — unless careful precautions are taken — also its shape.

The precise nature and extent of movement in a given piece depends, therefore, on the way in which it has been cut from the log; but all square sections tend to become diamond-shaped (if only

Above and **right** The largest kilns for seasoning timber are buildings in their own right. This small one is used by a firm providing high-quality raw materials for musical-instrument makers.

slightly) and round sections oval. Flatter sections
'cup' (lift up along the edges).

Further distortions include 'bowing' and
'springing' (curving in the length) and twisting.
These in particular point to the fact that the
dynamic balance of a living tree embraces stresses
which are ready for release when it is felled. Once
it is cut into sections, the restraining effect of opposing forces is removed; loss of moisture introduces further tensions which can have all sorts
of effects, such as 'shakes' — natural splits of
various patterns (although these can also occur
before felling). Here again, a great deal depends
on the species.

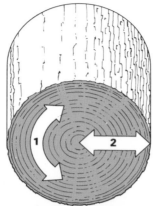

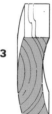

Above *The greatest
shrinkage in any piece occurs
along the rings, or tangentially
(**1**). Radial shrinkage is
commonly about half as great
(**2**). The difference means
that loss of moisture pulls
wood out of shape as well as
reducing its size. The pattern
of distortion depends on the
position which the particular
piece occupied in the tree (**3**).*

Left *Longitudinal shrinkage is
negligible. However, endgrain
picks up moisture with
especial ease, which is why
the ends of the timber have
been treated after cutting.*

Above *Most timber is seasoned and stored before it reaches the user.*

Below *Ways of grooving a panel into a frame to allow the panel to shrink and swell with humidity changes.*

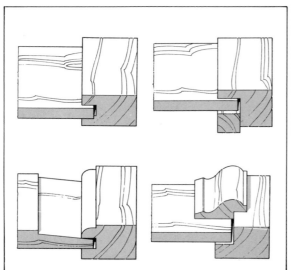

Seasoning

The procedure which has been developed to counter all these problems is seasoning: the deliberate release or extraction of moisture from felled timber. Drying makes wood stronger (down to an MC of 4 or 5 percent), lighter, easier to work with conventional tools, more receptive to finishing treatments, and less prone to decay (the dangerline is about 20 percent). Dry timber is also more stable, because swelling takes place less readily than shrinkage, and in any case drying causes a certain permanent loss of moisture — which means that wood will not swell back as far as it has shrunk.

By far the chief aim in most cases, however, is to reduce the MC to within about 2 percent of the EMC required by the environment where the finished article will be situated (it should be drier rather than wetter). This is especially vital in the case of furniture. If you were foolish enough to make a chair from green timber and immediately place it in a comfortably warm house, the reduction in its MC would cause all its components to shrink a great deal, loosening its joints; and the suddenness of its drying would almost certainly cause severe distortion and probably splitting.

Those are the reasons for and aims of seasoning. It is not, therefore, a matter of simply allowing or encouraging evaporation. The essential thing is to control the rate at which evaporation happens.

Traditionally, timber has been seasoned by leaving it outdoors — covered to protect it from extremes of weather, and carefully stacked so that the air can circulate around it. Except for the smallest logs, it is generally cut into large boards first.

This allows it to reach an EMC with the surrounding atmosphere at a leisurely pace, usually reckoned at one year for every inch (25mm) of thickness in the case of hardwoods. If left even longer, the wood will not shrink noticeably further but — at least in many woodworkers' opinion — its internal stresses will continue gradually to even themselves out: the wood will settle down. This subtle process partly accounts for the esteem in which 'air-drying', as it is known, is often held.

The operation has two sizable drawbacks, however. One is its slowness. The other is its inability to dry timber below an MC of approximately 20 percent (an average figure which varies by 3

Left *A kiln of the type used by major suppliers (**below**) to season large amounts of timber quickly.*

percent or more according to the region and the season). Once it has reached its EMC, it will dry no further. Yet the EMC required for domestic interiors is no more than 14 percent or so — as little as 8 percent for some centrally heated rooms.

To solve these problems, artificial seasoning methods have been developed. These involve placing the timber in a special chamber. Kilns, used for large-scale seasoning, in effect dry the timber by extracting its moisture as steam. Dehumidifiers, which are becoming popular for smaller-scale users, work by the gentler but slower method of heating, condensing and draining the moisture from the chamber's atmosphere, decreasing its humidity so the wood follows suit.

Not surprisingly, all this bears heavily on furniture design. Since movement is by a percentage and not by a constant amount, it affects wider pieces more than narrow ones. However, no piece is immune, and it is rarely possible to guarantee that whatever you make will always remain in surroundings of the same humidity. Therefore you must plan for movement, at least to a certain extent. The chief rule is never to fix a wide component in such a way that it cannot freely expand or contract across its width (movement along the grain being negligible). You cannot, in fact, stop it shrinking — but, if prevented from narrowing, it will become liable simply to split instead.

Though briefly stated, this maxim has wide implications, today just as much as in the past.

Moreover, even a design which caters very cleverly for possible changes in size can rarely make much allowance in, for example, the fitting of drawers — and the change in humidity between, say, workshop and living-room may cause them to rattle or stick. Moreover, while seasoning is intended to minimize distortion in shape, and as far as possible to prevent it from recurring, such changes in humidity may trigger that as well.

Even assuming the timber you buy is air- or kiln-dried (as is almost certainly the case), the problems are not over. Ideally, it should then be cut down to its finished sizes (in width and thickness as well as length) — and after that not only stored for six months or so, but also worked, in the place where the finished item will be used. This, of course, is rarely possible. You will probably have to be content with buying it as early as you can, reducing it fairly quickly to something near its intended sizes, and waiting until the last minute so that any changes in size or shape or both can take place before, rather than after, the components have been cut or the item assembled. But the furniture-maker can still expect trouble if his workshop is damp, because his tables, chairs, cabinets and the rest will still leave the workshop with an MC above that needed for most modern buildings.

Bear in mind that changes in humidity may take a day or two to have any noticeable effect on timber, and much longer to complete their work.

MAN-MADE BOARDS

Artificial panel products are a staple of industry, especially the bulding industry. Four types matter to the furniture-maker: plywood, blockboard, chipboard and fiberboard.

While there are cabinet-makers who use only solid timber, most accept that these new materials are indispensable. They come in large sizes; they are largely free of timber's unpredictability — and they do not shrink, swell or warp much. They will usually stay the same size under all atmospheric conditions: at any rate, changes will probably be imperceptible. Note, however, that thin boards are more prone to warping than thick ones.

Above *Some of plywood's particular advantages are well displayed by Bob Pulley's Flexichair. The deep cuts provide springiness in the seat and back; the uniform strength of the material (ensured by its laminated construction) makes the design practical.*

Plywood

Veneer is a piece, or rather sheet, of wood less than about ⅛in (3mm) thick, and usually nearer to 1/16in (1.5mm) or 1/32in (0.8mm). Plywood is made by gluing three or more veneers together in layers called 'plies'.

Except in one particular variety, the grain of each veneer runs at right-angles to the grain of those immediately above and below it. Because the veneers are thin and well seasoned, and the glue is strong, this prevents the usual movement from taking place as humidity changes. Moreover, while solid timber breaks much more easily along the grain than across it, the opposing grain directions in plywood make it equally strong both ways.

The exception is 'drawer-side' plywood, used in the furniture trade for making drawers, in which the grains of the plies all run the same way. The main reason for this is to eliminate the stripy effect on each edge which is the result of alternating bands of endgrain and side grain. With ordinary plywood, where this is always apparent, there are two choices: either to leave the edges exposed and even make them a feature, or to conceal them in various ways.

Plywood is available as thin as 1/16in (1.5mm), which is very useful for bending into tight curves. The thickest available is usually 1in. In fact, most plywood thicknesses are given in millimeters, the range being 1.5, 4, 5, 6, 9, 12, 18, 19, 22 and 25. You may also find 6.5, 9.5, 12.5, 15.5, and 18.5 — especially on American and Canadian boards, since these dimensions correspond more closely to the imperial fractions which are still in official use here.

The number of plies (always odd, to combat warping by ensuring uniform tension on either side) varies even in boards of the same thickness. In some types, only the two face veneers are thinner than the rest, all the inner veneers being the same thickness; in others — 'stoutheart' plywoods — the middle (core) veneer is thickest. Apart from the question of appearance, this matters chiefly because uniform veneers make the edges easier to work with planes, chisels and the like, and slightly easier to sand. Such boards also tend to be stronger.

Plywoods for furniture fall into two broad categories: those which are meant to be hidden, given an opaque finish, or veneered or laminated by the buyer, and those whose face veneers are of attractive timber which is meant to be displayed.

The first group is headed by boards from Finland which are faced with birch, and often composed of birch throughout. Birch is rather pale and uninteresting, but its very close grain means it can be coated with opaque lacquer or paint without further preparation — and an unblemished piece may even lend itself to a clear finish.

Boards from Africa and the Far East are generally faced with nondescript tropical hardwoods such as gaboon and lauan. These are fairly soft and coarse-grained, which usually means more work at the finishing stage.

American and Canadian boards, among others, are faced with softwoods such as Douglas fir and southern yellow pine. These boards are really intended for external cladding and similar uses.

Generally available in the second group are plywoods faced with oak, sapele, teak and afrormosia; other veneers are less widely available. These are more expensive — but for many purposes you can save by getting a board with the decorative facing on only one side, instead of both. The latter type is often stamped to indicate the quality of the face veneers — as indeed are many ordinary (non-decorative) plywoods. 'A/B' means there is a top-grade veneer on one side and a

Below *Michael Reed's cabinet and shelves again make especially striking use of plywood.*

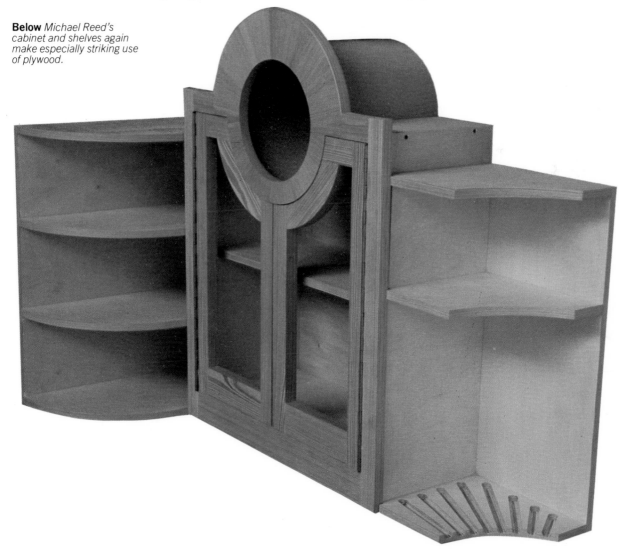

second-grade veneer on the other. 'B/BB' denotes a second-grade veneer coupled with a third-grade. C, CC and X are lower grades; so are WG and CP. Grade BB and those below it (plus occasionally B) allow knot-holes; these are usually plugged in the factory, often with oval patches.

Blockboard

Blockboard also has veneered faces. Beneath them, however, is a core of solid wood, usually softwood; this consists of separate pieces laid side-by-side. Good quality ('five-ply') blockboard has two veneers on each face.

Blockboard is somewhat cheaper than plywood, comes in similar thicknesses, and is even stiffer. However, it has the disadvantage of occasional gaps where the core lengths of wood do not meet. Its construction can also result in an undulating surface unsuitable for fine work.

Blockboard comes with a similar range of face veneers to those used on plywood. Its edges, however, are rarely considered acceptable for show, especially if gaps are present.

Laminboard is very much like blockboard. Its core, however, consists of much narrower strips of hardwood; these features make it stronger and stiffer, but more expensive and less easy to obtain.

Chipboard

Chipboard or 'particleboard' is often dismissed — but those who specify and use it know that it has its own well-earned place. Made from fragments of wood held together with plastic 'resin' glue, it is not as strong as plywood or blockboard: it breaks more easily. But it is just as stiff and stable, and much cheaper. Thicknesses are similar.

When chipboard is used in furniture, it can be given a clear finish in the odd case where that might look right. More usually, however, it is painted, coated with opaque lacquer, or veneered. Best for clear finishing, and essential for painting, opaque-lacquering and veneering, is a grade of chipboard meant primarily for furniture, since this will have fairly fine particles at and near its surfaces. Some of these 'fine-surface' and 'superfine-surface' boards will accept paint or opaque lacquer directly. Others need painting and filling first to avoid a rough texture — but ready-primed and filled types are available.

What is more, some chipboard comes ready-veneered. The range of decorative timbers used is much the same as on plywood and blockboard. Overall thickness is standardized at ⅝in (16mm). A problem here, as with other factory-veneered boards, is that the veneers can be extraordinarily thin. This makes it all too easy to expose the board itself with an accidental blow, or even by sanding a little too heavily.

Chipboard's main shortcoming lies in its edges. Even furniture-grade boards have large particles towards the middle of the thickness. In the edges this variation is readily visible: they are always at least slightly coarse and crumbly. It is hardly ever desirable to leave them as they are — particularly since they absorb water very easily. The faces soak it up a little more slowly. The damp area almost immediately swells and begins to fall apart. The implications for, say bathroom furniture are obvious, although there are moisture-resistant (but not waterproof) grades of chipboard. Lastly, the plastic resin content makes chipboard notorious for blunting both hand and machine tools very quickly.

Fiberboard

Fiberboards are made from much smaller fragments of wood than chipboards are. Most fiberboards contain no glue; instead, only heat and pressure are used in their manufacture.

The best-known fiberboard is hardboard. Ordinarily this is never more than ½in (12mm) thick, and usually about ¼in (6mm). It is, therefore, not generally used as a constructional material in the same way as other boards are, although it is very dense.

It has one face smoother and harder than that of any other board (except for plastic- and metal-laminated ones), and one rough face. 'Duo-faced' hardboard has two smooth faces; this is sometimes achieved by bonding two standard boards back-to-back, which allows generally greater thicknesses — up to ⅝in (15mm). 'Tempered' or 'oil-tempered' hardboard looks like standard hardboard but has been treated to make it stronger, harder and more resistant to water.

The familiar pegboard with its regular round holes is a type of what is known as perforated hardboard. Others are pierced in all sorts of patterns; whether any of these have a place in your furniture designs is up to individual choice. The same goes

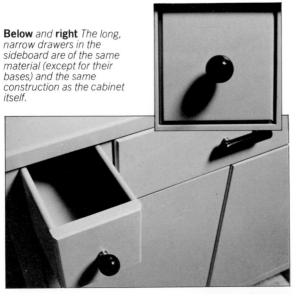

Below and **right** The long, narrow drawers in the sideboard are of the same material (except for their bases) and the same construction as the cabinet itself.

for the many hardboards which are embossed in sundry textures and 'pre-decorated' in an enormous range of finishes.

Medium-density fiberboard (MDF) is a fairly recent invention, still little-known outside the furniture trade, which has unique and very useful properties. Unlike other fiberboards, it is made with the addition of plastic resin. Although not quite as dense as standard hardboard, it has two very smooth faces, and comes in thicknesses right up to 2in (50mm). This quality turns it into a constructional material, and in that role it has one huge advantage: its edges, if cleanly cut, are smooth and uniform right the way across. They can usually be painted or opaque-lacquered without further preparation. If clear-lacquered, perhaps after staining, they will even in certain cases provide a close enough match for solid timber. These virtues make MDF almost irreplaceable for maximum efficiency in certain jobs; it is also quite cheap.

Below Medium-density fiberboard (MDF) was used for almost every part of this sideboard, described in full on pages 160-167.

Right _and_ **below right**
Colorcore is an expensive but versatile new plastic sheet material; it can be used singly, or laminated to give alluring effects. Its particular advantage is that its color is uniform throughout its thickness, unlike that of conventional high-pressure plastic laminates. It is used in the handles of this serving cart by Ward Bennett.

Below _Colorcore is also used for the drop-in top of this sycamore console table. Note the effect of the chamfered edges._

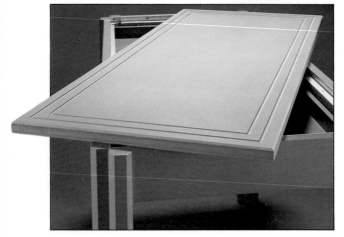

Plastic and paper facings

Plywood, blockboard, chipboard and fiberboard are all available with thin facings which require no finish. Four types are used for furniture boards.

The first is paper, and the second is a film or 'foil' of solid PVC (vinyl). On the whole these are the least hard-wearing of the four, and such boards are normally sold only to industry.

Plastic laminates, in contrast, have layered paper as their basic material, impregnated with phenolic and melamine plastic resins, with a final layer of melamine. (They should not be confused with plastic coatings and lacquers, which also often contain melamine; the latter are usually applied as sprays.) 'Low-pressure' laminates — the description refers to the method of manufacture — include relatively few layers, and are not particularly hard or tough until actually fused to a board. High-pressure laminates, on the other hand, have more layers, bonded to form a material which is extremely stiff and resilient in its own right. In fact, although they may then be factory-glued to boards, many are sold (unlike low-pressure laminates) for other uses. You can stick them to boards yourself. Because high-pressure laminates are thicker and made from heavier papers, their edges show as distinct dark lines,

With both types, it is a general rule to cover both sides of a panel. Laminating only one side tends to unbalance the board's natural exchange of moisture with the atmosphere, and thus initiate warping. The same goes for applying wood veneers. Worktops are an exception because of their thickness, their weight and the fact that they are firmly fixed — though many are backed with paper.

Needless to say, all plastic facings are available multifariously colored, patterned and textured. Often timber colors and figures are combined with a grain texture to imitate real wood, sometimes very convincingly.

Plastic-faced boards are most at home in the kitchen and bathroom, because they repel liquid and thus allow cleaning much more easily than most alternative materials and finishes. In kitchen cabinets, chipboard, factory-faced with low-pressure laminate to an overall thickness of ⅝in (15mm), is practically universal.

Above *In Milton Glaser's table, Colorcore is strikingly combined with solid oak. Man-made materials may often be enhanced by natural ones.*

BUYING BOARDS AND LAMINATES

The sheet materials mentioned here are only those of use to furniture-makers — a smallish proportion of the total; yet even they are not all available from any one source. As with timber and indeed other supplies, the best plan may well be to locate a handful of stockists who carry good ranges, familiarize yourself with those, and design your projects accordingly.

The commonest size for all boards is 8 x 4ft — or rather, its metric 'equivalent', 2440 x 1220mm. This varies slightly from brand to brand. 3050 x 1220mm (10 x 4ft) is standard for plastic laminates. Other lengths available are 9, 7, and 6ft (usually 2745, 2135 and 1830mm); other widths are 5 and 3ft (1525 and 915mm).

In the cases of plywood, blockboard and veneered chipboard, the measurement given first is supposed to indicate the way the face grain runs. In other words, a 2440 x 1220mm board has its grain lengthwise (the usual way); on a 1220 x 2440mm board, the grain runs across. This can be very important when you are planning how to cut out components for the best appearance.

One particular material — chipboard faced with a wood veneer (teak, African mahogany or pine) or with low-pressure laminate in white, beige or imitation teak or pine — comes in widths from 6in (152mm) right up to 36in (914mm) in 3in (75mm) steps. Lengths are 8ft (2400mm) and 6ft (1800mm); thickness is ⅝in (16mm) for veneered, and 15mm for plastic-faced boards. Both long edges are concealed by a glued-on strip which more or less matches. There are better-wearing, better-looking and more carefully finished materials, and the chipboard edges must still be sealed or hidden if the boards are cut to width. But few materials are so convenient to buy — or so cheap, either absolutely or in terms of wastage.

Sheet sizes in general dictate careful design if leftovers ('offcuts') are to be minimized. Many small and medium-sized suppliers sell offcuts of their own; these are sometimes even taken from unusual types of board, for example those veneered with special timbers. It may be worthwhile to explore these.

All boards should ideally be stored flat. Failing that, keep them as near vertically on edge as possible. If they lean to one side, they may warp, perhaps permanently.

Lastly, plywood and all veneered and plastic-faced boards carry the risk of splintering out the veneer or facing when sawing, especially across the grain. The damage will occur on the side from which the saw-teeth leave the board. You can minimize it by using the right sawblade, by cutting at the shallowest possible angle, and — if you have the patience — by scoring through the veneer with a knife first.

APPROACHES

If you want to work in wood, you will have to equip yourself properly. This means organizing yourself in three distinct ways. A furniture-maker needs the space in which to undertake a project, plus the facilities with which to handle it; a sensible way of setting about it; and the tools with which to execute it properly.

THE WORKSHOP

It is almost impossible to make furniture (or indeed practice most other branches of woodwork) without a workshop: in other words, an area which is dedicated to no other purpose. In the absence of one, you may be prey to interruptions, which will sap your concentration and thus lower the standard of your work. You may have to clear away completely at the end of each session, which is time-consuming and again opposes any continuity of approach; you may have nowhere to keep your tools, which may mean they risk loss or damage; you will probably be unable to buy machines of any size; and routine procedures — sanding, for example — may be extremely difficult.

The workshop space should be as big as possible, for ease in handling large pieces of timber and board. It should have good light, artificial and preferably natural as well; you should make sure, too, that dust cannot escape into living areas.

The shop should also be as dry as possible, both to protect tools from rust and because damp timber will create many problems after a job is over. In addition, an environment that is too cold can make quite a few gluing and finishing operations more difficult.

As for equipment, the first requirement is a bench. In essence, this is a table for working on. Although fixed machinery in many cases makes it unnecessary, it is still nowhere near obsolete — especially for the amateur. It must be extremely reliable — strong and rigid; the top should be very flat, and deep enough (from front to back) to accommodate your work — but not so deep you cannot reach across. It should be a convenient height.

Excellent benches can be bought. If you make one instead, it is usually best to follow or adapt an exisiting design, because it will probably incorporate many sensible details. However, sheets of board can be used to achieve — more cheaply and simply — the stability which is customarily ensured by heavy joints in solid hardwood.

Common features of a workshop bench are a recess (a 'tool well') in the rear of the top, where tools and other items can be left without projecting above the level of the work surface; shelves or drawers, or both, under the top; and two vices. These vices are very important, because holding work firmly and conveniently is half the secret of a successful job. Often there is a proprietary metal vice fitted to the front of the bench, and another at one end whose purpose is to clamp pieces end-to-end, where necessary, in conjunction with a 'bench-dog'. This is a square wood, metal or plastic peg which fits into one of a series of holes in the bench top, so the workpiece pushes against it.

Frequently the leg or upright at the opposite end from the front vice has holes drilled in it. A round peg can be inserted into any of these to support the far end of a piece too long to be held in the front vice alone.

A variety of other devices have been invented to position and keep work where you want it, while allowing the free execution of whatever task you are performing. A few are available in the shops, but many more exist only as individual ideas (often in magazines and books) for you to copy or adapt. Some make use of an existing bench vice, and some are fixed to or through the bench-top. The unceasing flow of such inventions testifies to the frequency and variety of the problems encountered. Some are for steadying thin boards while planing, some are for gripping intricate carvings, some are for holding cylindrical pieces, and so on. In certain cases — and this is true of other tasks as well — engineer's tools and equipment may provide answers.

Despite all these aids, ripping (sawing timber along the grain) and working large boards are usually too awkward to do on the bench, even with simple tools. An invaluable accessory here is a pair of portable sawhorses, on which you can rest the workpiece with plenty of overhang. A sawhorse also comes in handy for heavy cross-cutting (sawing across the grain). However, its legs traditionally slope in two directions at once. If this threatens to present problems when making it, a pair of folding trestles is one fair alternative.

Storage is another basic need: for hand tools, portable power tools, finishing treatments, fixing hardware — and materials, or at least those required for any project in hand. Being systematic

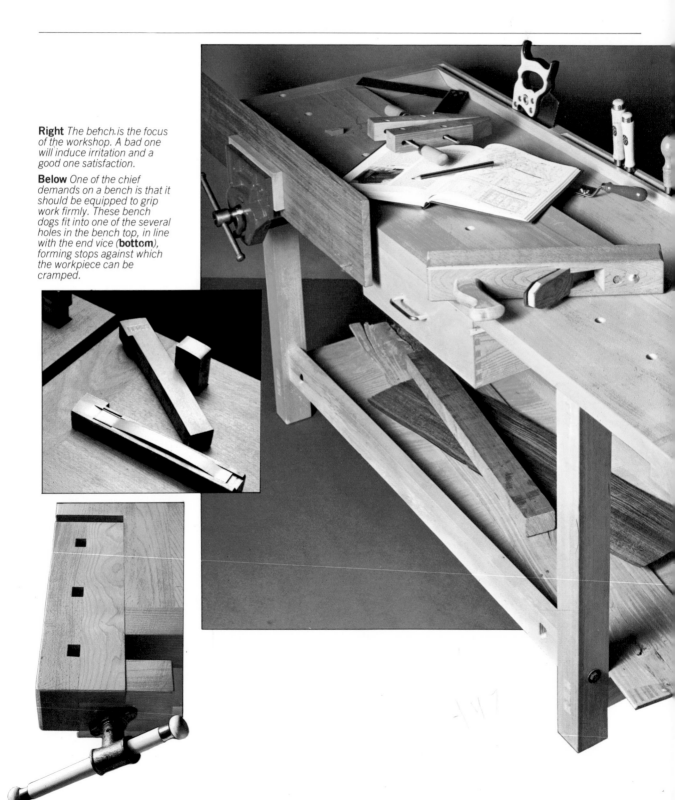

Right *The bench is the focus of the workshop. A bad one will induce irritation and a good one satisfaction.*

Below *One of the chief demands on a bench is that it should be equipped to grip work firmly. These bench dogs fit into one of the several holes in the bench top, in line with the end vice (**bottom**), forming stops against which the workpiece can be cramped.*

Above *The rarely seen vice clamp works by jamming. It fits into holes in the leg or top.*

Below *An impressively long and heavy version of the conventional front vice. This one will hold longish pieces securely along the whole of their length — a common requirement which is not always so easily met.*

saves time spent searching; it can even save money, because it means you are less likely to buy something you already possess. A project can also be planned more efficiently if you can readily see what you have in stock.

A variety of odds and ends which have come or may come in handy will also demand storage space. Part of the craftsman's job is to seek, recognize and even invent whatever will make his work better and more efficient — whether it be a special hinge, a plywood template for cutting a curve, or an individual finishing recipe. If he depends solely on what he can get in the shops, he is neglecting the fundamental skill of thinking creatively around a problem.

It is also a waste to throw away any but the smallest offcuts of timber and board, except perhaps in a periodic clear-out. Many of them will find a use — but, again, not unless you can locate them. Short pieces of wood are best racked horizontally, with their ends pointing towards you.

Health and safety

Do not ignore safety. Many woodworking tools are dangerous. Specific precautions, especially when using machinery, are detailed in the appropriate parts of this book; but the rule is to pace yourself and concentrate. No one has ever caused an accident while fully alert to all that he or she was doing. Adopting this outlook heightens standards in general, too.

While the substances used in the average woodworking shop carry few risks to health, especially for those who are only in contact with them for relatively short periods, some people are affected by the dust from certain timbers. The particles can be very fine indeed. If you feel ill while working with a particular wood or woods, consider the alternatives. You may be able to use another material, or another process (for example, planing instead of sanding) which will create less dust or no dust. Alternatively, different types of protection are available; they range from a simple mask of flexible metal which covers mouth and nose, with an elastic strap and a replaceable soft filter pad, to an expensive but highly effective 'air helmet'. In addition, there are extraction systems for small as well as large shops. Essentially large vacuum-cleaners, these will not eliminate dust from the air completely.

Workbench

A workbench must be sturdy and stable. It should also be sized to accommodate the individual worker (especially in terms of height) and the work that will be done on it. It should include as much storage and as many clamping facilities as possible. Another common feature is a 'well' at the rear, in which tools can be placed so that they do not protrude above the level of the work surface; some benches, however, are designed so that you can work from both sides.

Traditionally, benches are made from hardwoods like beech, and many such excellent models can be bought. But they are expensive, and a home-made version can be detailed to your exact requirements. This one, designed by Peter Milne, is made from chipboard and ordinary softwood. The chipboard provides the weight and rigidity of the classic pattern at a far lower cost.

The work surface is made from edge-glued pieces of softwood, while most of the underframe is simply screwed together. The heavy front rail is doweled and bolted. The work surface and tool well are removable.

A particularly useful feature is the absence of framing underneath the front of the work surface. This means items can be clamped to it easily.

*This bench is fitted with two woodworking vices from the variety available (**above**).*

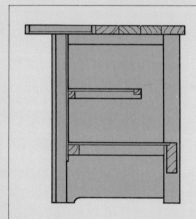

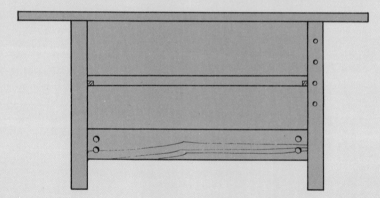

*Plans for bench (**above** and **right**) are not dimensioned; dimensions will depend on the space available and the preferred working height.*

*Square mortices are cut in the top to accept bench dogs (**right**), while the holes in the right-hand leg accept a peg which supports the far end of any long piece gripped in the front vice at the left-hand side (**above right**).*

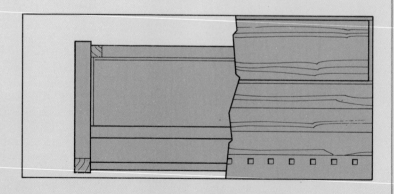

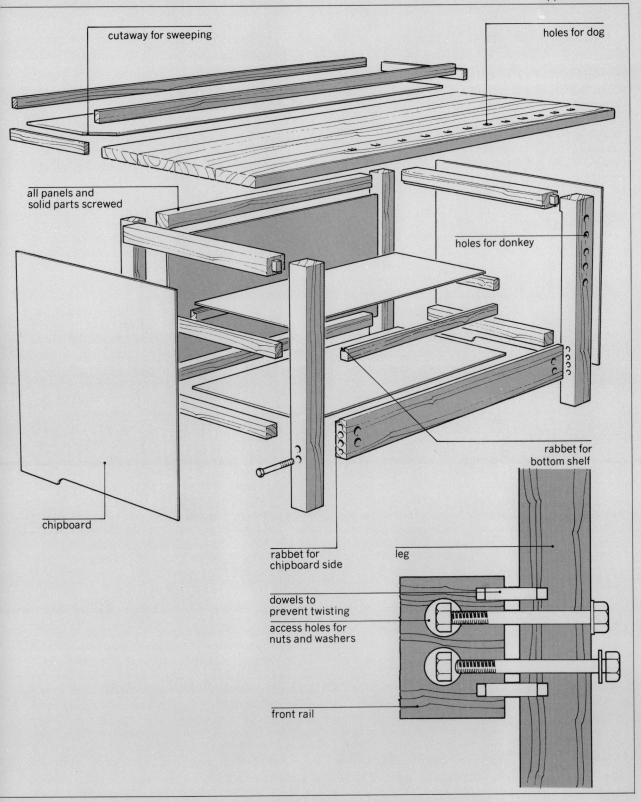

cutaway for sweeping

holes for dog

all panels and
solid parts screwed

holes for donkey

chipboard

rabbet for
bottom shelf

rabbet for
chipboard side

leg

dowels to
prevent twisting

access holes for
nuts and washers

front rail

DESIGN AND PLANNING

Design enters into every stage of work — from choosing a project to the final steps in finishing. It is not a separate activity, limited to preliminary work on a drawing-board.

Some people, in fact, aim to let each piece evolve — in size, shape, structure, color, texture and even function — rather than proceeding according to a definite plan. Often the figure and other characteristics of the timber itself are allowed to suggest final details.

Others start with a partly formed idea and perhaps a rough sketch. Still others, including most professional designer-craftsmen, make formal and complete scale drawings before starting, leaving little or nothing to future decision.

What counts is the finished result, and the different approaches frequently indicate different outlooks and even different beliefs. But even the systematic approach is only a technique of expression. The creative process itself can start anywhere.

It can start, for example, at the end. Perhaps you have been wanting to try your hand at stenciling, and are thinking of making a piece which invites a repeated motif. Suppose, too, that the living-room always seems to be carpeted with toys, and you have a limited budget because you have just bought a portable circular saw. One project that would naturally spring from these conditions might be a painted toybox made mainly from chipboard. The cheap material, best cut with a circular saw, is a natural choice for the job because it will be painted — enlivened rather than devalued by the stenciled pattern from which you began.

In other words, every detail of a finished piece can be determined by any number of needs, wants and habits: by workshop space, by comfort, by skill, by tools. The more of such considerations you list, the fuller the brief you will give yourself, the easier your task is — and the better the job will be. What really matters is that the details should be deliberate, and not just included by accident or default.

Putting the design on paper helps to ensure that. For extremely straightforward projects, a clear sketch with annotated measurements may be adequate. For anything more complex, however, a proper scale drawing is more or less vital — particularly because it will starkly reveal points you have not considered.

Technical drawing has reached a very high level of sophistication, but the basics are well within the reach of even a beginner. Textbooks will tell you that a drawing must be executed in certain ways — but in reality it is only a tool. If it is for your own use, the important thing is that it should tell you clearly what you need to know.

The first essential is a truly square or rectangular board, and a T-square whose crossbar locates over its edge so you can draw parallel lines — or else a 'parallel-motion' board: one with an integral sliding straight-edge which serves the same purpose. A triangle, a scale-ruler, a pair of compasses, and a pencil and eraser are the other most essential items of equipment.

The aim is to produce accurately scaled drawings — usually at 1:4 (imperial) or 1:5 (if using the metric system) in the case of furniture. This means that 1in on the planned object is always represented by ¼in on the drawing (2mm represents 1cm).

But drawing to scale can represent quite a few complications and invite many refinements. The basic procedure is to draw a view from above (a 'plan'), a view from in front (a 'front elevation') and a view from the side (a 'side elevation') — plus 'sections' where necessary: drawings which show how the object looks if cut open vertically or horizontally. Because a plan combines the horizontal dimensions of the front and side elevations, you can work more quickly by drawing elevations respectively above or below the plan, and to one side of it.

If, however, a drawing is comprehensible without all these aspects, omit one of them. If it needs a further section, or a full-size or half-size drawing of a particular detail, add that. If you only need to draw half the object, stop there. If it helps you to draw the outline in a bright color, do so.

Moreover, there is no point in wasting time drawing small details — for example, the exact widths of grooves or tenons — if they can easily be settled later and do not affect anything else. In any case, certain features, such as the exact profiles of moldings and shapes of handles, are sometimes best decided once the item is partly made and you can see how the various alternatives will look.

Curved shapes, apart from arcs (parts of circles) and combinations of arcs, must be drawn full-size at some stage, because you cannot use a scale drawing as a pattern from which to cut them. Arcs can be drawn with a pair of compasses.

Beware, too, of angles. If a desk measures 2ft (600mm) horizontally from front to back, that will be the size shown on the plan drawing. But a sloping top — shown on the side elevation — will measure more than 2ft. If the sides of that top were angled inwards too, they would be longer still.

School geometry, however, will get you by in most situations. Where it fails, an elementary textbook will soon tell you how to draw most shapes you are likely to need, such as hexagons and ovals. Indeed, a short session of experimenting with a ruler and compasses will often prove very useful.

If you have an aptitude for perspective drawing (easier to acquire than most people believe, the secret being simply to practice and to strive for accuracy), you will probably find it most helpful in visualizing and comparing your ideas. If not, experience is your best guide to what will work and what will not.

The other point about formal drawings is, of course, that they make it easier to buy supplies,

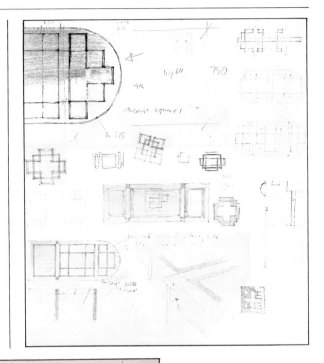

*First thoughts (**top**) should be as free-flowing as possible; you never know where the right idea will come from. But they will usually need harsh refining before the item is completed (**left** and **above**).*

because you know exactly what you will need.

In addition, the nature of timber dictates particular methods of construction and working. Reflected in the design, these in turn partly dictate the classic method of planning a woodworking job.

Because the strength of timber is highly directional, its 'length' is not necessarily its longest dimension; rather, it denotes the direction in which the grain runs. A piece 6in (150mm) wide by 1in (25mm) long will break far more easily than a comparable piece 1in wide by 6in long. The former is entirely composed of 'short grain', a term applied to any timber measuring less along the grain than across it.

Short grain is, therefore, to be avoided in all but exceptional circumstances. Where lines meet at right-angles, or nearly so, and where they are

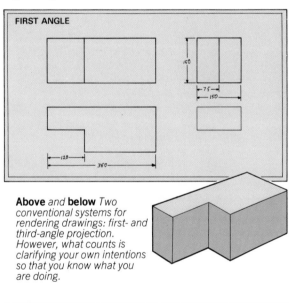

Above and **below** Two conventional systems for rendering drawings: first- and third-angle projection. However, what counts is clarifying your own intentions so that you know what you are doing.

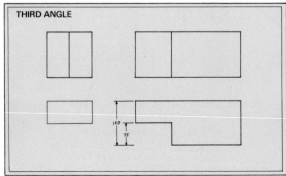

Reading drawings
A drawing is a tool. Although professionals represent objects in certain conventional ways, these vary widely. You need adopt only what you find useful, and you can adapt when the need arises. Besides, any drawing by the home craftsman is almost certain to be superseded in the workshop. Several details of this table were changed and several expanded after the drawing was made. Nevertheless, it is worth understanding the basic idea, since a clear drawing will make sense of a complex project.

comments on materials, finishes and fixing

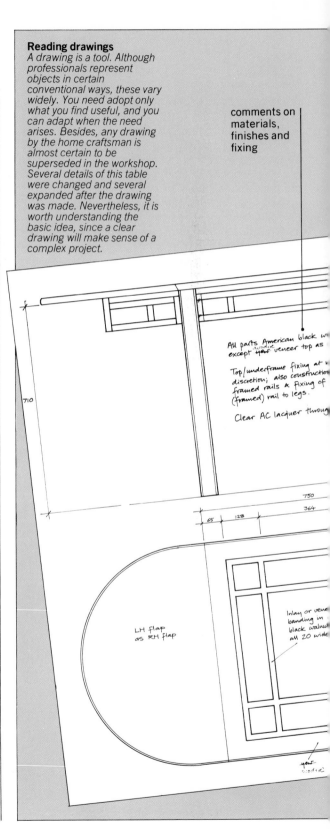

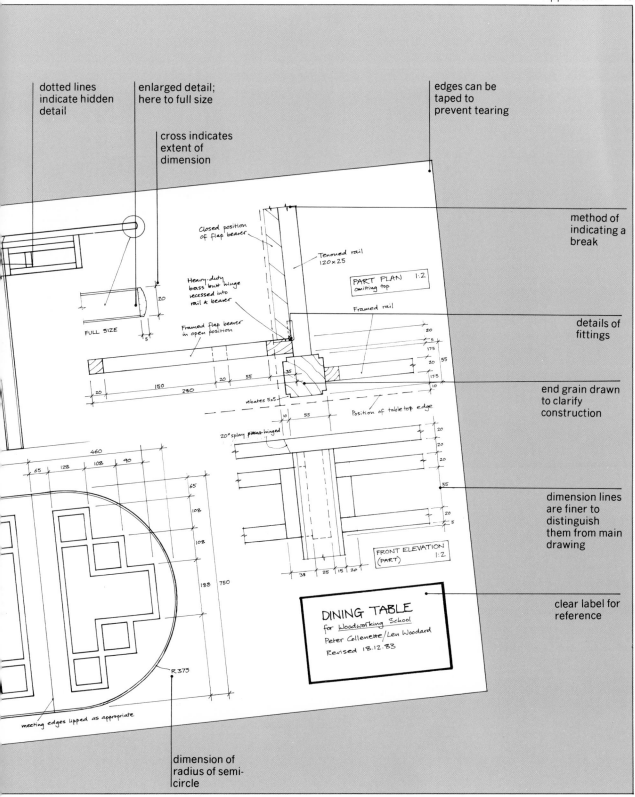

dotted lines indicate hidden detail

enlarged detail; here to full size

cross indicates extent of dimension

edges can be taped to prevent tearing

method of indicating a break

details of fittings

end grain drawn to clarify construction

dimension lines are finer to distinguish them from main drawing

clear label for reference

dimension of radius of semi-circle

Closed position of flap bearer

Tenoned rail 120 x 25

PART PLAN 1:2 omitting top

Heavy-duty brass butt hinge recessed into rail & bearer

Framed rail

FULL SIZE

Framed flap bearer in open position

20

5

150   20   55

280

20

rebates 5x5

35

20
5
17.5
20   55
17.5
10

Position of table top edge

10   55

20°splay piano hinged

20
20
20

55

20

FRONT ELEVATION (PART)   1:2

460

65   128   108   90

65

108

108

108

188   750

35   25   15   20

R 375

meeting edges lipped as appropriate

DINING TABLE
for Woodworking School
Peter Collenette/Len Woodard
Revised 18.12.83

Design considerations

In woodwork, as in other areas, design is essentially problem-solving: a two-fold process which involves first understanding what the problems are, and then integrating their solutions. These illustrations (and on pages 54-5) show the particular approach of Peter Milne, a professional furniture designer who runs his own workshop. They are grouped to illuminate four common problem areas: the availability of machines and skills; material; cost and form.

Available machines and skills

The hall table (**1**) was designed around the sizes of cutters available for the router, used here to create stopped grooves.

Skill is, among other things, a matter of coordinating construction. This reception desk for GECO International (**2**) was designed so that it could be sub-assembled to avoid extensive gluing up at the last minute, and to ensure that all its components fitted correctly.

3

Materials
The straightforward yet sensitive use of a quality material is displayed in this elegant table (3). If you possess a full understanding of their qualities, materials can direct the design process.

Good design also involves using the right materials for each job. An example is the combination of woods used in this octagonal table made for Wrexham Lager Brewery (4). The top is white oak with a star-pattern veneer, chosen for its appearance and smooth finish; the lipping is brown oak to resist chipping; and the base is chipboard, chosen for constructional soundness.

4

steeply curved, the designer almost always endeavors — often unconsciously — to see how the shape can be made in a way which will exploit the strength in the long grain instead. This may involve using two or more components, such as a leg and a horizontal 'rail'; bending a piece; making it up by lamination; or cutting it from an artificial board — to name only four basic alternatives.

The point is that the woodworker automatically thinks of wood in lengths, not blocks. Cutting a piece to length is distinct from reducing it in 'section' (width or thickness or both).

After completing a design, therefore, the maker groups together (at least mentally) all com-

ponents of the same wood, then those of the same and similar sectional size, and finally those of the same length. He may note what other operations need to be performed on each, for example grooving, drilling and so on. He groups man-made boards by type and thickness (which cannot of course be reduced), followed by length and width.

The result, transferred to paper, is a 'bill of materials'. This enables the maker to work out how much of each material is needed, then to rip and plane the timber to the right sectional size — in batches of like width and thickness if that is more efficient — before finally crosscutting each piece to length. The procedure can be adapted for

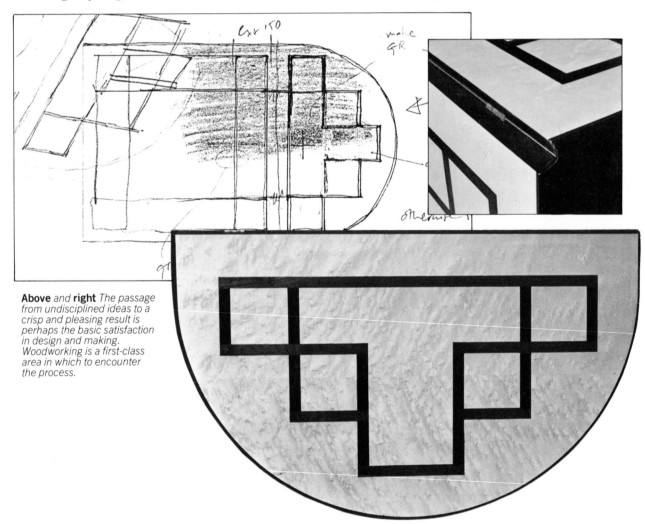

Above and **right** The passage from undisciplined ideas to a crisp and pleasing result is perhaps the basic satisfaction in design and making. Woodworking is a first-class area in which to encounter the process.

buying and working dimension stock ready-sawn or planed by the supplier. For accurate work, ready-planed material will usually need to be planed again, and a consequent allowance made.

It is usual to plane one face of each piece flat first, marking that as the 'face side', and then to plane an adjacent edge exactly 'square' (at right-angles) to it and equally flat before marking it as the 'face edge'. These surfaces establish a basis for further work, and all marking should ideally be done from them. Boards are dealt with separately.

It is usually sensible to do as much further work as possible, for example, cutting joints (in effect making up a 'kit'), before assembling any parts. Many projects do in fact break down into three quite distinct stages, namely, cutting, assembly and finishing, with each one completed before the next is started; but this is by no means always the case. Sometimes measurements must be taken from assembled structures, and often components must be finished, or at least sanded, before assembly because they will be too awkward to tackle afterwards. Sometimes, too, glue-setting times — like the drying times of finishes — impose their own schedule.

Personality will play its part in deciding exactly how things are done. But the methodical approach is the one used by professionals.

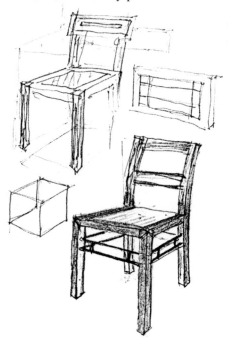

Above and **left** Chairs are notoriously difficult to visualize, because they often incorporate compound angles and because of the elevated viewpoint from which they are usually seen: neither is easy to catch in a drawing. At left are a few of the sketches which preceded the item above.

5

Design considerations: cost

Costing is an ever-present consideration for the professional designer and maker. For the amateur, too, an awareness of this factor can be helpful, because it encourages more concise work. Careful costing implies making the best use not only of materials and tools but also of time.

The oak table with a slate inset, weighing several hundred pounds (**5**), and the small jewellery box weighing only a few ounces (**6**), actually cost about the same amount to produce. Oak was chosen for the table because it involves relatively little wastage. The small box was made of English walnut and ebony; it has wooden hinges and a magnetic locking system.

Another design feature resulting from cost and time limits is the 'gap detail', exemplified by the blue line in this laminated table-top (**7**). The idea of this is to make a feature of something that would be too difficult to execute perfectly: in this case, the glued joints.

6

7

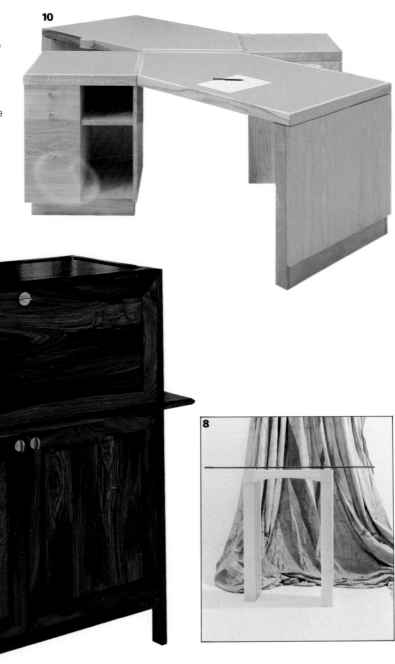

Form

*These examples owe much of their design quality to Peter Milne's interest in what he calls 'the dynamics of form'. The calm lines of the table (**8**) are achieved by delicately resting a 12mm glass top on a sycamore frame. The writing-desk in rosewood (**9**) displays a tension by cutting one shape into another. The lino-topped partner's desk in ash (**10**) has a plastic quality and sense of movement not traditionally associated with cabinet-making.*

Joints

There can be no definitive list of woodworking joints, because new variants are constantly developed to meet particular situations. A few of the commonest are shown here to give an idea of the range that is possible and indeed necessary.

Factors dictating the shape of a joint include its appearance, the tools available, and of course the configuration of the pieces being used. It is worth remembering that, in general, a joint's strength depends partly on the area of its glued meeting surfaces.

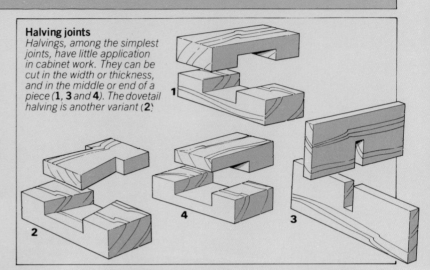

Halving joints
Halvings, among the simplest joints, have little application in cabinet work. They can be cut in the width or thickness, and in the middle or end of a piece (1, 3 and 4). The dovetail halving is another variant (2).

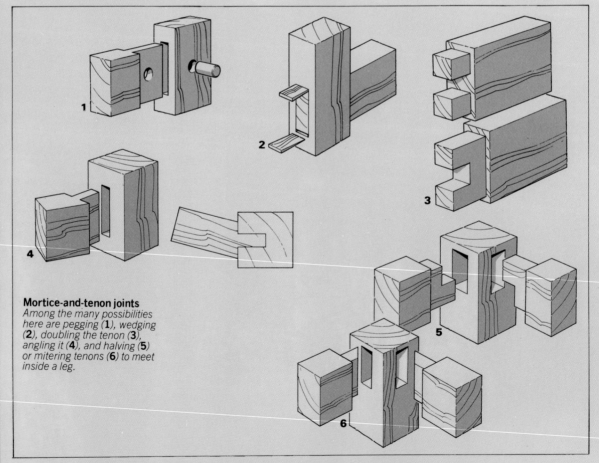

Mortice-and-tenon joints
Among the many possibilities here are pegging (1), wedging (2), doubling the tenon (3), angling it (4), and halving (5) or mitering tenons (6) to meet inside a leg.

Panel joints

These joints for connecting panels can all be used on solid timber as well as man-made boards, provided the grain runs the same way on each piece. That will prevent splitting due to moisture movement. Housings are shown far right.

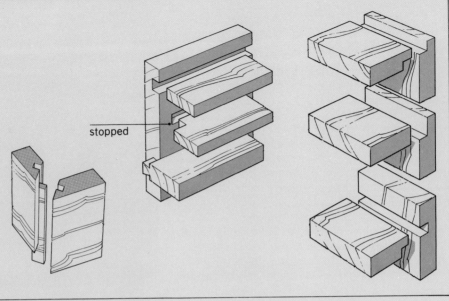

stopped

Corner joints for solid timber

The dovetail (through, 1, or lap, 2) and the comb joint (3) are rightfully classic. The keyed miter (above) is useful for the odd light job. A miter alone is almost never strong enough.

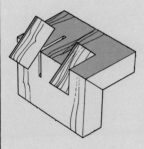

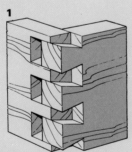

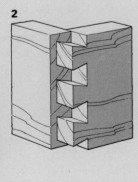

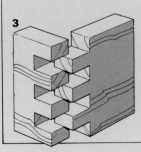

Bridle joints

The bridle is a basic joint, and in the appropriate situation it is indispensable. It can be pegged with dowels like a mortice-and-tenon.

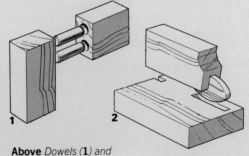

Above *Dowels (1) and biscuits (2) are two ways of reinforcing butt joints in frames or panel structures. Both provide considerable strength.*

TOOLING UP

Of all the factors which determine the type of work you do, available tools are by far the most influential. Power tools and machines can accomplish very few, if any, tasks that hand tools cannot. Nevertheless, they work so much faster and in such different ways that they effectively provide an entirely different set of options and require quite separate attention. Like man-made boards, they frequently allow and dictate their own constructional methods.

In theory, the beginning woodworker nowadays need acquire almost no hand tools at all, starting instead with a set of small power tools or even fixed machines. In machine shops it is common to see a huge bandsaw started up and run for five seconds just to cut a piece of molding in half. Few, however, will want to go quite so far at the start; and besides, it is often necessary to reach for a hand plane to 'clean up' a joint that does not quite fit — while some hand tools (the tape measure, for example) are basic to any kit.

Power tools mean simplifying a job so they can tackle it, because hand tools — especially chisels and gouges — do have certain unique capabilities. This simplification takes time. Besides, hand tools can be moved about quickly, and will often perform a 'one-off' task in less time than it would take to set up a machine for the purpose. The professional will 'design out' such one-off tasks, so that the machines can be exploited to the full; for the amateur, time is not necessarily money.

If power tools make their own demands, however, so do hand tools. Woodworkers who have no others will find all sorts of operations just too awkward; in particular, they will probably be restricted to buying dimension timber if they are unprepared or unable to get pieces specially cut.

Portable power tools can accomplish a great deal if you buy good ones with a reasonable capacity, and for certain jobs they are unrivaled. A power jigsaw, hand-held, is often the only tool for cutting a shape out of the middle of a board that is too big for the fixed bandsaw. A portable circular saw is invaluable for cutting large sheets into manageable pieces, especially if you have no table-saw — or no one to help you maneuver such sheets through it.

All power tools, however, have their limitations; chiefly in accuracy and in the size of material

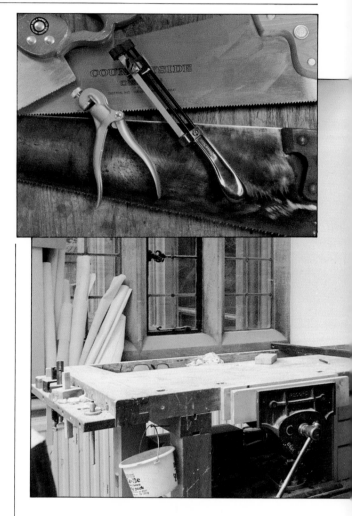

they can deal with. These limitations are still present even when they are turned into fixed machines, as most can be, by means of 'tables' and stands. For example, some power planes can be fitted upside-down into purpose-made mountings, forming miniature if rather dangerous versions of the larger jointer. But they will still only plane narrow pieces of wood.

Some such conversions can represent good value; everything depends on the amount and type of work expected of them. If they are unequal to their tasks, large fixed machines are the answer. They are expensive, but they certainly make woodwork easier. Of course, that may not be your aim.

Left *Tools for keeping saws in top condition — just one of the ancillary skills a cabinet-maker can learn and may even enjoy.*

Below *The serious woodworker will make quite sure of obtaining the right tools and equipment essential for good work.*

Many people say that buying cheap tools is a false economy. They are right. Even a relatively costly item, such as a jack plane or router, should be giving faithful service when the money spent on it has long been forgotten — but a cut-price one is likely to be causing trouble instead. So, especially if your budget is tight, buy a good tool once a month rather than a cheap tool once a fortnight. You can do excellent work with only a few tools if you know how to maintain and use them. You will also buy more wisely if you allow yourself time to discover the tools of which you most feel the lack, and exactly what you will require of them.

Luckily, too, the products of the leading manufacturers — certainly their hand-tool ranges — are on the whole thoroughly well-made and reliable. There is no need for an intensive search unless you happen to want something that is particularly unusual.

However, there is no denying that tools — especially hand tools — can arouse remarkable passions. Standardized patterns are a relatively recent development, and they cannot please everyone. Each has his or her own preferences and working habits, and these make demands that can sometimes only be satisfied by very particular models or variants — or even by home-made tools and other devices.

A browse through the shop or catalog of a tool dealer (new or secondhand) will almost always be repaid — in fascination if not in immediate usefulness. But there is sometimes a temptation to become a tool-collector instead of a craftsman, and it bears repeating that using simple tools properly will produce work of more value than using fancy tools ineptly.

Sub-contracting

You may easily develop a design that calls for one or more operations outside your capacity: large-scale veneering, for example, or turning, or molding complex profiles. It may even be only the amount of work involved that seems too daunting to tackle.

Either way, if the details concerned matter enough not to design them out, there is no reason why you should not do what many professionals do: pay someone else for the work. You may be agreeably surprised, or at least not deterred, by the quotation you are given. Almost any woodworking job, from rabbeting a piece of plywood to making up a complex pattern in marquetry, can be contracted out in this way.

Some districts are better in this respect than others, and it may take some searching before you locate what you want, but it is worth a try. Many timber merchants cut boards to size for a fee; this can save you trouble, and guarantee accuracy which you might find it hard to achieve yourself. Some also offer other machining services, as do many small-to-medium joinery and furniture manufacturers. Indeed, quite a few components — notably hardwood cabinet doors and traditional types of leg — are available ready-made for the amateur as well as the trade.

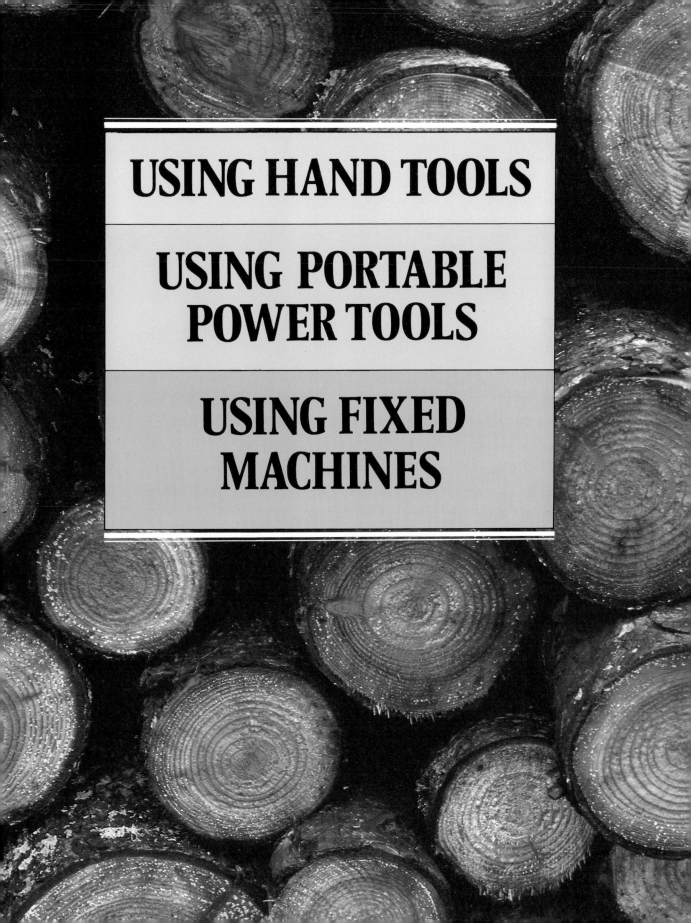

USING HAND TOOLS

USING PORTABLE POWER TOOLS

USING FIXED MACHINES

USING HAND TOOLS

T here is no denying that hand tools usually require harder physical work than power tools and machines, and often a higher degreee of skill and concentration in achieving accuracy. Nevertheless, they are assured of a place in every small workshop by their adaptability and their relative cheapness. In many cases they offer the quickest solution because they require little or no setting up — and much fine cabinet-making still calls for a great many operations which no machine can tackle.

Lastly, most people enjoy using them.

Setting out

The familiar steel tape measure is invaluable. The smaller sizes are more manageable and thus a better buy if you are only going to use them for cabinet work. But a tape is not quite as accurate as the traditional folding rule, once always of boxwood but now made in plastic as well.

Marking from a tape or rule with a pencil or even a knife can, however, introduce inaccuracy. A marking gauge has a sliding 'stock' which is pressed against an edge or surface, while its sharp point 'scribes' a line on the material. If the same setting is used, for example, to mark out both halves of a joint, they will automatically match — and several operations (measuring, 'ticking off' the measurements, and squaring them across the pieces) will be bypassed.

A cutting gauge has a small blade, wedged in position, instead of a point, so it will mark cleanly across the grain without tearing. A mortice gauge has two points, adjustable in relation to each other as well as to the stock, with which both sides of a mortice and its matching tenon are marked out at once. A pencil gauge has a hole for a pencil, instead of a point.

Most gauges are of wood, but you can get metal ones. Patterns are even obtainable which have four separate points, so that you can preserve four separate settings during a job — a good idea because re-adjustment destroys the consistency which is the chief idea behind using a gauge in the first place.

A plain, steel straight-edge will come in very useful if you have one, but it is not cheap. A straight-edged piece of plywood or blockboard, ideally but not necessarily faced with plastic laminate, is a better substitute than a length of solid

Back saws
*A selection of back saws, ranging from bead or gent's saws (**1** and **2**) and even finer-toothed patterns (**3** and **4**) to the dovetail saw (**5**). At least one back saw is essential for fine cabinet-work. As with any tool, comfort in handling is an important factor in choosing.*

timber because it is unlikely to warp. These instruments can gauge flatness and straightness.

So can a square — whose normal use is, however, in marking cuts at right angles to an edge or face. Plain ones are L-shaped, usually with a brass-faced wooden stock and a steel 'blade': small 'engineer's' squares, made entirely of metal, are much used by wood machinists — for checking rather than marking. A miter square has its blade at 45° to the stock. A combination square has a sliding metal stock with one face at 90° and one at 45°. You can use the sliding facility, like that on a gauge, to take dimensions without measuring, but the instrument is more easily damaged than traditional squares are. The sliding bevel resembles a square but can be set to any angle.

Knives

On the whole, a knife or special sharp-pointed scriber is better for marking than a pencil because it gives a thinner and clearer line. All sorts of small knives are available; some blades have to be sharpened, others replaced. Marking knives are meant for that specific job, while many other types are used especially in veneering and carving.

The drawknife has a handle at both ends. Especially associated with country woodworkers, who have used it for such jobs as shaping chair components, it is simply gripped in both hands and drawn along the timber towards the worker. It is capable of great precision when skillfully used.

The inshave is a drawknife bent into a U-shape, traditionally employed for hollowing chair seats.

Saws

Saws for hand use fall into three categories — of which 'hand saws', confusingly enough, form only one. Although some modern types blur these distinctions, saws in general can be discussed in more or less their order of appearance during a job; that is, working from the coarsest to the finest (and, incidentally, from ripping to crosscutting). The deciding factor is the number of teeth per inch (TPI) or 'points', which increases as the length and width of the saw decrease.

Some modern saws have their blades coated with 'non-stick' plastic, and possess plastic instead of wooden handles. Special 'hard-point' teeth are also found, introduced largely for cutting man-made boards.

Hand saws

A rip saw is, as its name declares, for ripping. This can be quite heavy work — but hand-ripping may still be a better alternative than, on the one hand, having timber ripped to order or, on the other, investing in a bandsaw or table saw.

Apart from its coarseness — 4½TPI is normal — a rip saw is distinguished from all others by the shape of its teeth: they are square across, with their leading edges at right-angles to the blade, so they cut with a chisel action.

A crosscut saw's teeth, on the other hand, slope both backwards and forwards, and their points are angled to sever the fibers of the wood. It has 7 or 8TPI, and can be used for ripping too — though it is naturally rather slower at that than a rip saw.

A panel saw has 10TPI, of the crosscut type. It is the nearest thing to a general-purpose hand saw.

The occasional pattern of hand saw can now be bought with fine teeth at the front and coarser teeth behind them. Saws which cut backwards as well as forwards are another development, as are 'universal' teeth — a compromise pattern, designed for both ripping and crosscutting.

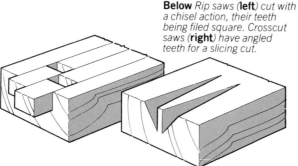

Below Rip saws (**left**) cut with a chisel action, their teeth being filed square. Crosscut saws (**right**) have angled teeth for a slicing cut.

Back saws

To be manageable enough for fine cuts, a saw needs to be short, light and thin-bladed. But a thin blade buckles more easily when pushed forward. Most fine saws, therefore, have a 'back' — a U-shaped strip of metal which fits over the upper edge of the blade to keep it rigid. This of course means you cannot cut timber which is thicker than the distance between teeth and back, although saws with removable backs are available.

A tenon saw is so called because of its suitability for cutting tenons, but it is generally useful for all precise work. It has 12 to 14TPI, while the similar dovetail saw is even finer with 18 to 22TPI. The

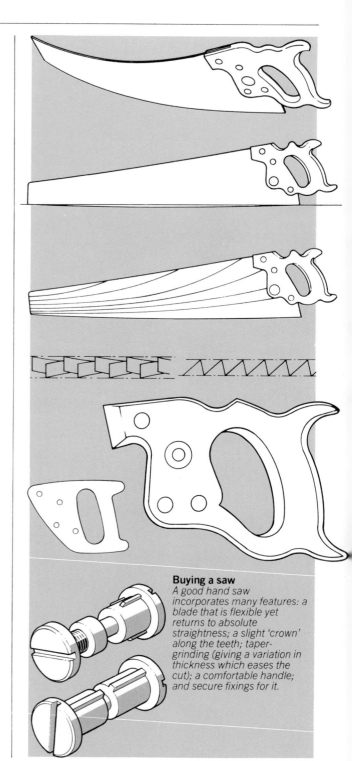

Buying a saw
A good hand saw incorporates many features: a blade that is flexible yet returns to absolute straightness; a slight 'crown' along the teeth; taper-grinding (giving a variation in thickness which eases the cut); a comfortable handle; and secure fixings for it.

Sawing
Sawing is a skill in its own right. The stance should be firm and the shoulder behind the saw (1). The index finger may be used as a guide (2). Note how the cut levels off (3).

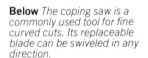

Below *The coping saw is a commonly used tool for fine curved cuts. Its replaceable blade can be swiveled in any direction.*

latter may have a pistol-grip handle, open at the bottom, which is easier on the hand with such a small tool.

Smaller still, however, is the bead saw, at 32TPI — also known as the gent's saw because it was once an upper-class hobbyist's tool. This is available with its handle offset to one side, a useful feature where your hand would otherwise get in the way. Like the smallest of all — the jeweler's, razor or slitting saw, which has so many points that their number is not specified — the bead saw has a cylindrical handle that protrudes straight back from the blade.

Small saws have less 'set' than large ones: that is, their teeth are not bent sideways to the same extent. This, coupled with the thinness of the steel itself, makes for a narrower cut or 'kerf'. Such fineness makes accuracy a lot easier to achieve.

Saws for curved work
Hand and back saws are only for straight cuts. Curves demand other tools. There are two groups: compass and keyhole saws, and frame saws.

The compass saw is, in effect, a very small hand saw with an extremely narrow blade. The keyhole saw, or padsaw, is smaller still, with a straight (instead of pistol-grip) handle from which the blade can be removed. The 'nest of saws' consists of a pistol-grip handle with three interchangeable blades. Sometimes, too, a keyhole-saw blade can be fitted into a handle which normally takes replaceable knife blades.

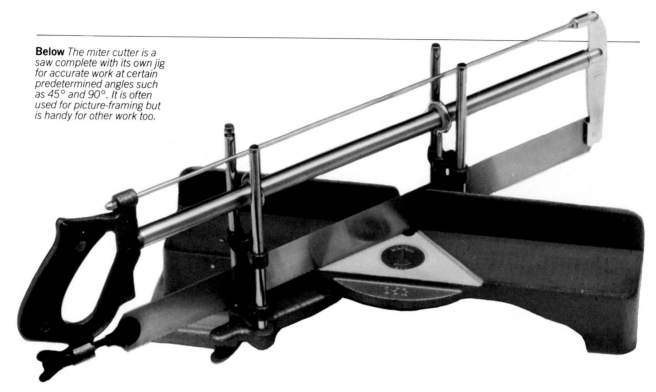

Below *The miter cutter is a saw complete with its own jig for accurate work at certain predetermined angles such as 45° and 90°. It is often used for picture-framing but is handy for other work too.*

These saws may come in handy at any time. Naturally, however, the narrow blade necessary to get round curves also buckles more easily than the wider blade on a hand or back saw. An ancient solution to this problem is to fit the narrow blade into a sprung frame which keeps it continuously under tension — 'stretched' — along its length. It will then flex less easily, just as a taut elastic band will not readily deflect.

A bow saw has a metal frame if it is meant for heavy work, such as cutting logs, but a wooden frame when fine blades are to be fitted. It is tensioned ('strained') by twisting a length of twine which runs between its two side pieces. It must be gripped with one hand at either end.

A coping or scroll saw, the most generally used frame saw, has a light metal frame; the extremely narrow blade is tensioned by turning the saw's protruding handle, and the tool must be held with both hands for a steady cut. The piercing saw is similar, but smaller. On both, the blades are replaceable.

The frame on such a saw does, however, impose a limit on how far in from an edge it will cut. The fretsaw's frame is made deeper than that of a coping saw in order to minimize this problem, but that

in turn makes it more cumbersome — although it has finer teeth. Both types allow the blade to be angled as necessary.

The hacksaw is a metal-framed saw designed to accept metal-cutting blades. It is useful to have at least a small one — a 'junior' hacksaw — for the odd occasion when you need to cut steel, brass, aluminium or the like.

Miter cutters

The woodworker should be able to cut accurately to any line marked. However, the marking itself may be awkward, e.g. on moldings with their variously curved profiles. To overcome this problem and ensure perfect cuts into the bargain, back and frame saws are available ready-fitted into metal mountings which enable the workpiece to be firmly positioned, while the saw cuts at a predetermined angle. Most types offer a setting of 45° or 90°, and some also allow certain other angles to be selected — commonly 60° and 67½°.

These are, of course, ideal for miters. Those who do a lot of mitering, most notably picture-framers, can invest in a miter guillotine; this is not a saw but a heavy, lever-operated knife, which provides even greater consistency and cleanness.

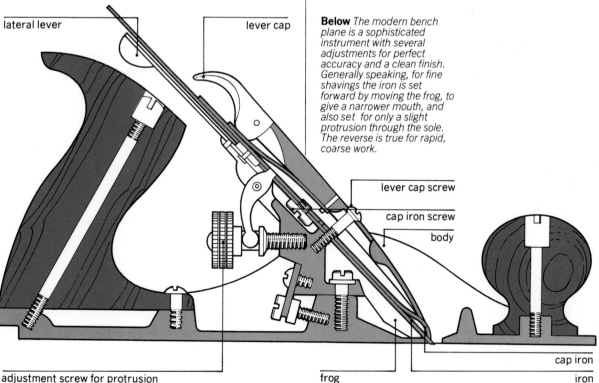

Below *A mitering jig into which a thin-bladed back saw can be inserted. It is also used for clamping the completed miter together while gluing.*

Planes

Like a saw, a plane reduces timber in size. It cuts, however, not with teeth but with a knife called an 'iron', which is mounted in a holder. This can only remove timber a little at a time — but it leaves a far smoother surface than a saw. In other words, it is a finishing tool, usually coming into use only after the saw has done its work.

The plane probably inspires more affection than any other tool, and has certainly evolved more and stranger variants. These can be confusing until you remember that, generally speaking, each has its own particular job.

One exception is the wooden plane. Many types of plane are available in either wood or metal, and — where the wooden variety incorporates all the adjustments that the metal one does — the choice is largely a matter of taste. Some people find that wooden planes allow smoother work and produce a better surface. Others are quite content with metal ones, which, of course, tend to be heavier (usually an advantage). Metal planes nowadays often have plastic instead of wooden handles.

Below *The modern bench plane is a sophisticated instrument with several adjustments for perfect accuracy and a clean finish. Generally speaking, for fine shavings the iron is set forward by moving the frog, to give a narrower mouth, and also set for only a slight protrusion through the sole. The reverse is true for rapid, coarse work.*

lateral lever

lever cap

lever cap screw

cap iron screw

body

cap iron

iron

adjustment screw for protrusion

frog

*The plane iron's alignment is visible in relation to the mouth (**above left**). The frog is moved by means of an adjusting screw (**above**), after loosening and before retightening its retaining screws (**left**).*

Every plane iron is mounted in such a way that it can protrude down through an opening, or 'mouth', in the plane's 'sole'. On simple wooden planes it is simply wedged in position, but on many modern patterns it is surmounted by a 'cap iron' whose function is to deflect the shavings as they come up through the hole. This prevents the iron from catching on them and digging into the surface. A 'lever cap' usually completes the arrangement by clamping the iron and cap iron in place.

Three adjustments, in varying combinations and effected by various means, are possible on most planes. They determine the protrusion of the iron, the size of the mouth (from front to rear) and the iron's lateral alignment. The first two in particular — together with the distance between the tips of the iron and cap iron — determine how thick a shaving is removed.

The harder the material and the more difficult the grain, the smaller the protrusion and the mouth should be. Extraordinary fineness is possible, and it is widely acknowledged among woodworkers that using a good plane, sharp and properly set for the job in hand, offers intense pleasure and satisfaction.

Using a plane
Using a plane takes practice
(**left**). *Check your results (the
tool itself provides a useful
straight-edge) and correct
your stroke as necessary*
(**below** *and* **bottom**).

Bench planes

General-purpose planes for flat surfaces, used
two-handed except in special circumstances, are
called bench planes. Their irons are mounted at
45°. Some metal patterns are available with soles
grooved along their length to reduce friction and
so enable easier cutting.

The jack plane, 14in (350mm) or 15in (375mm)
long, is foremost among them because it can be used for getting a piece straight (truing) as well as
final smoothing. The shorter smoothing plane is
specifically for the latter purpose, not being so
good for truing since it has more tendency to
follow any rise or fall in the surface; while the
larger fore, try and jointer planes — the last as long
as 24in (600mm) — are noble and massive tools of
rather less general usefulness.

Block planes

A block plane, much smaller than a bench plane, is
used one-handed. It has no cap iron; its cutting iron
is mounted bevel-upwards and at a lower angle
than that for a bench plane — usually 20° but on
some models 12°. Lower angles permit easier cutting of difficult materials such as plastic laminates.

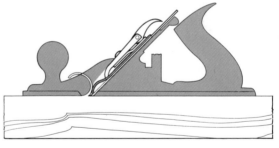

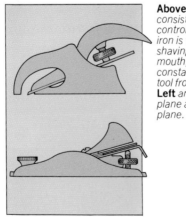

Above *The action of a plane
consists, in effect, of a
controlled splitting. The cap
iron is vital in breaking up the
shaving as it rises through the
mouth, keeping its thickness
constant and preventing the
tool from digging in.*
Left *and* **below** *A bullnose
plane and an ordinary block
plane.*

In fact, one primary job of the block plane is to shave endgrain, plywood edges and the like, although a finely set bench plane will do quite well.

Planes for rebating

A rabbet is a 'step' along the edge of a piece — a one-sided groove. It can be made with certain types of plane, and it is handy to have at least one of these.

The bench rabbet plane is simply a bench plane whose mouth and iron extend the full width of the sole. One variant has small blades which you throw away and replace when blunt — plus a 'fence' which guides it along the workpiece and is adjusted according to the width of rabbet desired. Both types are suitable for general duties as well as rabbeting.

Right *The bench rabbet plane's iron runs the full width of its sole so it can establish the corner of the rabbet. It may also be used for general planing.*

Below *Winding sticks offer a means of checking a surface for flatness. You sight along to see whether their edges are in line.*

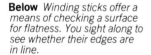

The duplex rabbet plane is a more specialized tool. It has a handle like that on a hand saw, and two alternative positions for the iron: using the one at the front, the plane will cut most of the way into corners (this is known as bullnose work). It also possesses a cutting spur which scores the material ahead of the cutter to prevent tearing when planing across the grain, and an adjustable depth stop (to prevent you from planing too deep) in addition to the side fence.

A bullnose rabbet plane is like a little block plane, but with a full-width mouth and iron which are positioned almost (but not quite) at the very front. A shoulder or shoulder rabbet plane is so called because it can be used to shave the 'shoulders' of tenons and similar joint faces to make them fit better — though it is not quite unique in this. A bullnose shoulder or bullnose shoulder rabbet plane is similar, but follows the bullnose configuration; on some models a second front section can be added to return it to the standard layout, and on some even the first front section can be removed to make a 'chisel plane', which will cut all the way into a corner. None of these planes incorporates a fence.

Generally speaking, the trick of using a rabbet plane is to establish the front end of the rabbet first and gradually work backwards.

Most bench, block and rabbet planes can also be used on their sides when necessary, e.g. to widen a rabbet, since their sides are ground dead square to

Left *There are specialized planes with interchangeable cutters for grooving, rebating and cutting certain mouldings. Though nowadays partly superseded by the power router, they can give excellent results if used with care. They are adjustable for both the position and the depth of the cut.*

Below *When working an edge with any plane, guide the sole with your fingers to help prevent yourself from creating an unintentional bevel.*

their soles. The side rabbet plane, unlike any other, will widen a groove.

Only you can decide which of these tools will earn its keep in your particular workshop.

Grooving and molding planes
Craftsmen formerly had sets of wooden molding planes, each with its sole and iron profiled to cut a particular shape. These can still be bought second-hand, and one or two are still made. The plough plane is a more recent invention which offers a partial substitute. It looks a bit like a catamaran, because of its skeletal body and large accompanying side fence. It can be fitted with one of several interchangeable 'cutters', much narrower than the usual iron, for rabbeting and making grooves. The latter may be square- or round-bottomed. It incorporates a depth stop as well.

A combination plane is similar, except that its cutters come in a greater variety of widths and shapes — and that, like the duplex rabbet plane, it possesses adjustable spurs to allow clean cuts across the grain. Both these tools are very ingenious, but some people find them fiddly. Their features need careful comparison with those of the power router.

The hand router or router plane, with a side fence and depth stop, is mainly used for jobs such as leveling and smoothing the bottoms of grooves and recesses.

Compass plane
*The compass plane (**above**) is an ingenious tool whose sole can be adjusted to conform (within limits) to any curve required, whether convex or concave (**right** and **far right**).*

Above *The spokeshave is in effect a plane for curved surfaces. It has a handle at each side.*

Shaping planes

All the planes just listed work only on flat surfaces, but others are made for curves.

The compass plane is not unlike a bench plane except for its sole, which is of thin and flexible instead of rigid steel. A screw adjustment means it can be curved, within limits, to follow any shape. It is big and expensive but capable of heavy work.

Smaller and lighter is the spokeshave, with its twin grips like the handlebars of a bicycle. It is not really meant for large surfaces. On metal patterns the iron's protrusion can be adjusted just as on other planes. Some models have flat soles and irons; some (radius spokeshaves) have convex ones, some have concave ones, and others even have both side-by-side.

Finger and palm planes

The curious enthusiast may encounter, among further wonders, tiny brass planes — some shaped like fish, porpoises and whales — which are held in one hand and directed with a fingertip. These are finger and pocket planes; palm planes also have a wooden knob to accommodate the palm of the hand. Many have convex and some have concave soles, and irons to match. Their general pattern has been favored by musical-instrument makers, but they do have other uses where space is tight and a top-class finish is required.

Scrapers

Taking shavings leaves a clearer surface than sanding it down, for sanding achieves smoothness at the expense of making tiny scratches. A cabinet scraper is a flat piece of steel used in final finishing to remove very thin shavings indeed by means of a burr or 'hook' along its edge.

Essential equipment in fine furniture-making, it is usually rectangular, though curved 'gooseneck' scrapers are available. It may be mounted in a body like that of a bench plane or spokeshave, to form a scraper plane.

The scratch stock works on a similar principle, but it is used for cutting molded profiles. Usually made in the workshop, it simply consists of a piece of steel (ground and filed to the desired shape) clamped in a timber holder which incorporates some sort of fence to guide it along the edge of the piece being worked.

Above *This scraper plane consists of a scraper mounted in a body like that of a spokeshave. The action is exactly like that of an ordinary scraper (**left**).*

Sharpening
*Sharpening a scraper involves filing away the old edge (**1**), smoothing the face and edge on the stone (**2**), 'consolidating' the metal of the face (**3**) and finally 'turning over' the edge to form a small burr (**4**). It is this burr which removes the shavings.*

Using a chisel
*Paring endgrain (**right**) is routine for a properly sharpened chisel. Note that both hands must always be kept out of the tool's path to avoid potential bloodshed.*
Below *A selection of bevel-edged and firmer chisels with various handles.*

Chisels and gouges

The chisel's uses are far too numerous to list. It is a simple tool, however, and its variations are mostly ones of detail.

The firmer chisel's blade has edges which are square to its faces, while the bevel-edged chisel's name describes it accurately. The former is more robust, but in practice the latter will do any cabinet-making job within reason.

The mortice chisel is a firmer chisel whose blade tapers in the thickness, making it stronger still so that it can chop and lever out the waste wood from deep recesses without risk of snapping. Even more specialized for this task is the swan-neck mortice chisel, whose curved blade allows easier access to the bottom of the recess.

'Paring' is the name given to chisel work which involves taking fine shavings without the use of a hammer or mallet. Special long-bladed paring chisels are available, though ordinary chisels will do the job quite well. Bent paring chisels have an offset handle.

Chisel blade widths vary from ⅛in (3mm) to 1½in (38mm) in increments of various imperial sizes, but not all patterns are available in the full range.

The chief variety among chisels is displayed in their handles. These come in several different timbers and plastics, and are fixed in several different ways to hit their blades. Only use a wooden mallet to hit wooden handles, never a hammer.

Gouges are primarily carving tools, but it is useful to have a couple for general jobs where a chisel's flat blade would be too clumsy. Cabinet-maker's gouges have straight, heavy, parallel-sided blades with a standard curve in the section; an in-cannel gouge has a bevel ground on the inside of the tip, while an out-cannel gouge has its bevel on the outside. Sometimes these are called 'firmer' and 'scribing' gouges respectively, but sometimes the term 'firmer' is used for both.

Files

Though usually thought of in connection with metalwork, files are extremely useful for the fine shaping of wood, since they often allow more control than any other tool.

Unfortunately, the terminology here is bewildering. 'Hand' files have flat faces and parallel edges, tapering only in thickness if at all,

while a 'flat' file usually tapers in width as well. Half-round files are flat on one face and rounded on the other; round files are basically cylindrical; three-square files are triangular in section; and square files are square in section. Pillar and millsaw files are types of hand file, while a warding file is a type of flat file. A termite file is a coarse round file.

File teeth come in three configurations — single-cut (the finest, with single diagonal lines), double-cut (with criss-cross diagonal lines) and curved. But their coarseness varies with size, and is also categorized separately as 'bastard', 'second-cut' or 'smooth'; coarser and finer grades are sometimes found.

Some files, usually with a unique zigzag tooth pattern, are sold specifically as wood files, but a half-round double-cut bastard type is the most generally useful for cabinet work.

Files must be thrown away when worn out, but file handles — of wood or plastic — are bought separately and therefore re-used. The file's sharp 'tang' is simply tapped in.

The exceptions are small 'needle' files, available in quite a few shapes (and often in sets), which need no handle.

A file card is a type of fine wire brush used for unclogging files and rasps.

Rasps and Surforms

Rasps are like files, but much coarser since they have single teeth instead of long serrations. Meant especially for wood, they come in 'hand', 'flat', half-round and round shapes like those of files. So-called wood and cabinet rasps are usually half-round, but not always. Coarseness, too, is graded like that of files. Needle rasps correspond to needle files, but you can also get very small double-ended rasps in a great many shapes: mostly curved in the length, these are known as rifflers.

More generally efficient than the rasp, however, is the perforated rasp, or Surform. This consists of a metal blade with sharp-edged perforations, fitted in a holder. Each perforation acts like a tiny plane, and consequently Surforms cut extremely fast. Their shapes correspond to those of bench planes, block planes, hand files, round files and decorator's scrapers; there is also a concave-soled pattern which is especially useful. A similar tool comes in one model only, but the shape of its sole is varied by means of an adjustable screw mechanism.

Making a Mortice-and-tenon Joint

The mortice-and-tenon remains the basic joint for frames. These pictures show how to cut it by hand, though you can use machines. Start by squaring the 'shoulder line' across the tenon piece with a knife (**1**) or pencil (**2**).

Set a mortice gauge to the width of a suitable chisel — usually about one-third the thickness of the mortice piece (**3**). Use it to mark right round the end of the tenon piece. Indenting the points on the shoulder line will prevent you from marking too far (**4**).

Use either a tenon saw or a larger one to saw along the grain, following the twin gauged marks and stopping at the shoulder line. When cutting, try to split the line you have marked (**5**).

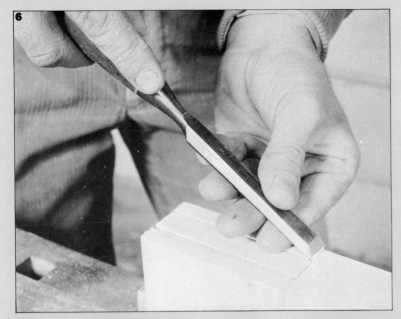

If you have marked the shoulders with a knife cut, an oblique chisel cut to meet it on the waste side will make a neat V-groove. This will provide a guide for the saw and leave a crisp, accurate shoulder (**6**). Cut the shoulders with a back saw, steadying it with your finger or thumb (**7**) and leveling off after your first couple of steep cuts (**8**). Finally clean up with a chisel (**9**).

haunch

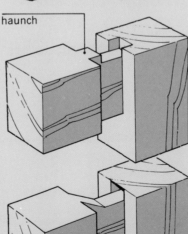

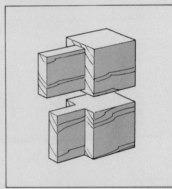

Types of mortice-and-tenon The mortice-and-tenon joint comes in many forms. It can be pegged or wedged for additional strength. Numbers and sizes of shoulders vary (**above**). A haunch (**left**) is sometimes included to prevent twisting; it is either square or 'secret' — the latter being cut at an angle.

The dimensions of the mortice are squared across and marked along (the gauge having been left at the same setting). It is easiest to remove most of the waste by drilling (**10** and **11**); follow up by paring the ends and sides clean with a chisel (**12**). All holes and cuts must be perpendicular to the piece if the joint is to align properly (**13**).

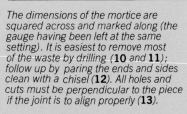

Tenons
*Tenons can be wedged for an extremely secure joint — either diagonally (**left**) or otherwise (**right**). Traditionally this was only done by joiners, who used wedges in windows, doors and the like. Now, however, the device is increasingly used by cabinet-makers, especially when the wedges are cut from contrasting timbers for ornamental effect.*

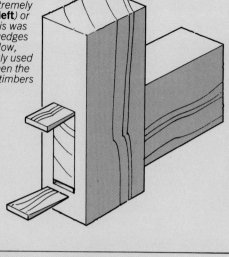

*The tenon should be a very tight fit in its mortice. Extra length (a 'horn') is often left on the end of the mortice piece (**14**) to prevent splitting when the tenon is inserted; it is cut off afterwards. With a through tenon, the final step is to trim its endgrain flush (**15**). A stub or blind tenon, on the other hand, does not pass right through the piece, so it is completely hidden.*

Making a Dovetail Joint

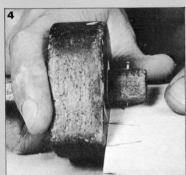

Just as the mortice-and-tenon is the classic framing joint, the dovetail joint is traditional for boxes. Like the mortice-and-tenon, it can rarely be used except in solid timber. As a rule, only unsophisticated versions can be cut by machine.

You may start with either component. Here the tails themselves are cut first, followed by their matching 'pins'.

The first step is to decide the tails' spacing. If the piece does not measure a whole number of units in width, it is convenient to slant a rule across it at such an angle that you can read off a number that will easily yield the sub-divisions you want (**1**). These can then be squared down to the end of the piece.

Once the spacing has been set out, the sloping sides of the tails can be marked with a bought or home-made template that hooks over the end of the piece (**2**), or with a sliding bevel.

For through dovetails (see opposite), set a gauge (**3**) to the thickness of the other piece and run it across the end of the tail piece (**4**). Then clamp the timber upright and saw down to the line with a dovetail saw (or a similar fine-toothed back saw), taking care to split the slanting lines accurately on the waste side (**5**).

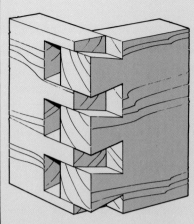 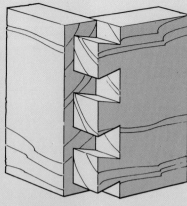

Types of dovetail
*Through dovetails (**left**) can be seen
from both directions. Lap dovetails
(**right**), usual in drawers, are half-
hidden; they are somewhat harder to
cut, and gauge marks should be kept off
the outer face of the pin piece.
Dovetail slopes vary from 1 in 6
('coarse') to 1 in 8 ('fine'), the former
usually used for softer woods and
rougher work. Spacings
need not be regular. Note the half-pins
at top and bottom, which make a tighter
joint than half-tails would.*

*Take out the waste between the tails
with a coping saw, or with a chisel (**6**).
Then remove the piece from the vice
and replace it with the other piece. Align
the tails on the endgrain of that and use
them to mark the pin positions with a
sharp pencil or scriber (**7**). Square these
positions along the faces of the piece
(**8**), and finally mark the pins' depth
across the grain with a gauge set to the
thickness of the tail piece.*

Make saw cuts down to the marked line to define the sides of the pins (**9**). To ensure tightness, cut to one side of each marked line instead of splitting it. Finish by chopping out the waste between the pins with a narrow chisel. Ideally the pieces should fit first time; if the joint is really snug, it will loosen slightly if taken apart and re-fitted (**10**):

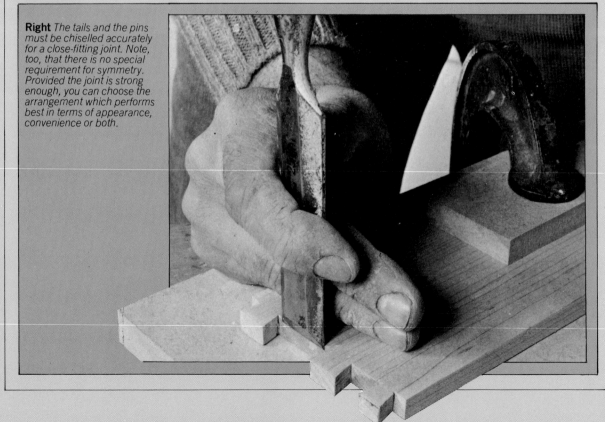

Right *The tails and the pins must be chiselled accurately for a close-fitting joint. Note, too, that there is no special requirement for symmetry. Provided the joint is strong enough, you can choose the arrangement which performs best in terms of appearance, convenience or both.*

Drills

Although virtually everyone seems to have a power drill, there are quite a few hand drilling devices still made.

Their convenience in handling, and the fact that they need no power supply, make little difference to the furniture-maker who will not be using them outside his workshop; nevertheless, some are quicker to use than a power drill would be for the comparable operation.

Twist bits will not work properly in a brace, though woodworking bits will. Those most commonly used, however, are auger bits, which have a deep, slow spiral, plus a screw point to center them accurately and pull them through the work. The Jennings pattern has a double-helical spiral, while the solid-center or Irwin auger bit has a single helix around a central shaft. The former is a little cleaner and more accurate, the latter a little faster.

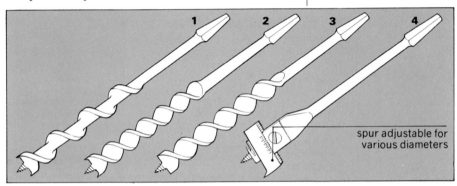

spur adjustable for various diameters

Left *Four bits for use in the brace: the solid-center auger (**1**), the Jennings pattern auger (**2**), the Scotch auger (**3**) and the expansive bit (**4**).*

Below *The brace is the traditional tool for hand drilling. It is very efficient, though naturally not as quick to use as a power drill.*

An awl is simply twisted to make a small hole, usually for starting a screw. A push drill, like an Archimedean or fretwork drill, revolves as you push its handle in. It requires special bits, called drill points, stored inside the handle. However, its maximum bit size is only about 3/16in (4.5mm). Larger holes require a hand drill or brace.

The hand drill works via a crank handle and gears. The breast drill is a hand drill with a curved plate at the top on which you can lean for extra pressure. Both tools accept twist and woodworking bits, which have straight shanks. Twist bits — primarily for metalworking — come in diameters from 1/64in (0.4mm) right up to 1in (25mm) or so. Woodworking bits have a steeper spiral which clears wood waste more quickly, usually a 'lead' or 'brad' point, which prevents them from wandering, and sometimes 'spurs' at the outside of the tip as well; however, they start at about ⅛in (3mm), so a full kit also includes twist bits to cover the smaller sizes. Woodworking bits are used for doweling.

The brace or swingbrace is rotated bodily, but usually connected to its chuck (the part that holds the bit) via a ratchet. The chuck either has universal jaws, which accept any bit, or alligator jaws, which take only bits with specially tapered shanks.

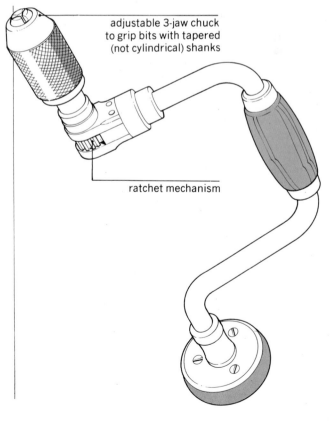

adjustable 3-jaw chuck to grip bits with tapered (not cylindrical) shanks

ratchet mechanism

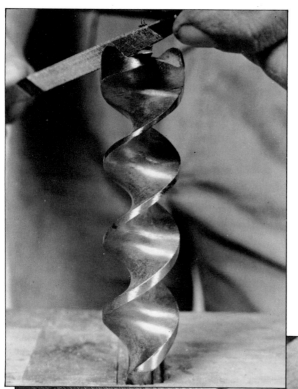

Most auger bits have two spurs, but some have one, and Scotch and Mathieson bits have none. The center bit is for making wide, shallow, round recesses which are flat-bottomed except for the central hole left by the screw point. An expansive bit does a similar job, but its diameter is adjustable.

You can also get turnscrew or screwdriver bits, which are especially handy for undoing stubborn screws.

Bits for braces range in diameter from ¼in (6mm) to ½in (38mm) — or to 3in (75mm) if you include the expansive bit.

Twist bits, woodworking bits and straight-shanked (machine) auger bits are also meant for use in power drills.

Left and **below** Auger bits must be sharpened with a fine file called a needle file, used very lightly. Only the cutting edges on the inside should be touched — never the outer circumference, or you will alter the bit's action.

Hammers and mallets

A clawhammer is absolutely essential for carpentry, but too heavy and unwieldy for cabinet-making. Far more useful is a Warrington-pattern hammer; this is lighter, and has a wedge-shaped 'cross pein' in place of the claw (whose function is pulling out nails). This pein is used for lightly tapping finishing nails to start them off, and it can come in handy for veneering and inlay.

Various weights are available, and the heavier ones drive the nails in faster. For really fine pins, you may find a pin hammer (also known as a tack or telephone hammer) is necessary. This is simply a very light Warrington hammer with a disproportionately long and slender handle.

The pinpush, pushpin or rampin is a device that

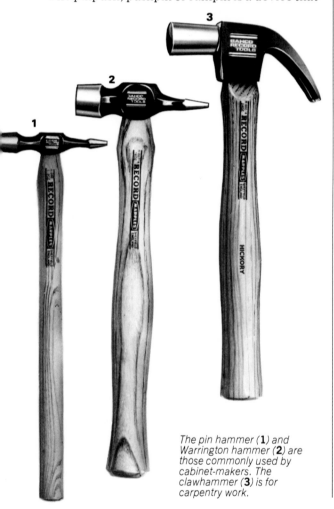

The pin hammer (1) and Warrington hammer (2) are those commonly used by cabinet-makers. The clawhammer (3) is for carpentry work.

looks like a screwdriver; you fit the nail into the hollow tip, and push hard on the handle to drive it in. Its advantage is that the nail cannot bend.

The main use of a wooden mallet — and it is a frequent use — is to tap the handle of a chisel when making heavy cuts. Most mallets are made of solid beech throughout, and have large, flat, rectangular faces.

If your joints are as tight as they should be, components will require knocking together at the assembly stage. You can always use a mallet or medium hammer, plus a block of wood to cushion the pieces against bruising, but a soft mallet is more convenient: preferably one with a rubber or rubber-faced head. Plastic and leather types also exist.

Screwdrivers

Screwdrivers are unglamorous but indispensable.

Perhaps the king is the Yankee or spiral ratchet screwdriver. This drives and extracts screws if you simply push — you need not turn it. But it can be extremely unwieldy, and for furniture a better choice may be the ordinary ratchet screwdriver. This requires turning, but its ratchet mechanism means you can return your hand to the same position after each turn without relaxing your grip on the handle. In practice this is a definite advantage. The Yankee can be set to perform as a plain ratchet screwdriver, and on both patterns the ratchet can be locked out of action so that you have the equivalent of an ordinary screwdriver.

More traditional types, which have no mechanisms, and wooden handles, are the cabinet screwdriver with its round handle; the London pattern, which has a flat blade — plus a flat-faced handle to stop it rolling off the bench; the crutch screwdriver, which resembles both but is shorter; and the 'perfect pattern', whose blade and handle form a continuous shape.

Very popular are sundry types and sizes of nameless screwdriver with plastic handles. Some, however, are more suitable for engineers, mechanics, electricians and others than for woodworkers.

Quite a few models, including the Yankee, have interchangeable tips, and some have completely interchangeable blades. This is because screw heads vary in size, and in whether they have a 'slot' or a cross-shaped recess cut into them.

Low Table

Making a low table
This low table is unusual in employing a panel construction. Apart from the glass top, the materials are relatively cheap.

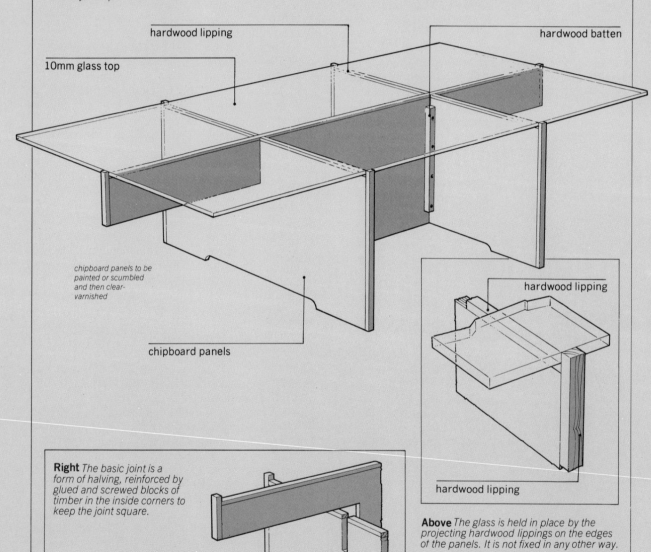

hardwood lipping

hardwood batten

10mm glass top

chipboard panels to be painted or scumbled and then clear-varnished

chipboard panels

hardwood lipping

hardwood lipping

Right *The basic joint is a form of halving, reinforced by glued and screwed blocks of timber in the inside corners to keep the joint square.*

Above *The glass is held in place by the projecting hardwood lippings on the edges of the panels. It is not fixed in any other way.*

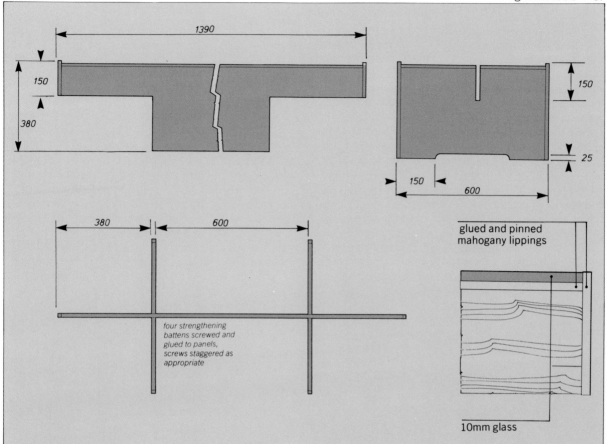

glued and pinned
mahogany lippings

1390

150

380

150

25

380

600

150

600

four strengthening
battens screwed and
glued to panels,
screws staggered as
appropriate

10mm glass

Miscellaneous tools

There are at least three other tools which you will find it hard to do without.

Nail sets, or punches, are small, rocket-shaped pieces of steel for driving nails or pins below the surface so that the resulting holes can be filled to disguise the fixings. After driving the nail almost all the way, you place the punch's slightly hollow tip on top of it and hit the other end with a hammer. Tip sizes vary, and it is best to provide yourself with two or three. Engineer's pin punches have flat tips, and may also be useful for some jobs.

A pair of pinchers is essential for extracting the nails and pins that refuse to go in properly.

An awl makes it a lot easier to drive small screws: you press it in and twist it to make a starting hole. Some have sharp points and round or square shanks (the latter being known as birdcage awls because they were used to make holes for canes in that trade); some have spade-shaped tips, so that they resemble small screwdrivers. Awls are also handy for making center holes before using a drill.

Right *The punch (**1**) is for setting nails or pins below the surface of the work. It is struck with a hammer. The awl (**2**) is very useful in making starting holes for small screws.*

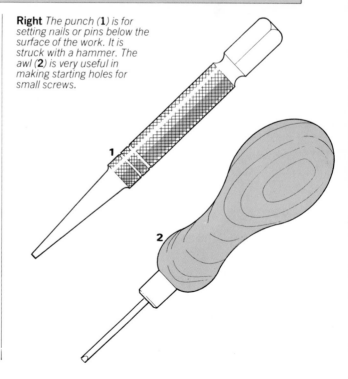

1

2

Clamps

The best tools in the world will not get you very far if you have no way of assembling the items you make with them.

Furniture can always be held together with screws and other hardware. This is ideal for 'knock-down' (KD) designs — those that allow dismantling. But it is frequently neater and stronger to use glue instead. And, since the two commonest woodworking adhesives, PVA and UF glue, take time to set, that means 'clamping' the joints tightly meanwhile.

It is proverbial among woodworkers that you never have enough clamps. This is because most types of clamp only exert pressure in one direction at a time and over a fairly small area, whereas a given piece of furniture may need gluing up in numerous places at once — and each 'glue-line' must be formed properly straight away. There are few second chances.

Some of the cabinet-maker's best friends are bar clamps — steel bars fitted with two 'heads' which you can place over the work. One head slides freely to accommodate differing sizes of job, and is plugged in position via holes in the bar; the other has a screw adjustment for final tightening. T-bar clamps have a T-section bar, which is even stronger and more massive.

But bar clamps are expensive, so alternatives are welcome. One is to buy only the heads (available separately) and fit them to a length of wood. The nearest cheap, ready-made alternative is a 'Rak clamp' of the 'beam' type; this has two freely-sliding heads, but its bar is serrated. A small screw locks each head into position and simultaneously tightens up.

Most clamps, however, have two fixed heads or 'jaws'. The familiar C- (or G-) and fret clamps tighten by means of a screw that exerts pressure on the work directly. But with quick-action and quick-release clamps, tightening also locks a second (sliding) jaw in position — as on Rak clamps, which are also available with one jaw fixed. Other clamps lock and tighten the sliding jaw by means of a cam or toggle instead of a screw.

Precise patterns, strengths and sizes vary, though none of these types has even the 36in (900mm) capacity of a beam Rak clamp, let alone the larger bar clamps or a T-bar clamp. Quick-action clamps are available up to 24in (600mm).

But remember that all clamps, no matter how long, are limited in the depth or width of work they can cope with.

Many cramps have removable plastic facings on their metal jaws, and cam clamps have wooden jaws, which may come faced with cork.

Edge-lipping or edge clamps have a second screw jaw at right angles to the usual one, while the hand screw is a traditional clamping device possessing two parallel wooden jaws linked by two screw threads — each with its own handle; it can be useful for tapered workpieces.

A totally different approach is offered by the web or band clamp, which is simply a tough, non-elastic strip of webbing, wrapped round the workpiece and tightened — rather like a belt — with a screw mechanism. This can take the place of numerous conventional clamps, and will often tackle awkward objects more easily too.

Below *The C-clamp is absolutely indispensable in any workshop.*
Bottom *The edge-lipping clamp is a much less usual variant.*

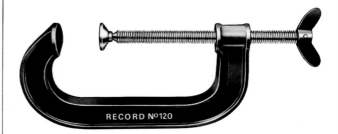

It has a particular application on mitered frames, which are best cramped on all four corners simultaneously. Picture-frame clamps, which have four L-shaped corner pieces connected by a length of wire or cord, do the same job. Others tackle each corner singly.

The infinite variety of furniture and the high cost of large clamps often mean improvisation. Web and frame clamps can be imitated on the tourniquet principle. The moving jaw of a bench vice, especially if it has (or can be fitted with) an upward-projecting dog, can supplant the moving jaw of a conventional clamp, the workpiece being held against a stop of some kind nailed to the bench-top. 'Folding' wedges (wedges which exert sideways pressure as they are knocked into a gap head-to-toe) can also be useful. Lastly, for really small jobs, there is no reason why you should not use elastic bands or bulldog clips.

Bar clamps (**top**) and the similar T-bar clamps (**above**) are staple tools for assemblies of any size. Both are shown with extension bars.

Left The band clamp is a versatile modern invention which is often handier than more traditional metal clamps. Alternatively, you can sometimes improvise with a tourniquet-style arrangement. Clamping often involves makeshift devices and set-ups of various kinds.

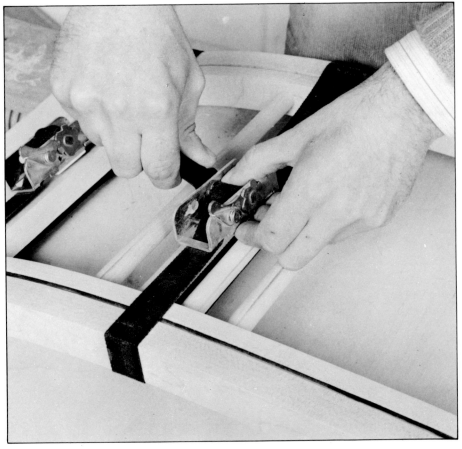

The Desk-top Cabinet

- *Moldings*
- *Solid-wood corner joints*
- *Drawer work*
- *Using exotic timbers*
- *Veneer-keying*

This little chest-of-drawers on its stand typifies design for pleasure. It has no great practical usefulness, but it is the kind of piece people like to give and receive as a present. It is made entirely of woods which are commonly termed 'exotic', yet whose cost in such small sizes is minimal by comparison with what you would have to pay a professional to do the work required. The actual making demands a fair degree of manual skill; not much of it submits easily to machine work — and inaccuracies in a job like this remove most of its point.

Features
The stand is ebony. The sides, top and base of the box, plus the drawer bottoms and runners, are padauk. Available in Burma, Andaman and African varieties, this wood can be scarlet and even orange when cut; but it mellows to a rich, deep red, irrespective of which clear finish you apply. Many timbers darken in this way.

The drawer-fronts, sides and backs, like the cabinet back, are of lemonwood — a timber which is so extraordinarily dense and hard that glue will scarcely penetrate it; too much clamping pressure merely squeezes almost all the glue out of the joint, so it falls apart at the slightest prompting. Some research was necessary to find out the real identity of this wood. There are so many species, and often so many names for a particular one, that confusion is very common — especially since the same name may be used for more than one timber, and since different countries, districts and sections of the trade do not share an agreed vocabulary.

Finished with several applications of oil, the item is a miniature exemplar of traditional solid-wood cabinetry. The carcase panels were

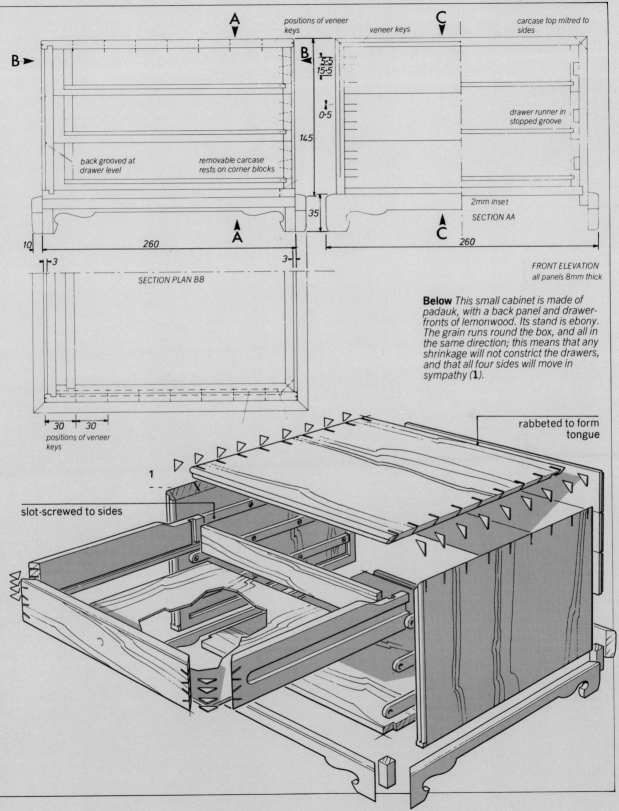

positions of veneer keys

A

B ►

veneer keys

C

carcase top mitred to sides

B ►

5·5
15·5

0·5

145

back grooved at drawer level

removable carcase rests on corner blocks

drawer runner in stopped groove

35

2mm inset

SECTION AA

A

C

10

260

260

3

3

SECTION PLAN BB

FRONT ELEVATION
all panels 8mm thick

30   30

positions of veneer keys

Below This small cabinet is made of padauk, with a back panel and drawer-fronts of lemonwood. Its stand is ebony. The grain runs round the box, and all in the same direction; this means that any shrinkage will not constrict the drawers, and that all four sides will move in sympathy (**1**).

rabbeted to form tongue

1

slot-screwed to sides

each made from two pieces because no single ones were wide enough. Such edge-gluing (with or without the aid of dowels, biscuits, tongues or loose tongues) is standard practice for making up large panels of solid wood.

These pieces were planed slightly too thick, but perfectly flat and square along one edge, then glued and clamped side-by-side — without softening blocks, so that the pressure would be applied as squarely as possible: this is very necessary for such a thin joint. Oversize cutting meant that parts which had been bruised by the clamps could be removed afterwards. Then the pieces were planed, and the insides scraped and sanded before assembly.

The grain runs round the box rather than from front to back. This means that any shrinkage or swelling will increase or reduce the depth of the box, not its height or width. If the opposite were the case, the drawers would be pinched or loosened as the wood expanded and contracted. Worse still would be a mixture of grain directions, since (if glue were used) one or more pieces would be bound

The shooting-board is a simple jig which ensures that you can plane the edge of a piece precisely square to its face by giving the plane a 'control surface' on which to travel (4).

eventually to split as the stresses — prevented from acting in concert with those in neighboring boards — found the weakest parts.

Since the cabinet would not necessarily be placed against a wall, its back is meant to withstand being seen. It imitates the front. It is not glued, so that it is free to move with changes in humidity.

Moldings
The double-reed molding on front and rear edges is of course for decoration. Most contemporary pieces use far less ornamental molding than traditional ones, but knowing where and how to incorporate it is still one mark of a good designer. Although a few people still have wooden molding planes, most rely for shaping either on the simple scratch stock (used here) or on the colossal variety of cutters for the router and for the shaper. Complex moldings often require several different cuts to build up the shape; sometimes it is even best to make them in more than one piece.

Timber merchants sell quite a few ready-made moldings in standard shapes and sizes, and using or ad-

Each side of the box consists of two pieces glued together. After their edges have been planed perfectly flat and square on the shooting-board (**2**), the pieces are placed side-by-side and given pencil marks for alignment (**3**) before gluing (**5**) and clamping (**6**). The excess adhesive (in this case white glue) is removed straight away (**7**), but the joint is allowed to set before the surface is 'cleaned up' with a cabinet scraper (**8**).

direction of shrinkage

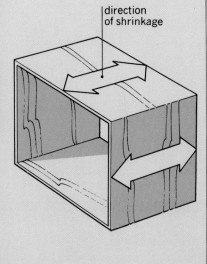

The scratch stock is a simple tool for making moldings. You simply grind and/or file the negative of the required shape in a piece of steel such as a cabinet scraper (**9** and **10**).

After shaping or sharpening the steel, clamp it with screws into a slotted wooden holder (**11**).
The tool is simply worked back and forth in a rocking motion until the profile reaches the depth you want (**12**). The 'fence' of the wooden holder should be kept against the edge or side of the piece for a straight cut.

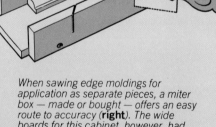

When sawing edge moldings for application as separate pieces, a miter box — made or bought — offers an easy route to accuracy (**right**). The wide boards for this cabinet, however, had their ends beveled at 45° on a home-made miter shooting-board (**13** and **14**). The scrap piece ahead of the component stops it from splitting out when planed.

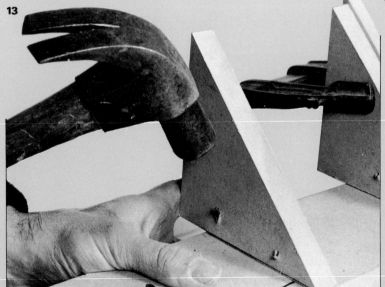

A block plane is handy for chamfering the drawer bases to fit into their grooves (15), and for the decorative chamfers on the back panel (16) — shown with pencil marks for alignment (17).

the joint completely.

A strong, neat alternative is the loose-tongued miter, in which a glued tongue, in paired grooves, takes the place of the veneer keys used here. With solid-timber components, the tongue must be of solid timber too — and short-grained, once again, so it does not restrict movement. The cross-grain will also make the joint stronger than a long-grain piece would.

The miter shooting-board, employed to plane the miters true, demonstrates how jigs can be just as useful in hand as in machine work to overcome the natural limits of manual coordination.

Keys are used on the drawer-fronts, too, the only difference being that they are angled (on a side view) to echo not only the appearance of dovetails but also a little of their strength. Again, however, this unusual and still fairly weak joint is feasible only because relatively little stress is expected. The keys in the box are of avodire (an attractive, yellowish timber something like satinwood) — except for one at each

apting these is sometimes a better answer than undertaking a laborious shaping operation yourself or buying a special cutter.

However, the number of timbers used is generally very limited, ramin being the chief one for small sections. Besides, applying a separate molded strip is not the same as shaping the edge of the component itself — as was done for this cabinet. Apart from the fact that the joins will show, the procedure requires its own gluing operation, plus pinning or clamping.

Corner joints in solid wood
The 'keyed' miters here are strong enough for their job. The miter itself is weak (gluing endgrain is not very effective) but the veneer keys provide sizeable gluing areas of face grain, and help to withstand any stress which tends to slide the joint apart. In a larger traditional cabinet, these joints would very likely be lap-dovetailed — often in conjunction with a separate top which would hide

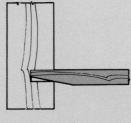

Below left *These drawers follow one of several traditional patterns, except for their unusual front corner joints (which echo those of the box itself).*

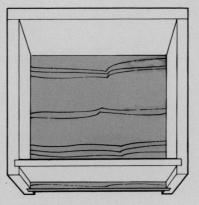

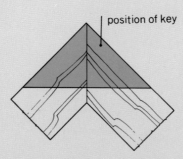

position of key

Veneer-keying provides a decorative corner joint with enough strength for a lightweight piece like this one. First, it is important to mark the keys' exact positions; a combination square is useful for marking the depth to which they will be inserted (**18**). Mark the extent (**19**) and 90 degree angle (**20**) of the saw cuts before making them (**21**). Check, too, that the saw-kerf will be neither too wide nor too narrow for the veneer (**22**). The keys themselves are cut oversize (**23**), and in such a way that grain runs diagonally across the mitered corner, which is vital for strength. To prevent splitting, the glue is allowed to dry thoroughly before the keys are shaved flush with a sharp chisel (**24**).

end of each joint, added for strength and to prevent the joints opening in these areas: these are in padauk so that they do not show. All the keys in the drawers are of padauk to match the box.

Another joint ideal for this purpose is the comb joint (sometimes called a finger joint, but that term is also applied to quite different configurations). The comb joint is like a multiple corner bridle: it consists of a row of small tenons on each component, arranged to fit between those on the other. It is very strong because of its large total gluing area, and easily cut by machine.

Drawer details

The upper edges of the drawer sides are relieved at the rear to ease re-entry of drawers into the box if they have been removed — more of a possibility for such a small cabinet than a larger chest-of-drawers.

The drawer-base (chamfered on three edges to fit the grooves in the front and sides) is fixed only by gluing along the front — not, of course, along the sides or back, for the ever-present reason: it must be free to

shrink and swell across its grain. Common practice would be not to glue it at all, but instead to pin it up into the lower edge of the back. Considering its thickness, and the hardness of the two timbers, gluing along the front seems the better alternative. The reason the grain runs from side to side in the first place is so that when the wood shrinks, the resulting stress cannot pull the component from its grooves.

A stack of three drawers like this, without intervening rails or panels, invites side-hanging. Grooves in the drawer-sides accommodate runners screwed to the carcase. Once again, glue cannot be used, and the screws themselves pass through slots instead of round holes, so that the boards can still move in relation to the runners. Lastly (and this is a vital detail) the screw gauge is a little smaller than the width of the slots, to enable slight vertical adjustment as well.

The drawer-fronts are mitered on the mitre shooting-board in the same way as the cabinet sides (25). 'Dry' (unglued) assembly establishes that the drawer's grooves and housings are a good fit (26 and 27).

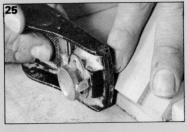

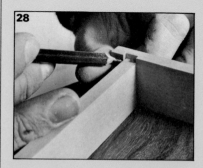

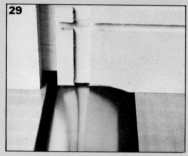

The drawer-sides are 'relieved' at the rear to allow easy re-insertion into the cabinet. After pencil-marking (**28**), the cut is made on the jointer (**29**), with a stop block ahead of the cutter.

The drawer runners fit grooves in the drawer-sides (**30**). They are screwed on through elongated holes, to permit moisture movement in the cabinet sides (**31**).

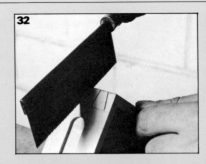

After each drawer is glued up (but before the base is slid into position), the front corners are veneer-keyed — this time at an angle, when viewed from the side: an echo of the more conventional dovetail joint (**32** and **33**).

MAKING A STAND

The stand consists of four equal lengths of ebony. The principal shape is cut with a bandsaw or jigsaw and refined with a file (**34**); the section is slightly rounded with a block plane (**35**) and checked against the drawing (**36**). The corners are mitered, glued and strengthened with small additional blocks (**37**).

USING PORTABLE POWER TOOLS

E ven professional furniture-makers with well-equipped machine shops find hand-held power tools useful, because there are often times when taking the tool to the piece you are working on makes more sense than the reverse.

Almost every powered tool, in either category, does more than just beat several equivalent hand tools at their own games: it allows you to approach the business of making in a different way, because it possesses and imposes a logic of its own.

In one respect, however, all powered tools resemble hand tools closely. They usually let you know — by feel and by the changing noises they make — when the material is too hard or otherwise difficult, when they are tearing it out rather than cutting cleanly, when the blade or cutter is blunt, and when you are trying to cut too fast. It is essential to develop a sensitivity in this area; otherwise you will pay the price in rough work, and possibly in tools and cutting edges which are damaged more than they need be in normal use. Mishandling power tools also adds to the risks involved; for example, a router cutter can break up in use if overworked.

Drills

Modern power drills have two common features whose usefulness is limited unless you plan to undertake work other than cabinet-making, because they are designed to help when tackling hard materials such as masonry and concrete. The first is the hammer or percussion facility — all drilling in timber should be plain 'rotary'. The second

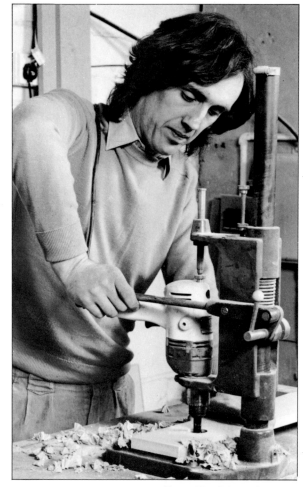

Above The drill stand is the basic apparatus for achieving accuracy when drilling. An ordinary power drill is fixed into it and lowered on a true vertical.
Left The principal bits for power-drilling: the woodbit (**1**), woodworking or dowel bit (**2**), Forstner bit (**3**), saw-tooth center bit (**4**), and twist bit, shown with an adjustable depth stop (**5**). At the upper right are two countersinks (**6** and **7**).

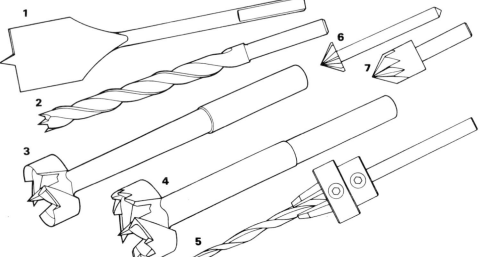

is variable-speed control, which is available in several forms. The speed may be continuously variable from 0 rpm upwards; there may be two, three, or four alternative gear ratios, or both systems may be combined, so that you can vary the speed continuously within the limits of each gear. Apart from their use in steel, glass and the like, low speeds are handy for screwdriving: but, on the whole, high speeds are best for woodwork. A reverse gear can also be useful, e.g. for extracting screws and driving certain attachments.

A medium-powered drill, say of 500 watts or so, should be quite adequate for cabinet work.

For the smallest holes, twist bits are the only option; above ⅛in (3mm) or so in diameter, woodworking bits are better. But from ¼in (6mm) upwards, the power-drill user has another alternative — spade or woodbits. These rather fierce-looking tools are designed for high-speed machine drilling only; they have an extra-long point, which centers them firmly even for angled holes, and they cut with a scraping instead of a boring action. Woodbits are available that have a single shank and interchangeable tips in a range of different diameters.

A great number of attachments and accessories are available for power drills. In general, these are second-best when compared with the corresponding 'integral tool'. If you want professional results, you are better off buying a circular saw than a circular-saw attachment for a drill, and better off buying an orbital or belt sander than an orbital-sanding attachment or a flexible drill-mounted sanding disk — to give only two examples.

There are three partial exceptions. One is the drill guide, a frame into which you fasten the drill to ensure that the bit enters the work at a predetermined angle (not necessarily 90°) and at no other. The second is the flexible drive — a tube with a chuck at one end, and a shank at the other that fits into the drill chuck. This has some use in reaching awkward corners.

The third is the hand shaper. This is used in conjunction with special cutters which, unlike ordinary bits, are capable of cutting along or across a piece instead of just into it. It is really a fence with a handle, fitting into the chuck — although at least one model can be fastened to the edge of the bench, forming a cheap (and inferior) alternative fixed shaper.

Below *The plug cutter removes neat pellets of wood which fit in matching holes, for example as a means of concealing screw heads and other fixings. The plugs can be taken from a contrasting timber.*

Shaping cutters come in two varieties, edged and rasp-toothed, and quite a few profiles, but their use is mostly restricted to edging work of one kind and another. That includes some very useful jobs, and the cutters work well enough if you do not expect wonders from them, but the whole set-up is essentially a cheap and less capable version of the router. The work it does is so vital to furniture-making that the purpose-made tool is usually a far wiser buy.

Bed

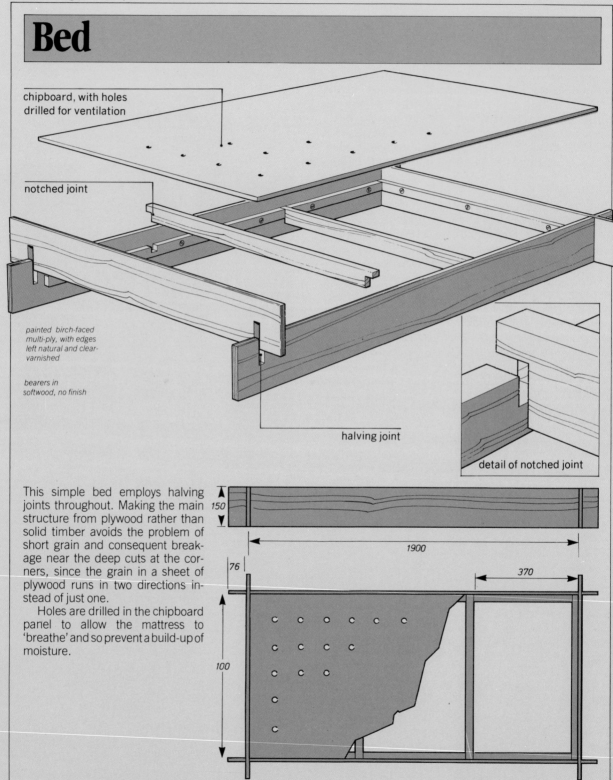

chipboard, with holes
drilled for ventilation

notched joint

painted birch-faced
multi-ply, with edges
left natural and clear-
varnished

bearers in
softwood, no finish

halving joint

detail of notched joint

150

1900

76

370

100

This simple bed employs halving
joints throughout. Making the main
structure from plywood rather than
solid timber avoids the problem of
short grain and consequent breakage near the deep cuts at the corners, since the grain in a sheet of
plywood runs in two directions instead of just one.

Holes are drilled in the chipboard
panel to allow the mattress to
'breathe' and so prevent a build-up of
moisture.

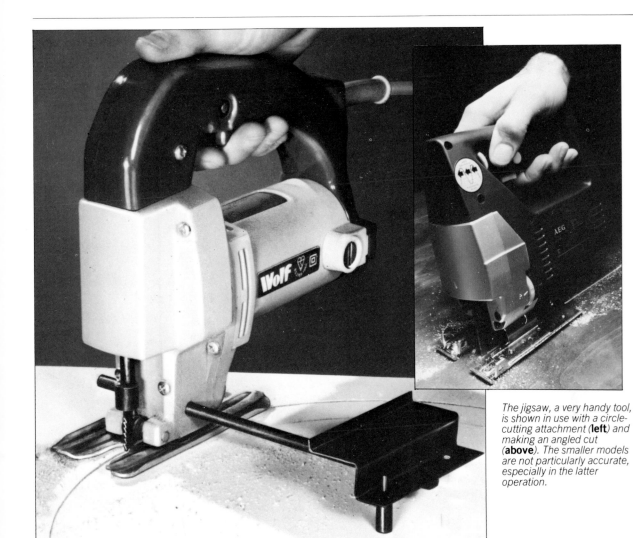

The jigsaw, a very handy tool, is shown in use with a circle-cutting attachment (**left**) and making an angled cut (**above**). The smaller models are not particularly accurate, especially in the latter operation.

Jigsaws

In its own narrow sphere, the jigsaw is a very useful tool indeed. Other saws excel at cutting in straight lines, but even there its maneuverability can be an advantage; and for cutting curves in thin components it has few equals. Unlike a frame saw or bandsaw, it is never limited by the length or width of the piece.

The jigsaw's oscillating blade cuts on the up-stroke. Some types can be used with one hand, others need two. Its main problems are deflection of the straight but thin and narrow blade during cutting — with consequent inaccuracy — and the fact that, if the workpiece is thicker than about 2¾in (69mm), no jigsaw will cut through it.

Like drills, many jigsaws nowadays have variable speeds; again, the lower ones are most useful for materials harder than wood, such as aluminum and plastic laminate. When working timber and boards, however, they can be a great help in starting cuts accurately — especially at the edge of a piece, where it is easy to go astray with the sudden vibration. On orbital-action jigsaws, the blade cuts more easily by swinging forward as it rises, and some models even allow adjustment of the degree to which this happens.

Most, if not all, models allow the sole plate to be tilted by up to 45°, giving cuts that are correspondingly angled away from the vertical. Blade deflection means, however, that it is unwise to expect accuracy from this. Many jigsaws offer a fence, designed to locate over the edge of the piece so you can consistently cut parallel to it and a certain distance in. But most cuts are freehand, and a very useful feature is a blower, which keeps the cutting line clear of waste material so you can see what you are doing.

Jigsaw blades are available in many tooth configurations — some for fast, coarse cutting of wood, some for slower and finer cutting, some more suitable for man-made boards, and others specifically for materials such as plastic, aluminum and even steel. Different profiles include extra-narrow ('scroll-cutting') blades for tight curves, and L-shaped blades which project forward beyond the front of the sole plate so you can cut right into a corner.

Circular saws

The portable circular saw, when hand-held, is probably more useful for cutting up large boards quickly than for any other job.

Its circular blade travels around within a casing, except where it protrudes through the sole-plate; and, even there, a sprung guard — like a continuation of the casing — covers it whenever the saw is not actually cutting. The amount of blade protrusion (i.e., the depth of cut) can be adjusted, to a maximum of over 3in (75mm) on the very largest professional models; the sole plate can be angled sideways, like that of a jigsaw and with rather more accuracy. Always provided, too, is a side fence, usually called a 'rip fence' because of its usefulness when ripping solid timber. This is not always as sturdy as it should be.

Circular saws cut upwards. They need to be fed through the workpiece at their own pace; they must not be forced, or the blade may 'bind' and stop revolving altogether.

Generally speaking, a portable circular saw must be guided with a 'fence' rather than freehand. Where this fence takes the form of a straight-edge clamped to the workpiece, you need to know the exact distance from the edge of the teeth to the edge of the saw's sole plate so you can position the fence accurately (**below** and **right**).

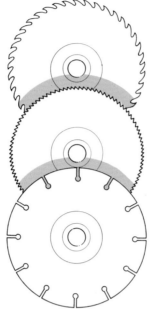

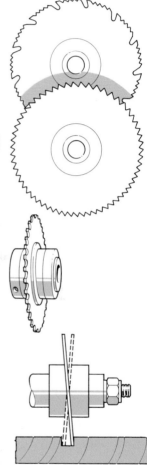

Sawblades

*Sawblades come
in several types for particular
jobs. In cabinet-making,
however, you are unlikely to
need more than one or two.*
Far left *Guard drawn back
to reveal the blade.*

Above *Some circular saws
(both portable and fixed)
allow the fitting of 'wobble
washers', which tilt the blade
and thereby make the cut
wider. The width of the
resulting groove or rabbet can
be precisely adjusted.*
Left *With circular saws, as
with other power tools, heavy
industrial models are often a
better buy than light-duty
'home handyman' makes.*

As with almost every powered tool, all sorts of ways exist in which you can extend and vary the saw's workload. Straight-edged guide pieces, clamped in place, help to ensure accurate cuts where the rip fence is no use — and because, unlike the jigsaw, the circular saw need not protrude right through the material in order to cut, it can be used for grooves and rabbets.

The main types of blade available are rip, crosscut, combination (mixing rip and crosscut features), hollow-ground or planer (for especially clean cuts) and tungsten-carbide-tipped (TCT). Tungsten carbide is much harder than steel, so edges or teeth which are made from or tipped with it stay sharp longer than others. This is especially important when cutting board materials, since most contain resin glues which blunt steel cutting edges of all types.

'Wobble washers' can often be fitted either side of the blade to tilt it to varying angles, thus introducing a sideways movement which makes a wider kerf — meaning that grooves and rabbets can be cut in one stroke, or 'pass'.

Power planes

The portable power plane is not to be confused with the jointer. It does the same job as a hand bench plane, and most types are also capable of rabbeting. It has a rotating 'cutter block', usually with two knives, in place of the hand plane's iron, and it removes timber correspondingly faster; the larger-capacity models take off up to 1/8in (3mm) or so in a single pass. Widths of cut vary too.

Naturally, the power plane is too large for many specialized planing jobs, but it can make very quick work of basic sizing, making it less essential to have timber sawn to almost the desired section.

Some models have replaceable cutters; on others the cutters need sharpening. A bag or other attachment for collecting the waste does help to avoid mess, but bags fill very quickly.

Biscuit jointers

In recent years the furniture trade has spent a great deal of time seeking the best way to join pieces of board together. One admirable solution uses the 'biscuit' or 'Lamello'. This is a thin, flat piece of compressed beech with a profile like that of a rugby football. It fits into a pair of recesses (one in each component) whose bottoms have

Below *Marking up for biscuit-jointing. A line is drawn across the first panel, and the recesses cut (**1**). Then their positions are transferred to a home-made 'square' (**2**) and thence to the second panel (**3**).*

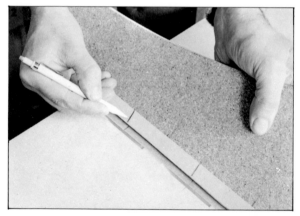

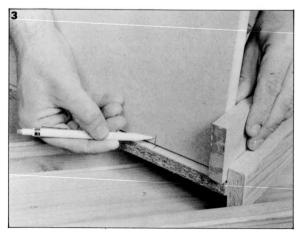

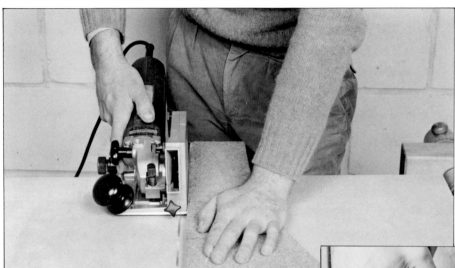

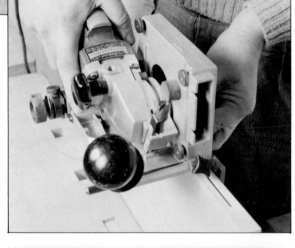

*The biscuit jointer is a circular saw with a very small blade. The handle is lowered for the cutting of each individual recess (**left** and **below**). The biscuits of compressed beech are inserted (**bottom**) before assembly; the method allows some adjustment along the length of the joint, which is very useful.*

curves to match it. Glue makes it swell, and the result is a strong and invisible joint.

One big point in favor of this technique is that the recesses need not be positioned with perfect (and almost unattainable) accuracy; a certain amount of re-alignment is possible after the pieces are fitted together. This is not the case with most other methods — even the most nearly comparable, namely doweling.

The biscuit jointer is the tool that makes the recesses, by means of a small circular saw blade. It looks different from a circular saw, and operates by plunging into the work while stationary. It has a depth setting and fence, and can also be used to make grooves.

There is no denying that it is a specialized tool, but — particularly if you anticipate making cabinets from sheet materials — the advantages of biscuit-joining make it well worth looking at.

Routers

Sawing and planing are not usually the router's job. However, just about everything else is. It is capable of cutting almost any joint, whether in timber or boards, and can also tackle a tremendous variety of decorative work. In many cases it has no substitute. And, more than any other power tool, it allows and encourages ingenuity in the user.

Its spindle, pointing straight down through its sole plate or 'base', rotates extremely fast (at

Below *The router can be guided through and along the work in a number of ways. The fence attachment may be used for grooving (**1**) or edging (**2**). For edging, however, it can be dispensed with if you use a cutter which has its own integral guide pin or pilot (**3** and **4**) or bearing guide (**5**). Often such cutters are used with templates, to which the work is fixed (**4** and **5**). The template guide bush (**6**) is a special attachment enabling you to use an ordinary cutter for edging if you provide a template of suitable size. Another option for straight cuts is simply to run the router base against a straight-edged piece clamped to the work.*

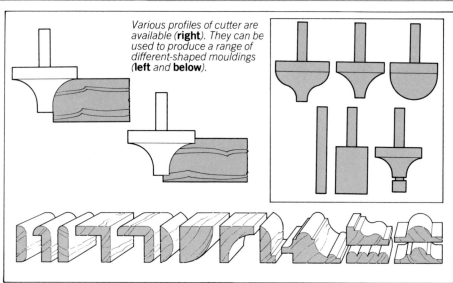

*Various profiles of cutter are available (**right**). They can be used to produce a range of different-shaped mouldings (**left** and **below**).*

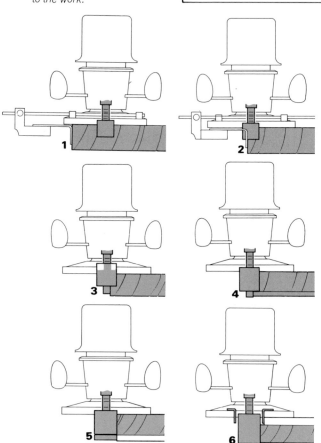

about seven times the top speed of the average drill). On the end of the spindle is a chuck that accepts cutters; these are available in a truly enormous variety of patterns. All share one characteristic: they cut sideways as the router is slid across the surface by means of its handles.

Naturally, the depth of protrusion (i.e., of cut) is adjustable. Fixed-base routers must be switched on before the cutter is lowered into the workpiece till the router base rests on it. More convenient, however, much less dangerous, and nowadays much more common, is the plunging router, whose spindle is on sprung mountings. This means you can position the tool on the workpiece before switching on and 'plunging' the spindle to make the cut; precision is thus far easier to achieve.

The power of a particular router firmly dictates the amount of material it can remove in a single pass without your slowing down the motor and impairing the cut. A good rule is not to cut deeper than the diameter of the cutter you are using. Cuts which cannot be made in a single pass can always be made in two or more, the depth being increased each time. It is often possible to cut right through a piece, in effect using the router as a saw.

It can also be used as a drill, to cut fairly shallow but exceptionally clean holes. However, its main uses can be categorized as either for grooving or for edging.

Cutting a groove is one of the simplest routing jobs. A circular saw, of course, is also capable of this, as are hand plough and combination planes — which forms a good demonstration of the principle that there is almost always another way of doing things. Very few woodworking jobs are the exclusive province of one tool, and many can be tackled by half a dozen or more.

For square-bottomed grooves, a plain 'one-' or 'two-flute' cutter is fitted (the terms refer to the number of cutting edges). Grooves of other shapes can be made with many other cutters, provided they have a 'bottom cut' — that is, they are not designed solely for shaping edges. Many cutters will perform either task.

In all work with portable power tools, especially the router and circular saw, a very great deal depends on how the tool is guided as it is fed into and through the workpiece. Only rarely does

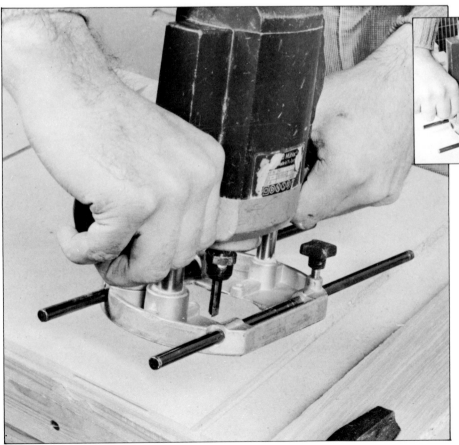

*The router's depth of cut is adjusted by leaving a gap between the adjustment bar and its stop. This gap can be set to correspond to a particular thickness (**top**). After the depth is fixed, the machine is switched on and 'plunged' to cut into the work (**left**), then moved along to produce a shaped cut such as a groove or molding (**above**).*

freehand work produce any accuracy. In the case of fixed machines, the question is the reverse — how should the workpiece be guided as it is fed into the tool? A real grasp of the router's possibilities is essential if you are to exploit it to the full.

An adjustable fitted fence helps to solve the problem in the case of the jigsaw and circular saw (and even some hand planes). A straight-edge fixed to the work does the trick where the fitted fence would not. Both these devices are also used with the router. A fitted fence is standard equipment; on some models it possesses what is called a screw feed, fine or micro-adjustable, which makes it much easier to set to the exact position you need. A router base also has at least one flat side, so that it can be run steadily against a straight-edged guide if necessary.

However, the router will cut round curves — and, unlike the jigsaw, it produces not just a thin kerf but a broad swathe, whose width equals the cutter's diameter and whose exact shape depends on the cutter's profile and setting. These capabilities demand guiding arrangements to match.

*A bearing guide (**above** and **top**), fitted to the cutter itself, can be used to produce an edging cut which exactly follows a template. The template is fixed to the workpiece or vice versa. This is ideal for repeating the same result. Different-sized bearing guides mean varying the relative sizes of template and workpiece. An alternative is a home-made curved fence (**right**), secured to the existing fence attachment and used for following a curved edge. In this case the cutter has no bearing guide or guide pin because the fence ensures it follows the edge.*

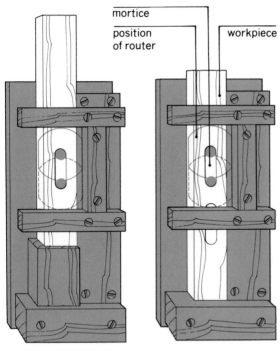

mortice

position of router

workpiece

Above *This jig enables two identical slot mortices to be routed in different positions. The router slides against the right-hand batten and*

between the two stop battens: the packing piece is removed for the second cut. A straight cutter would be used.

Many models offer a special fence or roller for following curved edges. It is also possible accurately to rout recesses of any shape and almost any size by fastening several guide pieces, where necessary, around the sides of the intended cut, so that the router can run against them throughout. The size of the router base dictates exactly how far away such pieces must be positioned; a few experiments will soon give you exact measurements.

Where guiding arrangements like this take the form of a single home-made device — which can be re-used to produce any number of identical cuts — they are called 'jigs'. Some types of jig, especially those made in one piece, are called 'templates'.

Quite often the size of the router base may make it awkward or impossible to use as a means of keeping the tool aligned against the guide. A template 'guide bush' protrudes through the base like a small sleeve for the cutter, and is excellent for following even guides, jigs and templates which incorporate tight internal curves. In all routing work, however, it must be borne in mind that the rotary cut makes absolutely sharp internal corners impossible. No internal corner, in fact, can ever have a radius smaller than that of the cutter (or the template guide, if you are using one). If sharp corners are essential, it is generally a simple matter to chisel them square.

Several metal jigs and templates are available ready-made. Most noteworthy is that which enables you to cut a simple but, nonetheless, usable version of the dovetail joint, or else the comb joint.

When shaping edges, you will need an independent guide, such as a batten or template, if you plan to cut away the edge's whole width, replacing it with a new edge further in. If, however, you will be leaving some of the existing edge intact, merely altering its profile (for example, rounding it over, or cutting a groove along it), you can use the edge as a guide instead.

There are two methods of shaping edges. One is to employ the fitted fence in the normal way. The other is to remove the fence and use a self-guiding cutter: i.e., one of which a certain portion, either above or below the cutting edges, is held sideways against the edge of the work, just like a fence. On the most sophisticated (and expensive) patterns, this portion takes the form of a collar that revolves on roller bearings — at your feed speed instead of the cutter speed, thus avoiding friction burns on the edge of the workpiece.

When edging, it is important to feed the router so that the cutting edges first make contact with the work at the point on their circular travel when they are moving in the direction you are cutting — otherwise the tool may be thrown to one side. The spindle turns clockwise, seen from above. So that means you must keep the edge on the left. Even when grooving or recessing against a straight-edged guide, it helps to have the guide on the left to withstand the kick which may develop.

Cutter manufacturers, and some retailers, distribute very useful illustrated lists and charts of their ranges, which, incidentally, include a number of special cutters for trimming the edges of plastic laminates after they are stuck down.

All cutters are either of high-speed steel (HSS) or, at least partly, of tungsten carbide. Sharpening the latter is not a task for the average home workshop, but it needs doing far less frequently.

Mirror

In this mirror, conventional mitered corners are replaced by bridle joints (open mortices) — pegged with dowels of a contrasting timber, or a timber stained to contrast.

A router is essential for the execution of this particular design, since two rabbets are cut after the frame is assembled. After clamping the frame in position, one method would be to surround it with guide pieces against which the tool could travel, and which would stop it cutting too far at the corners.

The depth and width of the rebates must be carefully fixed so they do not encroach upon the joints.

4mm mirror glass
4mm plywood

shoulders of joint chamfered

matching decorative groove

35

50

380

dowel in contrasting wood

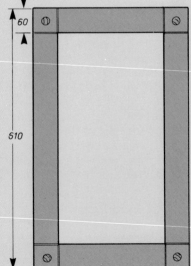

60

510

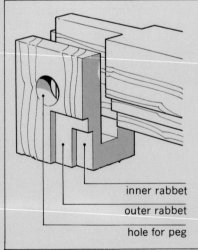

Left *Detail of corner bridle joint shown from the rear. The inner rebate is to hold the mirror in place; the outer to secure the backing. Mirror glass is always cut slightly smaller than the frame in which it fits to prevent cracking.*

inner rabbet

outer rabbet

hole for peg

Power-tool conversions

Despite their obvious differences, hand-held power tools and fixed machines do the same basic jobs. It is the distinctions of detail which need looking at. For one thing, accuracy is enhanced by not having to manipulate the tool itself, with its noise and vibration. Even though most portable tools can be used with fences and guides, pushing timber against a fence (as on a fixed machine) is a lot easier than keeping a moving fence pushed against a piece of timber. And, conversely, fixed machines are not limited in weight or power by human concentration or strength. This means they can be far more stable and more efficient.

The conversion of hand-held power tools into fixed ones naturally bypasses the latter advantage, except insofar as the mountings themselves are heavy and rigid (qualities which you should always look for). But it can be a useful compromise — especially since in every case it provides a 'table', whose presence makes any operation easier. Do make sure that any mounting you buy will accommodate the tool you possess.

Drill stands

A drill stand is a holder into which you fit a power drill so that it points downwards. You feed the bit into the workpiece by pulling a lever.

Not only does this enable far more accurate work than is normally possible when holding the drill by hand, minimizing discrepancies in jointing; it also enables you to fit certain types of cutter that will hardly work otherwise, such as the Forstner bit, the end mill and the saw-tooth centre bit, which bore wide flat-bottomed holes; the last two are universally used when fitting concealed hinges, and all can drill overlapping holes.

The other is the mortice chisel and bit — an invaluable tool which has the distinction of drilling a square hole. It consists of a hollow square-sectioned steel tube, its lower end sharpened on all four inside edges, within which revolves an auger bit. When this is plunged into a workpiece, the auger removes the bulk of the waste from the hole, while the chisel pares the sides clean and true. A series of these holes very quickly makes a mortice which is in no way inferior to a hand-cut one. Purpose-built mortising machines are also available which use the same bit (others work on different principles).

Circular-saw tables

A table for your circular saw allows you to fix it upside-down so that the blade sticks up through the surface. Tables are made for most, if not all, makes of saw; they vary in quality, and especially in rigidity. You can always make one yourself, but it would be wise to work from an existing design to ensure safety. The most important points are high stability and a secure mounting for the saw, but numerous other details also count.

Any saw table should include a rip fence parallel to the blade, so you can align workpieces for ripping — and, if it is to be much use, a sliding 'crosscut fence' at right angles to the blade, against which you hold the piece while moving it forward into the blade for a truly square crosscut.

The uses of a saw-table conversion are identical with those of an integral fixed table saw.

Power-plane inversion stands

Some power-plane manufacturers produce a small stand which enables the tool to be mounted upside-down, with its sole used as a table. It is most important that there should be a guard for the cutters, which are highly dangerous when exposed.

Router conversions

The portable router can be mounted rather like a circular saw, with its spindle pointing up through a cut-out in a table. Again, this can be bought or made. The arrangement produces the equivalent of the fixed shaper machine.

At least one of the smaller routers can be mounted in a drill stand, to resemble the industrial 'overhead router'. This provides quite a few useful options, especially when using templates. However, most routers are not convertible in this way.

Power-tool safety

Do not allow yourself to get over-confident just because power tools are portable and easy to use. Adopt wise habits and stick to them. Chief amongst these is to see that the tool is only switched on while it is actually cutting: never while you are adjusting it. Do not lay it down while it is still running, either. Before starting, make sure your workpiece is secure and all guides, adjustments and the like are firmly tightened. Minimize the unexpected: every move should be planned and performed without haste.

Dining Table

- *Making a table frame*
- *Woodturning*
- *Veneering, marquetry, inlay*
- *Adding lippings*
- *Bending wood*

The appearance of this piece parallels its construction: both exhibit subtle yet definite variations from tradition. Examples include the way the underframe is made, and the joints between flaps and main top.

Features
The table seats two with the flaps down, and four or six with the flaps up. The positions of the legs are most important because they effectively dictate where people can sit. Elbow-room (here reckoned at about 30in (750mm) each) is allocated with this in mind.

All the solid parts are American black walnut. The frame is basically a conventional arrangement of four legs and four rails, mortised and tenoned together. However, it includes some interesting details designed during making.

The design for the simple pattern on the veneered and inlaid top took several hours to reach its final form. It serves to introduce a whole realm of decoration quite independent of surface finishes (although a similar effect could in fact have been achieved by scrupulous masking while staining, painting or lacquering).

The sub-frame
The mortices for the solid end rails were made on the slot-mortising machine. Because their depth puts them beyond the capacity of most routers, the best alternative for the home workshop is either to use a hollow-chisel mortising attachment in a stand-mounted drill, or to cut them by hand (drilling a series of holes first).

The double tenon is a means of ensuring maximum strength without removing too much of the leg. Cutting chunks out of a piece will always weaken it, even if another piece will fill the spaces.

The side 'rails' — and the flap bearers — are frames made from relatively small pieces, tenoned

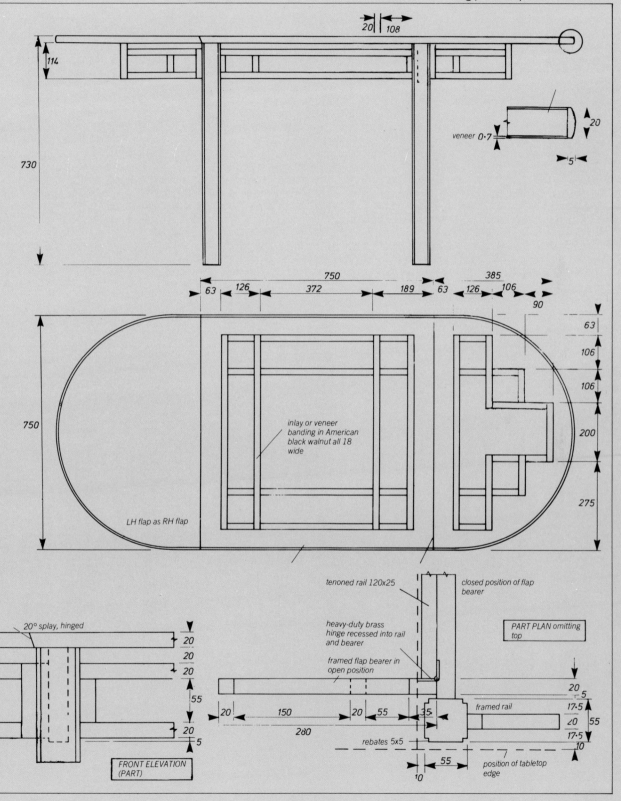

20 | 108

114

730

veneer 0·7

20

5

750 | 126 | 372 | 189 | 63 | 126 | 106

385

63 | 126 | 106 | 90

63
106
106
200
275

750

inlay or veneer banding in American black walnut all 18 wide

LH flap as RH flap

tenoned rail 120x25

closed position of flap bearer

heavy-duty brass hinge recessed into rail and bearer

framed flap bearer in open position

PART PLAN omitting top

20° splay, hinged

20
20
20
55
20
5

20 | 150 | 20 | 55 | 35

280

framed rail

20
5
17·5
20
17·5
10

55

FRONT ELEVATION (PART)

rebates 5x5

10

55

10

position of tabletop edge

together. This was done for visual effect, to echo the pattern on the top. The uprights at each end of these frames are wider than the rest so that the ends can be fashioned into tenons after assembly (the extra width disappears inside the joints).

Woodturning
An unusual feature is the spigot, turned on both ends of each horizontal to lengthen it and peg the tenons in position, thereby adding a little extra rigidity. It serves to introduce the whole business of woodturning, which is a very distinct branch of woodwork.

Unlike any other machine, a lathe works by moving the piece (in fact revolving it), while you shape it with hand tools supported on a tool rest alongside. The cost of a small lathe is comparable with that of other small fixed machines. Most of the tools themselves are hefty relations of ordinary chisels and gouges; a third type are known as scrapers.

Turning involves many considerations and a set of unique skills. It will, however, only produce items which are wholly or partly round in section — whether relatively long and thin, like table legs, or relatively wide and flat like dishes. If your designs do not incorporate such things, you will not need a lathe; if they do, turning may be the only answer. Often the best plan may be to get such components made by someone else. There are quite a few people whose woodworking is limited to turning alone; the craft has a fascination all its own. To learn the basics, you can rarely do better than to attend one of the short courses advertised in woodworking magazines: often these occupy only a single weekend.

Veneering, marquetry and inlay
The top is made from MDF, veneered on both sides before cutting to size.

A knowledge of veneering is more or less indispensable for the furniture-maker — though quite a number of people specialize in country-type pieces which incorporate only solid timber. Historically, veneering has been very important; it remains the prime method of achieving certain very attractive effects.

Below *This table's underframe and flap supports are of solid American black walnut. The top is MDF, veneered in bird's-eye maple with walnut inlay and lippings.*

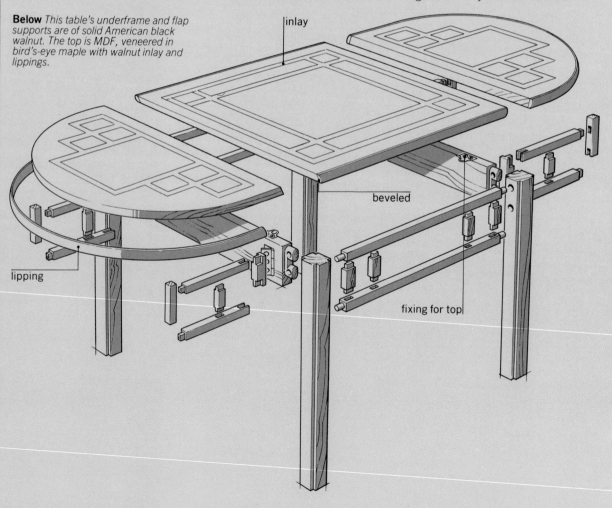

Veneer thicknesses range from a tiny 0.1mm to as much as 6mm for plywood cores. However, the average decorative veneer is 0.7mm thick in Europe and 0.9mm thick in the USA; these are the types you are likely to be buying.

Veneers vary from the very plain to the richly patterned and colored. This depends firstly on the species; a great many are available, and certain timbers and particular figures come primarily, or indeed only, in veneer form. The second vital factor in determining the figure is the way in which the veneer is cut from the log: usually either by peeling or slicing. Peeling produces a continuous sheet like, say, a roll of carpet. Almost all peeled veneers go into plywood — but the

The end rails' double tenons are rounded with a rasp to fit the mortices (1), which have been cut on a slot-mortising machine. Once they are fitted (2), the position of the second mortice is marked on the tenon (3).

technique is also employed, for example, to obtain the decorative 'bird's-eye' figure in maple (used on this table).

Slicing, however, will produce 'leaves' of veneer, each one repeating the figure of its neighbor with minute variations which build up throughout the complete bundle. This repetition can be used in all sorts of ways to make patterns.

A burr is an irregular, bulbous excrescence which occurs on trees of several different species. When sliced it displays a wildly swirling grain much prized in veneer work.

Lastly, you can buy dyed veneers.

The only place to obtain veneers is from a veneer merchant. All of them sell bundles; some sell individual

The mortice position is squared across the double tenon and holes drilled through it accordingly (4). These will accommodate the ends of the front and side rails, which will thereby lock the end rails in place. This effective variation on the conventional set-up is suggested by the fact that each side rail is itself a frame, whose projecting ends can be turned into pegs. It allows maximum tenon lengths and therefore maximum strength. To make each composite side rail, small tenons are first marked on the uprights (5).

leaves, but not usually from the middle of a bundle because that would break the sequence. A few firms sell small pieces, particularly of exotic veneers. In every case, as with solid sections, you should inspect before you buy, because timber varies so much — and because that is the only way of getting to know the species, figures, widths and lengths available.

Veneers can be 'laid' (glued down) on to both solid timber and man-made boards. On plywood, blockboard and veneered chipboard, the veneer's grain should run at right angles to that of the face veneer on the board — the idea being to prevent any small splits from appearing in the veneer as it moves in sympathy with the groundwork in changing humidity. On plain chipboard and MDF the question does not arise. Hardboard is not usually used for veneering.

Veneering over joints is not a good idea, in case any slight movement eventually shows through — but it is sometimes done. General practice,

The tenons are cut across the grain (**8**). They fit into slot mortices cut with the router (**9**). Note that the uprights at each end of the frame are wider than those further along; this is because they will be used inside the joints with the legs. Pieces are dry-assembled to check fit (**10**).

The tenons are marked in width (**6**) before being cut down the grain (**7**).

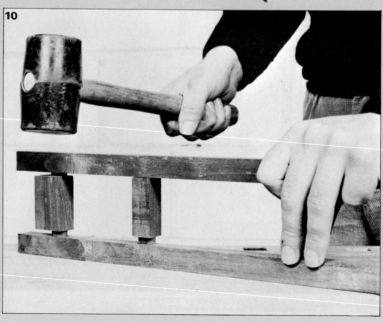

*Small spigots are turned on the lathe in the ends of the horizontal members, to the same diameter as the holes drilled in the double tenons (**11** and **12**). Then the ends of the assembled side rail are saw-cut to form shoulders (**13**).*

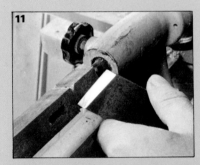

too, is always to veneer both sides of the groundwork, otherwise the veneered side will tend to assume a concave curve. The only exceptions are thickish sections of solid timber, and even then it is best to veneer on the heart side — that nearest the original center of the tree (you can tell the heart side by looking at the way the rings go on the endgrain). The idea is to counteract the natural cupping on the other side caused by shrinkage along the length of the rings.

In many cases, the backing veneer can be cheap and plain — as, for example, on the center section of this table, which will never normally be seen from underneath.

Broadly speaking, there are four methods of laying veneers in the home workshop: by caul, with a hammer, with glue-film and with contact glue.

A caul is simply a stiff, heavy piece which acts as the top layer of a sandwich. You spread glue (white glue is usually adequate) very thoroughly across the ground, lay the veneer on top, cover it in plastic sheet as a barrier for surplus glue, lay the caul on top of that, and clamp the whole lot together — using as many clamps as you can find, plus plenty of strong,

rigid battens to ensure close contact between veneer and ground over the whole area. It is also possible to caul-veneer both sides at once.

Hammer veneering usually involves 'sizing' the panel first with thin glue, letting it dry and sanding it; dampening the veneer a little with tepid water to make it more manageable; spreading Scotch glue on its underside; laying it down; and squeezing out the excess from the edges. The tool used for this, the veneer hammer, is generally home-made, and is not a hammer in the usual sense at all. It is pushed over the surface with as much pressure as you can muster (a little glue is a useful lubricant here). The important thing is to get the veneer to lie extremely close and flat, and thus to ensure suction, which will boost the inherent strength of the glue.

Since it goes off very fast, you will need a warm domestic iron to run over the surface and thus re-activate it during the job. A warm room and a warm hammer all help to keep it workable for as long as possible — but in any case it will only be a matter of a minute or so before it starts to jell. It is important to have all your needs to hand — hot glue, hammer, water, rags, iron — when you start, because speed is essential for a good job.

Veneering with Scotch glue does work, and work well, but it is a messy, touch-and-go procedure for the beginner. Methods differ drastically from one person to another, and there are all sorts of further considerations. The water in the glue (let alone any you use for dampening) will cause the veneer to expand at least slightly, with consequent risk of warping in the groundwork and even small splits in the veneer when it contracts. Water also thins the glue, and its presence in the mixture itself requires you to use some other technique anyway if the groundwork is chipboard.

Scotch-gluing means plenty of scraping and sanding to clean up the surface afterwards, for the glue goes all over the place. A more controlled though less time-tested method is to use glue-film. You iron this on to the

A chisel is used to remove the waste (**14**) so that the end of the composite rail will fit snugly inside its mortice (**15**). A tight fit and clean, level surfaces are always essential for a strong joint.

The supports for the flaps are constructed in a similar way (**16**). Then a marking gauge is set to the thickness of a hinge leaf and used to mark the depth of the hinge recess (**17**) and its width from the center of the knuckle (**18**) on the end of each support.

groundwork, peel off its backing, position the veneer and iron over that. Like Scotch glue, it can be reactivated by using the iron again.

The fourth alternative, contact glue, requires less time or equipment than any of the others — but more care, because its action is instantaneous (or nearly so) and irreversible, like those of UF and white glue. After gluing the veneer and groundwork — leaving an absolutely even surface — and letting the glue go tacky, the best plan is to lay the former on the latter with a sheet of paper in between. Align the veneer precisely, pin it lightly at one side, withdraw the paper and press down with a roller or veneer hammer.

If the veneers are too small for the groundwork, or you are building up a pattern, the pieces will have to be jointed. (Complex patterning is known as marquetry.) Jointing must be done before laying if you are using a caul or contact glue, and during laying in the case of Scotch-gluing. With glue-film you can work to either plan.

Jointing before laying is a matter of

*In chiseling the recess (**19**), the grain is first broken up by repeated crosscuts before the waste is removed (**20**) and the base is leveled.*

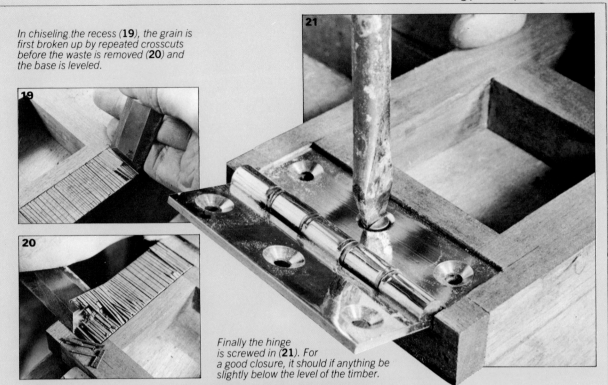

*Finally the hinge is screwed in (**21**). For a good closure, it should if anything be slightly below the level of the timber.*

cutting the pieces and taping them together tightly edge-to-edge with cellulose or gummed paper tape (afterwards peeled and, if necessary, scraped or sanded off). The smallest patterns can be edge-jointed with white glue. In all cases, straight edges are first made to fit snugly by lining up one piece on top of the other, clamping both between boards or battens so a fraction protrudes along the edge, and trimming the two at once — usually with a plane laid on its side.

Whenever you plane or cut veneer, you must pay especially close attention to the grain because the material's thinness makes it so very fragile. Cutting is best done in repeated light strokes with an extremely sharp knife; if you try to sever the whole thickness at once, you can easily tear out pieces or cause splits which follow the grain. Special tools are available for cutting and trimming veneers before and after laying.

To join pieces while laying, you stick one down, overlap the next, cut through both, melt the glue with an

*The width and position of the corresponding recess in the end rail can only be arrived at by measurement (**22**). It is cut in a similar way, but the chisel must be used bevel-down because the recess cannot be approached flat (**23**). It is inset from the leg by the thickness of the support.*

iron if necessary to release the waste strip underneath, and lay the top one finally with the veneer hammer. Then you tape across and along the join with paper tape, to stop it opening as the moisture dries out.

This principle is generally followed when laying decorative 'lines', stringings or bandings. These are, in effect, strips of marquetry-work which can be bought in many delightful varieties ready-made from veneer merchants. They range from 1mm-square pieces, in plain off-white and black, to pieces ½in wide and more which incorporate chevrons, chequers and other patterns in rosewood, tulipwood, ebony and the like. These are generally added by cutting back the main veneer after laying, and then gluing them down separately.

You can also buy ready-made marquetry ornaments, which come backed in brown paper. You stick the exposed side down and remove the paper later. Designs include shells, floral arrangements, urns and fan-like shapes; many are richly colored.

A combination square can be set to the intended depth of the recess and used to check the result (**24**).

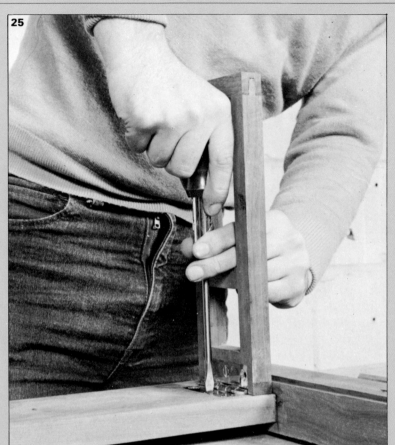

Both supports are fixed to each end frame (already assembled and finally glued) (**25**). With hingeing completed, the supports are checked for alignment and free movement (**26**). Naturally, it is important that they should line up and provide a perfectly level bearing for the flaps (**27**). Note the gap between them when closed.

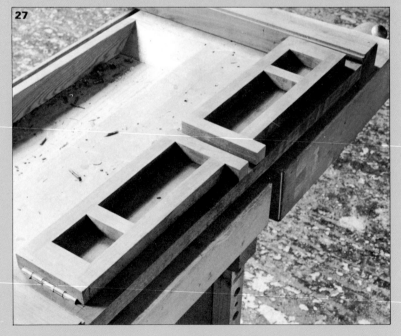

Although our own table-top could have been executed as a piece of marquetry, the technique we used instead comes under the heading of inlay — the recessing of decorative pieces into the material itself, rather than laying them on top. Once the boards had been veneered, shallow grooves were routed in them with an 18mm-diameter cutter — working off clamped-on stop blocks and straight-edges, not by eye. The corners were squared with a chisel, glue was applied, and strips of American black walnut were pressed in.

Lipping
Man-made boards often need a solid-timber covering for their edges — to prevent damage to boards and veneers, and also to improve the appearance. Numerous configurations are possible; a tongue-and-groove arrangement is generally strongest. This table-top exemplifies the two basic procedures: lipping before veneering (as was done along the hinged edges, later beveled for appearance and to avoid creating ledges for debris along the dropped flaps); and lipping after veneering, as was done around the curve.

Either way, an alternative to using solid wood is to veneer the edges. This procedure should present no problems on the long-grain edges of solid timber and blockboard. With endgrain, however, and with other boards, you must make sure the edge is smooth and dense enough for the veneer to stick properly: you may have to plane it, sand it, or both.

For obvious reasons, the caul method is not much use for veneer-

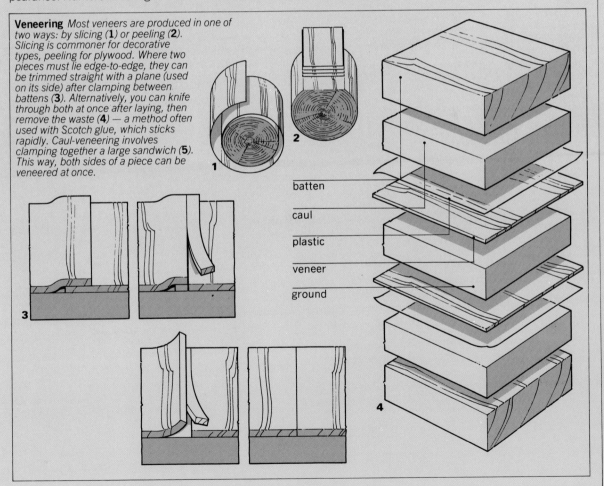

Veneering *Most veneers are produced in one of two ways: by slicing (1) or peeling (2). Slicing is commoner for decorative types, peeling for plywood. Where two pieces must lie edge-to-edge, they can be trimmed straight with a plane (used on its side) after clamping between battens (3). Alternatively, you can knife through both at once after laying, then remove the waste (4) — a method often used with Scotch glue, which sticks rapidly. Caul-veneering involves clamping together a large sandwich (5). This way, both sides of a piece can be veneered at once.*

batten
caul
plastic
veneer
ground

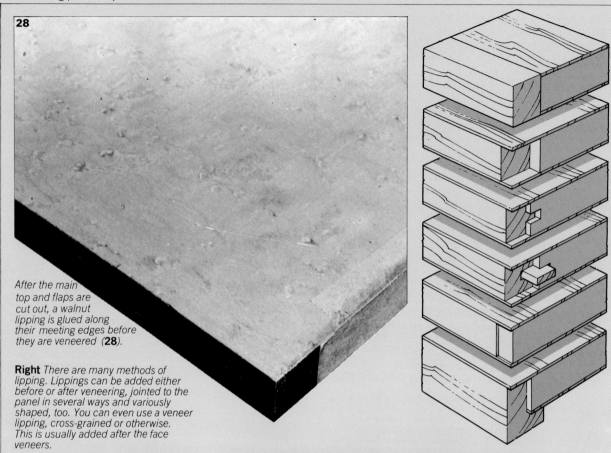

After the main top and flaps are cut out, a walnut lipping is glued along their meeting edges before they are veneered (**28**).

Right There are many methods of lipping. Lippings can be added either before or after veneering, jointed to the panel in several ways and variously shaped, too. You can even use a veneer lipping, cross-grained or otherwise. This is usually added after the face veneers.

This lipping, fixed after veneering, was steam-bent in an open-ended pipe attached to a kettle (**29** and **30**). Some woods bend better than others.

Then, after a while, the clamp was any joint or other fixing. First its ends were cramped to bring it to shape (**31**). Then, after a while, the cramp was removed and an offcut placed next to the straight side of the panel(**32**). This enabled a band clamp to be used for the the final gluing. Lastly, the lipping's ends were clamped again, and a further offcut from the panel positioned and clamped to bring a difficult part of the curve up tight (**33**).

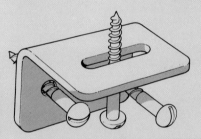

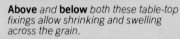

Above and **below** both these table-top fixings allow shrinking and swelling across the grain.

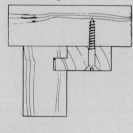

The grooves for the inlay strips are routed very carefully (**34**), using either the attached fence or guides clamped to the work — whichever the particular cut requires. Here, a clamp serves as a stop to end the cut in precisely the right place. The inlay strips are glued in (**35**) They should be a snug fit and slightly proud.

The inlay is trimmed flush with the surface first by planing (**36**) and then by scraping (**37**). This scraper is mounted in a holder like that of a spokeshave.

ing edges. If you employ Scotch glue, starting with a sizing coat on the edge may help adhesion; with contact glue and glue-film, you may need two applications of the coating concerned.

Bending
Some woods (notably ash, beech and elm) bend easily when steamed, and even, to a lesser extent, when immersed in hot water. The technique is far from being universally used, though some furniture-makers rely on it heavily (Windsor chair-making, for example, is largely a matter of bending and turning).

For lipping the table-flaps, however, this technique was ideal. Bending on a large scale or regularly, or both, means making a special steam-box, but a plain kettle-and-pipe set-up can work very nicely. American black walnut bends beautifully into a smooth curve without any splitting at all.

Working fast while it was still hot, the lipping was cramped around the flaps to let it take their shape, so that it would not spring back when positioned for final gluing.

Bent components which are not fixed along their whole length may, like laminated ones, have some slight tendency to straighten out even after drying and cooling. It depends largely on how long they are held in their intended shapes.

38

39

The lippings on the meeting edges are beveled with a plane to a marked line; the angle is checked with a sliding bevel (**38**). A router could also be used, but only with difficulty if an unusual angle were required. The curved lipping is shaped by eye with a block plane (**39**).

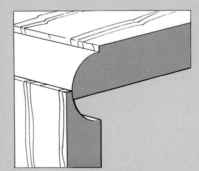

Above The rule joint is the traditional alternative to the detail actually used on this table. Easily cut with a router, it leaves an attractive appearance when the flap is down, and it does not trap dirt. A special hinge known as a rule-joint hinge is available for use with this arrangement.

USING FIXED MACHINES

Fixed woodworking machines can whistle through all sorts of jobs with magical speed. Their convenience makes a radical difference to the whole procedure; there is not doubt that, if you mean to spend some time working wood, you should look seriously at what they do and what they cost.

Buying machines, however, is not that simple. To start with, they are much more expensive than other equipment. Secondly, their functions overlap; as in the cases of hand and portable power tools, you will often find that the same task can be tackled in several different ways — on several different machines. Thirdly, capacities are important. A hand rip saw does its job no matter what, but it is no use trying to cut 7in (175mm) thick timber on a bandsaw which has a 6in (150mm) depth of cut.

Most machines come in both table-mounted and floor-standing versions. As a rule, heavier is better, but of course it also costs more.

Only consider buying a piece of machinery when you have a fair idea of exactly what jobs you want it for — and a fair understanding, in some detail, of how to use it and what it can do. If you can find someone who will demonstrate, seize the opportunity. Some machinery suppliers offer such a service, and (provided you keep an ear open for sales talk) it can be well worth taking the time to attend.

Woodworking machines are also extremely dangerous. Or rather, certain operations performed on them are dangerous — namely, those undertaken in ignorance or defiance of the relevant rules. And, unfortunately, it is all too easy to hurt yourself badly on a machine. Nevertheless, care based on understanding will keep you safe.

With most woodworking machines there are two hazards: the straightforward risk that your flesh will touch the blade (or cutter) — and another, perhaps worse because less obvious, which arises as follows.

In order to cut at all, any powered blade needs to be moving at a certain speed, which varies with the tool concerned. If you cranked a circular saw-blade round by hand, it would be useless. Paradoxically, however, actual cutting itself is relatively safe. The major risk comes when, for any reason, the cutting action is obstructed. A powered cutter such as a saw-blade is not going to stop moving, and its power has to go somewhere. If it cannot cut through the piece, it will simply hammer it: the teeth will deliver a number of very rapid successive blows — and the piece will be hurled away.

Above For ripping on the sawbench, the rip fence is fixed as a guide along which the timber can be fed.
Right Whether for ripping or crosscutting, the guard must be set so the workpiece can only just pass beneath it.

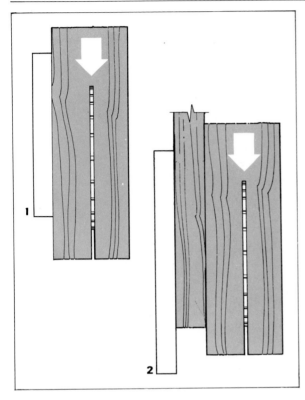

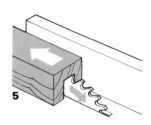

Ripping
Ripping can be perilous if not done properly. To avoid jamming and possible kickback, the fence must end opposite the blade (1) — or be fitted with an auxiliary fence which ends there (2). Careful feeding (3) and a push stick (4) are both indispensable. Grooving (5) is another possibility; it requires a sprung hold-down guard to replace the conventional one. For mitering (6), the work can be clamped to the crosscut fence to stop it slipping.

Circular saws

Take, for example, the fixed circular saw, or sawbench. Its blade sticks up out of a flat table. You feed (push) your workpiece into the blade. Solid timber can be ripped or crosscut, depending on which way you feed it.

At the point where the workpiece meets the cutter, therefore, the two must be traveling (paradoxically enough) in opposite directions. That way, the cutter can cut. If the directions of travel coincide, the cutter will meet an unmanageably large amount of material, which it will tend to reject.

The blade revolves down through the table on the side from which you feed it. The force tends to drive the workpiece securely down on to the surface. At the back edge, however, it revolves up from the table. If, for any reason, a piece starts to move towards you from the back of the blade, even a slight sideways pressure may cause the saw teeth suddenly to encounter a much larger area of uncut wood than they would during the normal

Right *In contrast to the rip fence, the crosscut fence slides back and forth, and is mounted at right-angles to the blade (though it can generally be angled to give cuts at other than 90°). For guaranteed accuracy, the workpiece can be clamped to the fence instead of just held on. By fixing a clamp or clamped-on stop block to the fence and butting the end of each piece against it before cutting, you can make repeated cuts to an identical length.*

feed. Faced with this snag in its cutting, the blade will react by trying to pick the piece up and throw it across the room at a speed of 100mph or so. That is dangerous.

There are three common causes of such hesitation and consequent reverse movement. One is feeding a piece that is simply too thick for the saw to cut comfortably, or at all. The second is a cut that starts to close up behind the blade — a very common risk with solid timber, and especially hardwoods, in which cutting often releases all kinds of stresses, with ensuing distortion. To counter this, a sawbench must have a riving knife immediately behind the blade: that is, a piece of steel (10 percent thicker than the blade, and following its curve) which wedges open the cut.

The third cause takes a little more explaining.

To rip solid wood to a given width or thickness, you need to push it along a rip fence parallel to the blade. Unless that fence ends exactly opposite the back of the blade, there is a danger that cut timber will be trapped between the two. It only takes a small nudge from the blade to push it askew, jamming it there — and, instantly and inevitably, to pick it up and throw it towards you.

Even if the flying piece does not hit you, it may hurt you indirectly by causing you to lose your balance, or your hand to move abruptly. Either way, that blade is far too close for anything less than perfect control at all stages of the cutting operation.

As an extra precaution, all sawbenches normally have a guard above the blade: not just to stop you putting a hand on it, but to keep workpieces where they ought to stay — flat on the table. Finally, too, push sticks (easy to hold, notched to fit over the piece, and always kept within reach) are essential for the last few inches of feed.

To crosscut a piece, you hold or clamp it to a sliding fence at right-angles to the blade (on bigger machines, an entire sliding section of the table), and push both forwards. There are several ways of ensuring a precise length by means of stop blocks and fitments attached to the fence or table, but the rip fence should never be used for this, in case of jamming.

The crosscut fence is often called a miter fence because it can be pivoted for angled cuts. Some saws allow cuts beveled the other way too, via a tilting blade or table; the former is the easier to work with.

Cutting large panels is still difficult on an ordinary-sized sawbench: it is best not attempted without a substantial 'run-off table', roller or rest at the same height.

By lowering the blade so it does not cut all the way through the piece, you can tackle a number of operations apart from simple sizing: grooving, rabbeting and tenoning, for example.

Saw-blades repay study. Some are of steel throughout, and some have tungsten-carbide-tipped teeth. Numbers and shapes of teeth vary, too. Broadly, there are three types — rip, crosscut and combination; and a good TCT rip blade will usually give you the best results all round. Tungsten is certainly far ahead of steel when it comes to staying sharp, especially while cutting man-made boards.

Radial-arm saws
Obviously, really long pieces are too unwieldy to crosscut on the sawbench. The radial-arm saw is unique among small fixed machines because, although its frame is stationary, its blade moves. It sits on a long bench and overhangs the workpiece like a crane; you pull it towards you to cut. Clearly, the maximum distance of travel limits the width of workpiece that can be dealt with.

The procedure has a natural appeal, perhaps because it parallels hand work. Radial-arm saws are also cheap. As their name implies, they will cut at other than right-angles. They can also be turned through 90° and fixed so that you can push pieces through them for ripping.

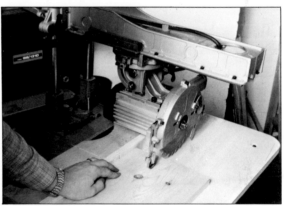

*The radial-arm (or 'pull-across') saw's basic operation is the crosscutting of a stationary workpiece (**top**). But it can also be used for ripping (**center**) and even as a form of shaper (**below**).*

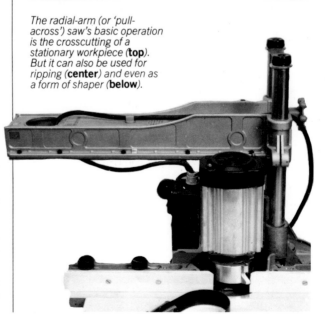

Jointers/planers

Of all machines, perhaps the jointer — sometimes called a surface or overhand planer — possesses the action most impressive to the newcomer. You pass a length of wood (rarely an artificial board) across a rotating cutter-block, which removes an amount pre-set by the distance the block protrudes up past the front or 'infeed' table. A handful of passes transforms a rough-sawn surface into a clean, smooth one from which the character of the wood shines out.

Much wood-machining follows a sequence similar to that of hand work: cutting roughly to length if necessary, perhaps on the radial-arm saw; ripping, usually on the sawbench; and jointing on the jointer. After obtaining one flat surface — the face side — it is then usual to joint an adjacent one as the face edge.

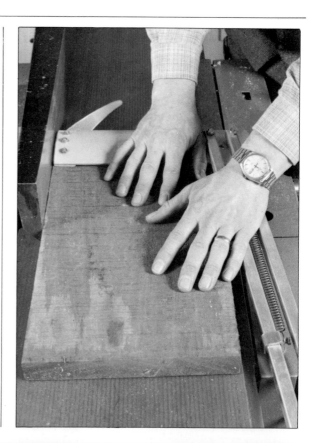

On the jointer, the workpiece workpiece is passed over a rotating cutter-block (**right**). It must be fed against a fence, steadily and with care. Hands are always passed over the guard (**far right**).

With a short workpiece, it is safer to use a push-block (**above** and **right**). This has an extra block fixed to its rear engage the rear of the workpiece (**above right**).

The direction of feed must oppose the direction in which the cutter-block rotates — as with the sawbench, and for the same reasons. If it did not, the cutters could pick the piece up and throw it off instead of jointing it. As it is, they tend, if anything, to push it down safely against the table.

Also for safety, a guard covers the cutters. At least when face-jointing, you should always pass the timber under it and your hands over it. That way your fingers can never slip into the gap. In addition, firm control is just as vital when jointing as when sawing; to avoid kickback you should guide the piece steadily forwards, keeping it against the fence at one side.

Machine jointing has one essential aspect in common with hand-planing — you cannot ignore the grain if you want a reasonable finish. Before passing a piece across the jointer, check which way the grain runs and feed it accordingly to prevent it from tearing out. You must never use this machine across the grain. The piece may break.

To get a truly straight piece, you need to adjust the table heights correctly in relation to each other and to the height of the cutters. However, merely using the jointer will not ensure parallel sides or faces, even if they are straight and flat. For that you need a planer.

This machine incorporates a tunnel, with the cutter-block in the roof, and powered rollers which draw the timber along the floor. The height of the floor (the table) dictates the height of the tunnel, and you adjust it until it is a little too small for the timber.

The planer is generally used after the jointer: it takes the flat surfaces achieved in the jointer as a basis, and proceeds to achieve uniform thicknesses and widths. In other words, it brings timber to the exact sectional size you want. (You joint the width first, because you need the maximum bearing surface.)

Many small planers are combined with jointers: the two machines have a common motor and

The planer planes timber to a pre-set thickness (**below**). The feed is automatic: you simply push the piece in at one end (**right**) and retrieve it at the other (**bottom**).

cutter-block, with the planing table directly under the jointing table. The important dimension for both is the width of the cutter-block and table, which dictates the width of work that can be tackled.

Jointer cutters (knives), of which there are several in a block, need sharpening like all other cutters; though not impossible by hand, especially with the right equipment, the job is usually best handed over to specialists.

Bandsaws

The bandsaw is much favored because it is quiet and very useful.

Its blade is a long continuous strip of steel with teeth on one side, which revolves over an upper and lower wheel. It passes through a hole in the

*The bandsaw can be very successfully used for cutting straight lines as well as curves (**left** and **far left**). Many workshops use it routinely for ripping and cutting tenons (**below**).*

*When cutting curves, it is wise to begin with 'relief cuts' so the waste can fall away easily instead of trapping the blade (**below** and **bottom**).*

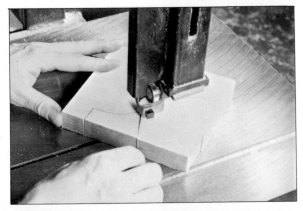

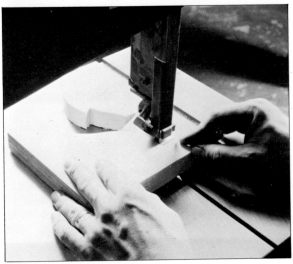

table, traveling downwards. Its relative safety consists in the fact that all the force is, therefore, directed through and on to the table, so it cannot fling material across the workshop.

Wide-bladed bandsaws are used in sawmilling and for other heavy work; the cabinet-maker's machine is the 'narrow bandsaw', whose blade is less than 1in (25mm) and usually less than ½in (13mm) wide. Important dimensions are the throat (the horizontal distance between the blade and the back of the machine, which dictates the size of piece you can cut) and the depth of cut — i.e., the distance between the table and the adjustable guide above it through which the blade passes.

The other point about the bandsaw is that it not only makes curved cuts (because of its narrow blade) but will also do much of the straight-line cutting otherwise performed on the sawbench. It has a fence for this purpose — although, in fact, it is also the only machine on which freehand cuts can be made safely.

It is important to get the blade tension right, working according to the supplier's advice. A loose blade will give a sloppy cut, whereas a tight one may distort the wheel assembly.

Shapers

Unlike the sawbench, planer or bandsaw, the shaper has its cutters mounted on an upright shaft. You shape or square off the edge of the work by pushing it across the table and past the cutter.

Work must be fed firmly and steadily past the opening of the fence which exposes the shaper's cutters (below): always against the direction of rotation, and always aligned by constant pressure on the fence (right).

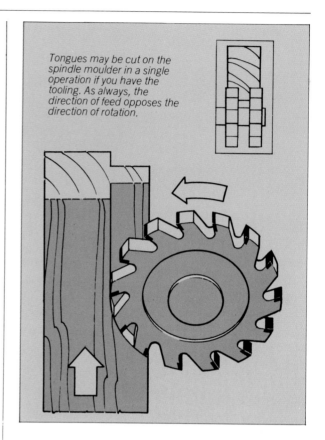

Tongues may be cut on the spindle moulder in a single operation if you have the tooling. As always, the direction of feed opposes the direction of rotation.

The machine may also be considered as a jointer on its side: the resemblance being that the fence, like the jointer table, is in two halves, one either side of the cutter-block. The two are lined up exactly (and fixed firmly!) for a true cut.

For even smoother operation, it is sometimes worth fixing a single 'false fence' of wood across the front of both; you start the machine, then push the fences back till the cutter strikes through the middle of the false fence and protrudes by the amount you want. A stop batten behind the cutter ensures accuracy.

Thirdly, you can use a 'back fence', positioned in front of the cutter and some distance away, setting the gap between fence and cutter to give your workpiece a precise dimension in addition to any edge shaping.

A further possibility is to use a ring fence: not straight at all, but a circular collar which surrounds the shaft and stands proud of the table surface. Curved workpieces are brought to bear

against this flange, and their edges shaped as if they were straight. This technique is not for beginners, but is most useful once you have got the feel of the machine.

The shaper is an alarming machine. In a way, that makes it safer because it keeps you alert. Here again, feed must be against the cutter's rotation — i.e., from the right. That way, the workpiece is cut into instead of being smacked outwards and propelled away, and the fence is on hand to keep it aligned.

The shaft is also adjustable in height. The overall result is that a shaper can do almost anything you like to an edge: square it, bevel it, chamfer it, rabbet it, tongue it, groove it, or profile it in whatever other shape you fancy. Provided you support the workpiece firmly in a suitable jig (or use the extra sliding table present on some models), you can also pass it end-on, for example, to shape endgrain.

The variously shaped cutters take three dif-

Left *The range of possible shapes is as great as the range of cutters which can be bought, or ground to shape in the workshop; in other words, infinite.*

Below left *The machine can also be used for shaping the ends of pieces. It is safest, however, to do this by clamping the workpiece to a special sliding-table attachment. This procedure can be used for making tenons, but the necessary cutters are expensive.*

ferent forms, of which only two are nowadays considered safe. A Whitehill block slips over the spindle. It has slots on opposite sides into which individual cutters are fixed. You can buy these bought ready-profiled, or grind them to the shape you wish. A solid-profile block, mounted in the same way, is an expensive, heavy-duty item whose cutting edges are formed in one piece with its body. Either pattern can be stacked up on the shaft, with suitable spacers, to make compound cuts.

Some small machines may still exist with 'french heads', designed to accept the third type of cutter. Here the shaft has a slot through it: the french-head cutter is simply a steel bar, both ends ground and filed to exactly the same profile, which is passed through the slot and held there by downward pressure from a nut on top.

The evident and real danger is that the cutter will work loose and fly out. This is by no means unknown, and the risk accounts for the demise of

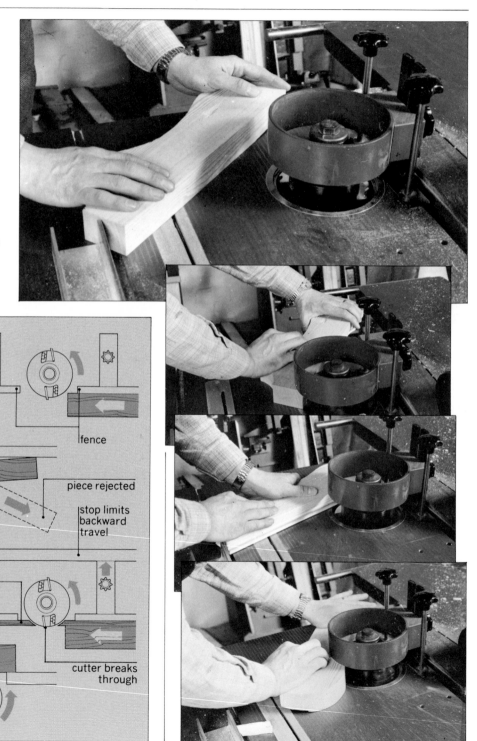

The ring fence on a spindle moulder (**right** and **below right**), with a corresponding circular guard above it, is used for profiling curved workpieces. The operation is not for the beginner. Even with the usual straight fence (**1**), moreover, there is a danger of rejection if feeding is careless (**2**). The false fence helps to ensure a continuously smooth passage, since the cutter only pokes through it (**3**). Cutting from the underside of a piece (**4**) is safer than from above; it also means a slip is less likely to harm the work.

1

fence

2

piece rejected

stop limits backward travel

3

false fence

4

cutter breaks through

french-head cutting in industry. The procedure does, however, have the advantage that the cutters can be fairly quickly and cheaply made up to individual requirements once you know how. They also differ from the other two types in that they work by scraping: the edge must be 'turned over', rather like that of a cabinet scraper.

A sanding drum, or bobbin, is another useful item that can be fitted to a shaper.

Straight fences are adjustable from side to side as well as back and forwards, and should be positioned as close to the cutter-block as possible without actually touching it (always re-check this if you fit a larger-diameter cutter). This minimizes the chance that either your hand or the work will be drawn between the cutter and fence.

Vital accessories on the shaper are hold-down and hold-in clamps — fixed respectively above and in front of the cutter area, and sprung so they keep the work firmly in position against the table and the fence while you feed.

Once more, the danger is perhaps less from the cutter itself than from a workpiece which has become a deadly missile. Nonetheless, the hold-in ensures you need never push directly towards the cutter. Push sticks and holding jigs are also essential, especially when you come to the end of a cut. That goes for the sawbench, jointer and bandsaw as well. Never underestimate the risks these machines present, and never treat them casually. If a planned operation calls for fingers to be brought close to the blade or cutter, think again.

The sawbench, jointer and planer are unsuitable for small pieces; these may bring your fingers too close to the blade or cutters, they are harder to manipulate, they may get trapped and possibly ejected, and they can usually be worked more effectively by hand anyway. However, they can be cut on the shaper, provided you use a jig to hold them: in effect, making them larger and thus more manageable.

Mortisers

Mortising accurately by hand, even with the help of a drill, is one of the more laborious tasks in cabinetry. Mortising machines, though specialized, therefore have a strong appeal.

Two types are worth noting here. One is the hollow-chisel mortiser, available as a machine in its own right, as well as a drill attachment. The

Below The hollow-chisel mortice attachment can be fitted to a power drill for stand-mounted operation.

other is the slot mortiser. This uses a bit rather like a router cutter, mounted vertically or horizontally. It drills into the work, which is moved from side to side; the result is a straight, square mortice with round ends. Usual practice is to round over the tenon to fit.

Universal machines

Since the basis of every woodworking machine is an electric motor, an obvious economy is to use the same motor for several functions.

So-called 'universal' or 'combination' machines allow circular sawing, jointing, planing, shaping and slot mortising, in various permutations, one by one but on the same machine. Surprisingly, they are not always an inferior alternative to buying a set of individual machines. Some are robust and possess large capacities. The decision comes back very rapidly to the nature of your requirements. The main point to watch is the ease, or difficulty, with which you can move the machine from one function to another. You do not want to have to lose a setting on, say, the saw just because you need to do some planing; it will have taken time to get right, and you may need it again afterwards.

Above *Like a larger version of the drill stand, the purpose-built chisel mortiser is operated by means of a lever.*
Right *Universal woodworking machines can provide a good solution to the problem of getting well equipped — though the larger ones are not cheap. They combine several functions, typically circular-sawing, planing, jointing and shaping. When buying, a particular point to investigate is the convenience (or otherwise) with which functions can be changed.*

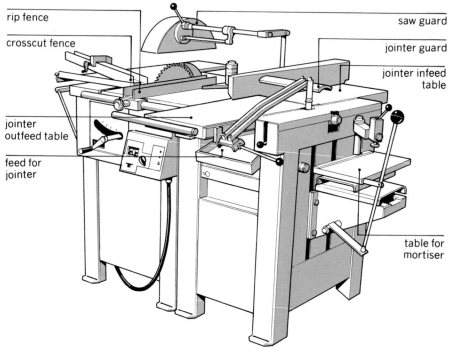

rip fence
crosscut fence
saw guard
jointer guard
jointer infeed table
jointer outfeed table
feed for jointer
table for mortiser

Left *The first step in any woodturning job, after preparing a square- or octagonal-sectioned block and fixing it in position, is to revolve it by hand to check that it can turn unobstructed.*
Below *Preliminary roughing-out of the cylinder is accomplished by means of various special gouges. All turning tools are supported on the tool-rest while cutting; they have long handles for control and leverage.*

Lathes

The lathe is not expensive when compared with other machines, and it does allow you to tackle jobs which would otherwise be impossible.

Important features to examine when choosing a lathe are the length of workpiece it will accommodate, and whether it is solid and stable; vibration makes woodturning extremely difficult. The swing — that is, the maximum diameter of workpiece that can be handled — need be no more than 16in (400mm) or so.

Using the special chisels, gouges, scrapers and parting tools is a matter of motion and feel. The best plan is to experiment for a while before taking one or two lessons from an experienced turner. This should provide an understanding of the problem areas, followed by practical (as opposed to merely theoretical) indications of how they may be dealt with.

Woodturning, it is worth noting, is a driving passion for many people, for whom it possesses a fascination far beyond its immediate practical value — at least in terms of cabinet-making.

Intricate shaping can also be carried out by manipulating gouges of different types and widths, and by the use of the skew chisel; this is like an ordinary wood chisel, but with an angled nose and a bevel on both sides. Woodturning is a skill of its own, with difficulties and refinements which can only be appreciated in practice, as shown by this sequence of turning an egg- cup. The exact cutting angle, and correct sharpening techniques, count for a lot (**right**, **center** and **below**).

These pictures give some idea of the variety of woodturning tools and operations. A round-nose chisel can be used for roughing out (**1**). The skew chisel produces a fine surface (**2**), while the straight chisel is also favored by some (**3**). Either can be used to clean up endgrain (**4**) and for finer detail (**5**), while the parting tool (**6**) can be employed for deep cuts which sever the workpiece altogether when the job is finished. All manner of shapes can be worked (**7**).

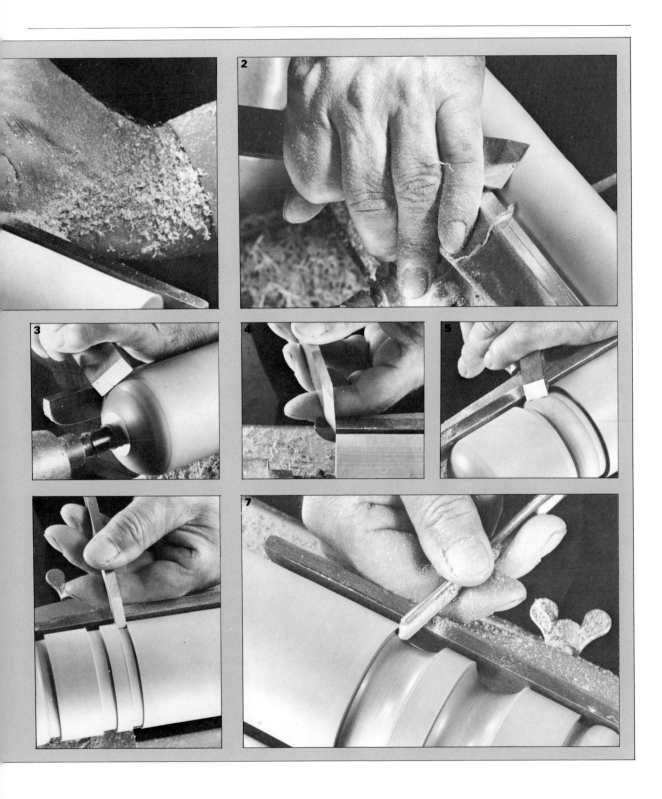

Writing Desk

- *Mortised-and-tenoned framing*
- *Dovetail joints*
- *Housed joints*
- *Designing and fitting drawers*
- *Mitreing*

The basic design for this desk was determined in a very short time: five minutes or less. The details took much longer, but the overall shape hardly changed at all.

Features
A comfortable height for sitting at, and a clear space into which knees and thighs can tuck in unobstructed, are two fundamental requirements this piece must fulfill. Shallow drawers and a suitable writing surface complete the brief.

The eventual finish was very much part of the initial idea, but once the piece was being assembled it became evident that several alternatives might have looked equally good. The solid-timber parts are maple, used for its hardness and density.

The construction has a fair amount in common with classic techniques, but differs in its use of the MDF base panel as part of the structure instead of just an infill. Traditionally there would probably have been a front rail running underneath the drawers. Instead there is only a cosmetic 'lipping' glued to the edge of the panel.

Mortice-and-tenon joints
The traditional and straightforward aspects of the design are the mortice-and-tenon joints between rails and legs.

Generally speaking, a mortice-and-tenon (the tenon is the piece that protrudes) is the best way of joining two pieces of wood at right-angles. Dowels are its principal rivals, but they are difficult to align. If properly designed and made, the mortice-and-tenon has a large gluing area and plenty of rigidity. Unless other factors intervene, the thickness of the tenon is usually one-third the width of the face in which the mortice is cut.

The traditional procedure for making such a joint involves squaring lines round both pieces to mark mortice-and-tenon length; marking tenon thickness and mortice width with the twin points of a mortice gauge (set to the width of a suitable

chisel conforming to the one-third rule); cutting the tenon with a tenon saw, first along and then across the grain; and chopping out the mortice with a chisel.

Tenoning is fairly easy; it can also be done on the bandsaw, circular saw, router, radial-arm saw and even the shaper. The most difficult part is probably making the mortice square and clean. One short cut is to drill a series of holes first, using a chisel only for finishing off. The router is a useful alternative for shallow mortices; like the specialized 'slot mortiser', it leaves a mortice with rounded ends. You can either square them off with a chisel, or round the ends of the tenon to match.

When mortising near the end of a piece, common practice is to leave extra length to be sawn off only after the joint is glued up. Such 'horns' prevent splitting when the tenon is inserted.

The joint comes in an impressive

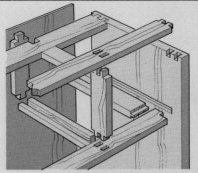

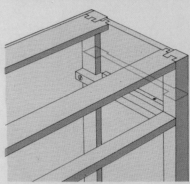

*Traditional cabinet construction ensures that nothing can restrict moisture-induced movement across solid-timber side panels (**above left**). Dovetailed rails connect these, and form the basis of a framework for installing drawers so that they run straight and do not tip up. The arrangement varies slightly where the side panel is inset (**left**).*
This writing-table has some similar features, but shrinkage is not a problem since its tenoned rails run lengthwise.

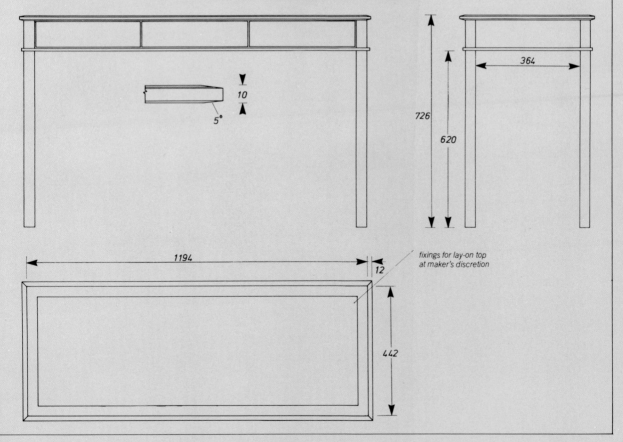

10

5°

726

620

364

1194

12

442

fixings for lay-on top at maker's discretion

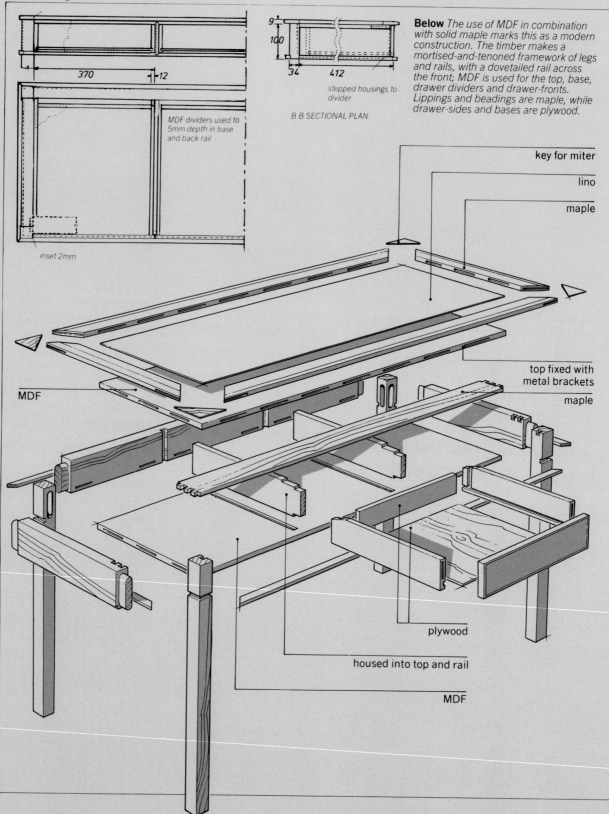

370 · 12

MDF dividers used to
5mm depth in base
and back rail

inset 2mm

9
100

34 · 412

stepped housings to
divider

B B SECTIONAL PLAN

Below *The use of MDF in combination with solid maple marks this as a modern construction. The timber makes a mortised-and-tenoned framework of legs and rails, with a dovetailed rail across the front; MDF is used for the top, base, drawer dividers and drawer-fronts. Lippings and beadings are maple, while drawer-sides and bases are plywood.*

key for miter

lino

maple

top fixed with
metal brackets

maple

MDF

plywood

housed into top and rail

MDF

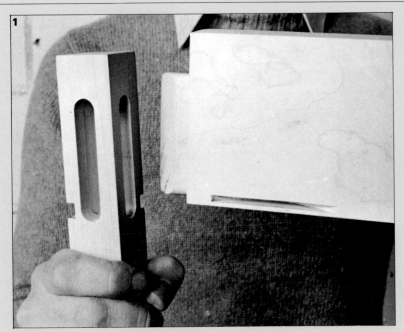

The tenons on the rails are mitered where they meet in the legs (**1** and **2**). A rabbet for the beading is worked in the lower edges of the rails (**3**) to align with the grooves across the faces of the legs (**4**). The beading is fitted (**5**) and mitered at the corners (**6**). Note that the rails are already recessed for biscuit-jointing to the base.

6

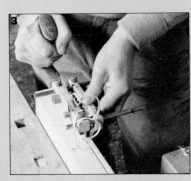

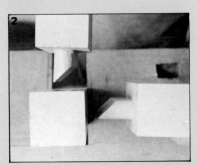

*Dovetails are cut in the front rail (**7**). Marking by eye is quickest, and the resulting variations — acceptable in hidden work — ensure that the rail only fits the right way round. The pins are marked onto the leg section (**8**) and then the exact depth is marked with the gauge set as for the tails (**9**). For this the leg and rail are cramped but not glued, so any error will not waste both.*

range of guises. To start with, it can vary in the number and configuration of its shoulders (the steps around the tenon). The tenon can be 'haunched' to stop it twisting. It can run right through the mortice piece, being cut overlong and planed flush afterwards; or it can be a 'stub' or 'blind' tenon, like the ones here. 'Through' tenons can be wedged from the far side in various ways. Both types can be pegged sideways with dowels ('draw-boring' is the technique of drilling the peg-hole through the tenon slightly further back than that through the mortice piece, so that inserting the dowel or dowels tightens the joint). Pegs and wedges can both be decorative, especially if cut from contrasting woods. The dining-table project includes 'double tenons'; twin tenons, on the other hand, are paired but completely separate.

Where tenons meet in a leg, they are often mitered, as here. They can also be halved over each other.

The bridle joint is a useful variant of the mortice-and-tenon: it is more or less the same in reverse, and thus ideal for T-joints where the top bar of the T is thinner than the other part.

Frame-and-panel construction
The ordinary paneled house door (not the 'flush' type) is a good example of traditional frame-and-panel construction. It is not a single solid sheet, but a composite structure which consists of a frame surrounding a panel, usually thinner. The panel fits in a groove round the inside of the frame, or in a rabbet where it is usually held with a strip of wood added afterwards.

The corner joints of such frames are usually mortised and tenoned. Careful consideration is needed to ensure that the groove or rabbet complements the joints, or at least does not interfere with them. It can be cut before jointing by several different means, or sometimes afterwards with a router.

There are many decorative possibilities in terms of shaping the edges of the frame, or panel, or both.

Design gaps
The outer surfaces of leg and rail are not flush. There is a 'step' of about 1/8in (3mm) between them, and it demonstrates an important point.

Sometimes it is both necessary and possible to get two components absolutely flush, usually by planing and sanding after assembly. If, however, it is not necessary, there is no reason to give yourself the work — and work there will be, because almost every assembly in woodwork contains at least small discrepancies, quite detectable by hand if not by eye. What is more, discrepancies often arise inexorably after flushing off, because of movement caused by changes in moisture content.

Frequently, therefore, it is best to introduce a gap, or other disjunction, in the first place — of a size which proclaims it to be deliberate and not a mistake.

A common trick with pieces which nominally lie flush is to run a small groove or molding of some kind down the joint to distract attention from the discrepancy that will inevitably be there.

Dovetails
The other important structural joint for solid timber — in this writing table as elsewhere — is the dovetail. This has a locking ability possessed by few

others, which is why it is used at the front and often the rear corners of traditional drawers: it withstands great stress in a particular direction. It also joins the corners of boxes.

In a drawer, the dovetails are cut in the side and their mating 'pins' in the front. In a through dovetail joint, the endgrain of the tails is visible at the front, whereas lap dovetails are shorter than the pin piece is thick. The miter (or secret miter) dovetail joint is a clever, intricate and very demanding variant which, when complete, is invisible.

Making dovetail joints is a fairly complex procedure, but some general points are worth outlining from the start. First, the pieces need not be the same thickness, although their ends must be square to their edges. Secondly, dovetails can vary both in slope (from 1 in 5 to 1 in 8) and spacing. Thirdly, there is always a pin at each end of the joint, rather than a partial tail, because this helps to prevent any twisting in the pin piece.

The dovetail principle can be used with quite a few other joints (for example, housings, bridles, halvings) where you want to increase strength by adding locking properties.

Housings
The drawer dividers here are housed into the back rail, the base and the

Once the pin recesses are chiseled (10), the side frames are assembled (11). Then the housings for the dividers are marked and cut in the base (12 and 13) before it is biscuit-jointed to the back rail. Their positions are transferred to the front rail, which is housed likewise before the entire central 'box' can be assembled (14).

The base is glued and biscuit-jointed to the side rails at the same time as the mortice-and-tenon joints connect the back rail to the back legs. Then the front rail can be fitted (**15**). Lastly the beadings are glued (**16**). Clamps hold them into their rabbets.

Hanging drawers

Drawers can be hung in many ways. Two unconventional arrangements are top hanging (**1**), and using the base as a runner (**2**). Two ways of fixing a drawer-base are indicated (**3** and **4**). The crudest joint for a drawer's front corner is also shown (**5**); dovetails are the classic refinement, but others are possible. Even these pins, however, impart sideways (shear) strength where it is needed.

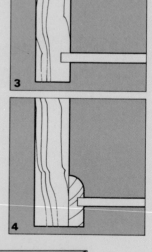

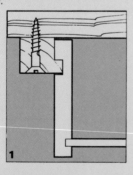

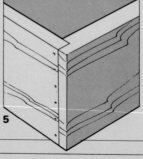

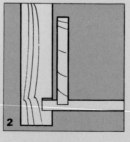

dovetailed front rail. A housing is simply a groove into which another component fits bodily (the method is standard for supporting shelves). A dovetailed housing has sloping sides so the housed piece cannot pull out. All the housings here are 'stopped', i.e., before they reach the edge of the piece, so that they are not seen. This means cutting a corresponding notch or shoulder in the housed piece.

The housings grooves in the base were cut with a radial-arm saw with a dado head, blocks being fixed to the fence so the piece could only be moved a certain distance before the groove was stopped.

Drawer construction and basic fitting
A drawer is a box for a special purpose. Dovetails offer only one answer to its contruction. Often it is enough to fit the sides into rabbets in either end of the front, glued and pinned. Here biscuits were used, and a very strong joint results.

Standard practice is to fit the back into vertical grooves in the sides, running the sides past for the purpose. The base either fits into grooves cut directly in the front and sides, or perhaps into a grooved molding (a drawer slip molding) pinned to them. Either way, it is generally slid in from behind after the rest of the drawer has been glued up, and pinned to the underside of the rear.

The front, sides and rear can be of solid timber or any board material — except chipboard, which is only suitable for fronts because its edges are fragile. Solid timber is more or less essential for dovetailing, though it will work in some plywoods and occasionally in blockboard. The sides of these particular drawers are cut from drawer-side plywood.

Drawer-bases nowadays are usually of ¼in (6mm) plywood; hardboard (generally with its face plastic-coated in white) is often considered an acceptable alternative.

Most drawers are boxes within boxes. The configuration used here is about the simplest possible. But, where the cabinet incorporates framing instead of just flat panels, com-

plications can result — because there must still be components which will act as guides to keep the drawers square and horizontal.

In all cases, the easiest arrangement is for the drawer to slide on its sides; if necessary, special front-to-back pieces must be incorporated (e.g., screwed to the cabinet sides) for support. Positioning two or more drawers side-by-side — as here — introduces further considerations: they will need dividers or other guides to stop them skewing sideways. Moreover, a drawer without a panel immediately above it will need 'kickers' to stop it tipping.

Many of these requirements are fulfilled at a stroke by side-hanging drawers. But there are still other methods; and new solutions will always emerge — too many factors are involved for all the methods ever to be cataloged once and for all.

Mitering
The writing table's top is made of plywood, faced in the workshop with lino (an excellent material for writing surfaces because it combines toughness with slight resilience). The lino is planed exactly flush with the ply: if it were oversize it would stop the maple edging from butting up

For an accurate fit, the drawer-fronts must be aligned in relation to the cabinet and to one another (17). A drawer should be an easy sliding fit, with no perceptible play either vertically or from side-to-side. To achieve this, it is best to make components very slightly too large for subsequent shaving (18).

properly, and if it were undersize there would be gaps.

The edging is biscuit-jointed to the ply; but first it is mitered. A miter is any joint made by cutting each piece at half the overall angle. Since most joints are at 90°, most miters are at 45°. There are a number of tools which enable mitering to be done accurately without having to mark out and follow the angle by eye. Accuracy is essential, for even ½° variation will be apparent — and most miters are for show.

A miter means that any profile in the pieces will flow straight round the corner uninterrupted. The laborious alternative is 'scribing': a term denoting any operation whereby a piece is marked and cut to fit round a shape, and especially whereby one length of molding is cut to fit over its neighbor.

For the sake of appearance it is crucial that the maple lipping biscuit-jointed round the top should be mitered (19). It must also be absolutely flush with the lino writing-surface; an offcut of lino is used to check this (20).
The lino sheet is glued on and trimmed flush round the edges before the joints are finally assembled. Then the decorative chamfer is formed on the lipping by careful planing (21).

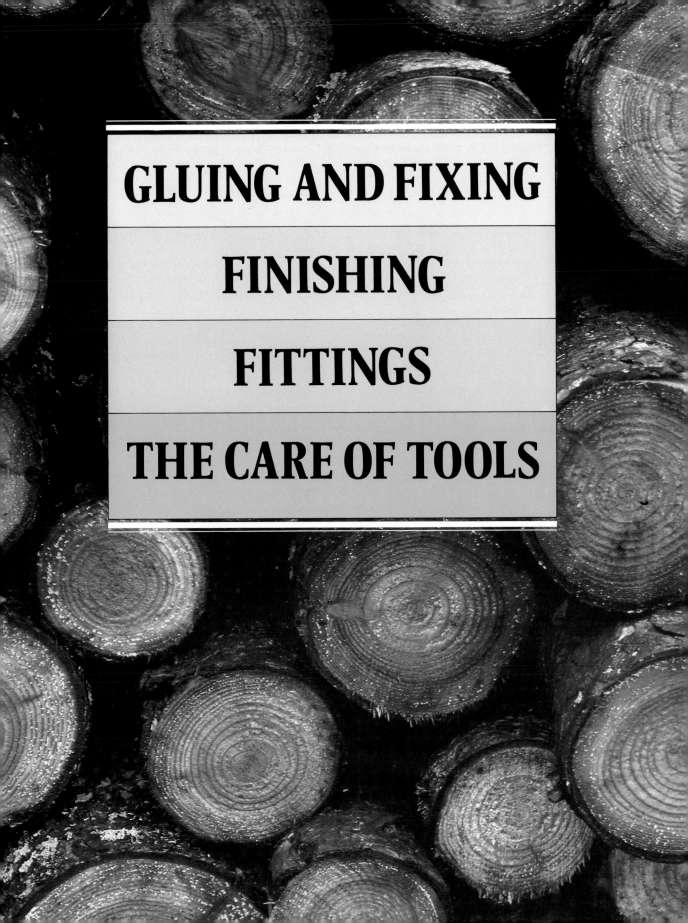

GLUING AND FIXING

FINISHING

FITTINGS

THE CARE OF TOOLS

GLUING AND FIXING

Traditionally, furniture was often held together solely by its joints, in many cases locked with wooden pegs. Nowadays this form of construction is only one option among several. The two principal means of making sure that components stay together are glues and fixing hardware.

ADHESIVES

There are at least five different types of glue in common use by amateur woodworkers. Each performs certain tasks better than others.

White glue

White glue, also known as polyvinyl acetate (PVA), is a thickish liquid, and probably the most useful and cost-effective all-round adhesive for

*White glue is the workhorse adhesive for general cabinet-making. For sound joints, it is sensible to use a brush for spreading it (**right**) and to make sure the area is completely covered (**far right**). The pre-requisite, however, is clean cutting.*

Urea-formaldehyde glue

Unlike white glue, urea-formaldehyde (UF) adhesive becomes completely rigid when it sets, and it fills gaps well. It is waterproof in all except extreme conditions.

This type of glue is also more expensive than white glue, and slightly more trouble to use because it must be prepared. Generally this means mixing a whitish glue powder with water — carefully, so as to avoid lumps and get the consistency right. Excessive thinness means weakness, so follow the manufacturer's instructions.

Once prepared, it takes much longer to go off than white glue. After application it is best left overnight to set fully. Again, heat speeds up this process.

woodwork. It is sold in almost every hardware store, and available from more specialized suppliers in large tins. It is used from the container.

Although it becomes too stiff to work with properly after ten minutes or so, it takes two or three hours to set or 'cure', so the joint needs to be held firmly together — for example, with clamps — during that period. It takes longer in cold conditions and less time in hot.

It is not ideal for joints which will come under continued stress, such as those in the average chair. This is because it never quite loses a certain elasticity, and may therefore 'creep'. It is also not especially good at filling gaps — sometimes a requirement if there is inaccuracy or roughness to be disguised. Most white glue is not water-resistant.

Animal glue

'Scotch' glue, made from hide and bone, is the cabinet-maker's traditional adhesive. It sets very quickly, and liquefies equally quickly with the application of heat.

These qualities make it extremely useful in hand veneering, although alternatives do exist. It can also come in handy when you are fixing something, such as a small decorative molding, that is too awkward or time-consuming to clamp, for the glue will set even as you position the item. In this case it is best to slide the piece to and fro till you feel the 'tack', in order to create suction and thus a stronger bond. This produces a 'rub' or 'rubbed' joint. (With very small pieces, white glue can be used for this.)

Traditionally animal glue comes as 'pearl glue' — small, hard beads which must be well soaked (ideally in a plastic container, so you can break it if the glue solidifies) and then gently heated until they melt. The glue must never boil or burn, or it will not stick. The best apparatus for heating it is, therefore, a double boiler, either bought — from specialist tool suppliers — or improvised. An improvised version could consist of an outer pot (which might be a tin can), partly filled with water and placed on a small gas or electric ring, plus an inner pot (which may be a glass jar on a block of wood) in which you put the glue.

Powdered, ground, caked and flaked animal glues also exist, plus liquid types which need less heating — and no preliminary soaking.

Ordinary Scotch glue is only liquid when very hot. It should be nicely runny, but not too thin. Although it starts to go off the moment it begins to cool, you can melt it again simply by applying heat — preferably in combination with moisture. Dried glue can be put straight back in the pot.

This adhesive is not waterproof at all, but it has a certain useful flexibility. It will also fill smallish gaps.

Hot-melt glues
The 'thermoplastic' nature of Scotch glue (the term refers to the fact that heat reverses the setting process) is shared by the modern group of hot-melt adhesives, mostly based on polyamide resins. Although much more common in industry, these are also sold for home use in two forms.

The glue gun is a pistol-shaped device into which you insert, from the back, a stick of solid adhesive. The gun heats the stick up, melting it, and ejects a 'bead' of glue from its nozzle when you pull the trigger. The glue sets in a few seconds — thereby recommending itself in situations where hand pressure is enough and is more convenient than clamping. In fact, however, it sets so quickly that you may be left with a thick deposit which prevents the pieces from coming together properly. In addition, it is not very strong.

Glue-film, by contrast, comes in thin sheets 36in (914mm) wide with a paper backing. Its particular application is in veneering, because an iron can be used to heat, liquefy and bond it. This avoids much of the awkwardness that might be experienced when brushing on Scotch glue.

Contact adhesives
Many people are unclear about the difference between contact (or impact) glues and other types. Contact glues must be spread over both surfaces — not just one, as with other adhesives — and allowed to become dry to the touch (which usually takes 15 minutes or so). Only then should the surfaces be brought together.

With most varieties, the bond is immediate on contact: hence the name. It is also extremely strong. There is no hope of any re-positioning. The glue is therefore useful, in the same way as Scotch glue, in circumstances where any clamping is difficult or impossible, but much less so where you need time to achieve accuracy. Although types which allow some re-positioning for a limited time are available, contact glues are never used for general woodworking. That is because they do not produce especially tight joints, since they allow no clamping and do not rely on suction. In addition, pieces cannot be slid together. Like white glue, they show some creeping under stress.

Scotch, white and UF glues are soluble in water until they have set; most contact adhesives are not, so brushes and spreaders must be cleaned in white spirit or a similar solvent. Water-based contact glues are, however, another recent development.

Epoxy-resin adhesives
The main use of epoxy glues is for joining dissimilar materials. They will certainly work in wood-to-wood and board-to-board joints — but for these purposes they are rarely a wise choice, being fiddly to use and relatively expensive.

However, for gluing steel to glass, brass to wood, aluminum to plastic laminate and so on, epoxy glues have no close rivals. The most familiar variety comes in paired tubes whose contents must be equally mixed to start the reaction which makes the adhesive set. The chemicals involved are very sticky and so need careful handling — especially since, again, water will not remove them (turpentine may, provided you do not wait too long).

The most common epoxy glues either set in about six hours (more quickly in warm conditions) or in less than half an hour in the case of the 'rapid' variety. Even with the latter, however, some arrangement is needed which will keep the halves of the joint firmly together meanwhile.

FIXING HARDWARE

Even today a strong feeling persists that metal fixings should be absent from the best work — that jointing problems should be solved without their help. There is something to be said for this approach, but the products are nonetheless available and each has its role. Decisions in this area will probably center on questions of appearance.

The range of metal fixings is enormous; included here are all the ones common in furniture-making. They should meet most requirements.

Nails

The cabinet-maker does not need large nails for assembling furniture (though they may well be needed for making jigs and the like), but there are a great many uses for small ones. The smallest of all are the so-called veneer pins and molding nails, so thin that they bend easily — especially in hardwoods. Drilling holes first with an extremely fine bit may prevent this tendency, as well as avoiding the splits which any nail can cause in certain circumstances. It is common sense not to drive a large nail into a narrow piece, or too near the end of a length. Some timbers (notably ramin) also split more readily than others. Another trick to minimize splitting is to blunt the point of the nail slightly before driving it, so that it punches a hole through the wood rather than parting its fibers.

Panel nails are slightly thicker than molding nails. Coppered versions are available, which are useful for preventing the corrosion that occurs by reaction when certain woods such as oak, sycamore and afrormosia are in contact with iron and steel.

Larger still are oval nails, oval in section. Lost-head nails, which resemble large panel nails, are round.

All these types — unlike the flat-headed nails used by carpenters — can be quite easily 'punched' so that their heads lie below the surfaces of timber and boards. All are sold by weight; for cheapness, they are best bought either loose or in large bags. Veneer, molding and finishing nails come in lengths as short as ½in (13mm).

Screws

There are countless varieties of screws — machine screws, set screws, socket screws, coach screws, self-tapping screws, and so on; but only two types

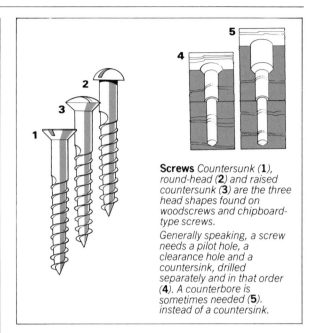

Screws *Countersunk (**1**), round-head (**2**) and raised countersunk (**3**) are the three head shapes found on woodscrews and chipboard-type screws.*

*Generally speaking, a screw needs a pilot hole, a clearance hole and a countersink, drilled separately and in that order (**4**). A counterbore is sometimes needed (**5**). instead of a countersink.*

matter much in woodwork, namely woodscrews and 'chipboard screws'. Both are sharp-pointed. Woodscrews are 'threaded' for about three-fifths of their length. Though they are still very familiar, chipboard screws now offer them strong competition. The latter do indeed hold better in chipboard, which is notoriously crumbly, especially along the edges; but they hold better in other boards and solid timber too.

The thread of a chipboard screw — which often, though not always, runs right to the head — has a shallower pitch than that of a woodscrew; in other words, it spirals less steeply, and therefore provides more turns and greater 'engagement' in the material over a given length. This would make for slower work except that the spiral is in fact a double one, so that the rate of entry is doubled.

The heads of woodscrews come in three main shapes. The commonest is countersunk: i.e., flat-topped and tapering at 45° into the shank. Countersunk screws require a corresponding countersunk recess to be formed in the material, to accommodate the head. The appropriate tool is a special bit called, unsurprisingly, a countersink, and available for both power and hand drills. (Do not expect screws to countersink themselves, because, as often as not, they will refuse to go flush with the surface.)

Alcove Cupboard

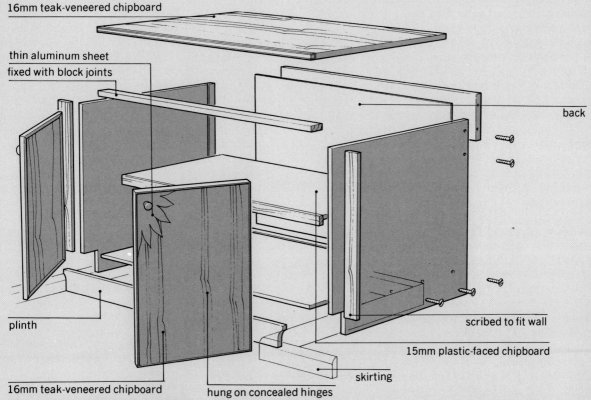

16mm teak-veneered chipboard

thin aluminum sheet
fixed with block joints

back

plinth

scribed to fit wall

15mm plastic-faced chipboard

16mm teak-veneered chipboard

skirting

hung on concealed hinges

The modern way of installing fitted furniture — items which are secured in position rather than free-standing — is to make up the carcase as a complete unit and then fasten that to the wall with relatively few fixings.

This principle (applied, for example, to kitchen units) has been used for this alcove cupboard. The plinth or kick-board is scribed to fit over the skirting, and 'scribing strips' cover any gap at either side.

The materials are largely plastic-faced and veneered chipboard, with aluminum sections and sheet being employed for some unusual decorative details. The carcase is fixed together with chipboard screws, which make quite a strong joint. The doors are hung on 'concealed' hinges.

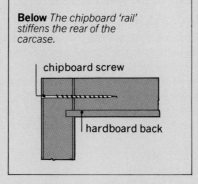

Below *The chipboard 'rail' stiffens the rear of the carcase.*

chipboard screw

hardboard back

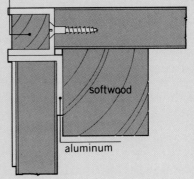

softwood planed to fit and epoxy-glued

softwood

aluminum

Raised-head or raised countersunk screws are similar except that their tops are slightly domed. Round-headed screws have pronounced domes which sit flat on the surface and so require no countersinking.

Chipboard screws are normally available only with countersunk heads.

The head of a screw, of course, is also cut away so that the screwdriver tip can engage in it. The cutaway may be a 'slot' or a cross-shaped recess. Raised-head and round-headed screws are mostly slotted, but countersunk screws of both thread types can be either slotted or recessed.

Some people prefer one type and some the other, but a different screwdriver (or at least a different tip) is required for each. And recesses themselves are of two very similar types, Phillips and Supadriv; for best results you should use a Phillips screwdriver for the former and a Pozidriv screwdriver (or Supadriva) for the latter.

Woodscrews, having been available for longer than chipboard screws, come in a greater range of materials. Steel is the most popular, but it can be plated in various ways. Brass, aluminum, stainless steel and even bronze are further alternatives. For the newer screws, the choice is usually between plain steel and steel which has been bright-zinc plated.

It is worth getting to know about screw gauges (thicknesses) and lengths. Gauges are numbered 0 to 32 in order of increasing size; the thicker the screw, the larger the diameter of its head. Gauges 4, 6, 8, 10 and 12 are the most generally useful, but 5 and 7 may also be needed sometimes. The precise diameters do not matter as long as you know which gauge is which — and can match each to suitable drill bits.

This last point is important, because all except the smallest screws require holes to be drilled before they are inserted. This may seem like a chore, but it avoids hard labor, and even averts the real danger of breakage. For fixings involving only wood and boards, two holes are needed. One is a pilot hole in the piece you are fixing into — its diameter rather less than that of the screw thread, so the thread can still bite. It should also be, if anything, slightly shallower than the total distance of insertion. The other requirement is a clearance hole in the piece you are fixing through; this should be a touch wider than the overall diameter of the thread — the fit need not be tight, since screws work by clamping.

For the same reason, you should always fix thin pieces to thicker. Where this is impossible, a neat solution is a counterbore: a hole which is wide enough for the screw head itself, and allows the screw to disappear completely below the surface to a depth at which it can clamp effectively.

A counterbore can be filled (and the screw thereby hidden) with a matching plug or 'pellet' — cut from the same material with a bit called a plug cutter. This exposes a cylindrical core that you snap off, lever out and glue in. Note that a plug, unlike a dowel, is cut across the grain.

Special bits are available for drilling pilot holes, clearance holes and countersinks all at once for certain lengths and gauges of screw. Some will make counterbores as well.

Another way of concealing screw heads is with plastic tops. Mirror screws have chrome-plated domes, fastened to the head after insertion via special mating threads.

Where concealment will not work, the answer may well be a screw cup or collar (usually of brass or steel), in which the head sits. Screw cups lie on the surface and act rather like washers; they are handy for fixing materials which are too thin to countersink, such as plastic laminates and thin plywood. Screw collars are counterbored into the surface.

Lastly, do not expect to find any combination of screw length, gauge, head type and finish which you happen to fancy; existing ranges do not cover all permutations. However, screws can be short and fat, short and thin, long and fat, or long and thin. In this they differ from nails, whose gauge generally increases with length.

With all screws, there is one further rule. Do not screw into endgrain, because the fixing is weak. If you must, drive a dowel sideways through the piece so that the screw will bite into that.

There is, of course, no telling when you may need fixings which are heavier or more specialized than screws, but a few other threaded fasteners fall directly into the furniture field.

Fixing into chipboard can be made less risky by first driving a plastic chipboard plug into a pre-drilled hole, and screwing into that. However, chipboard screws have overtaken this technique. The chipboard connector screw, or Confirmat, is a

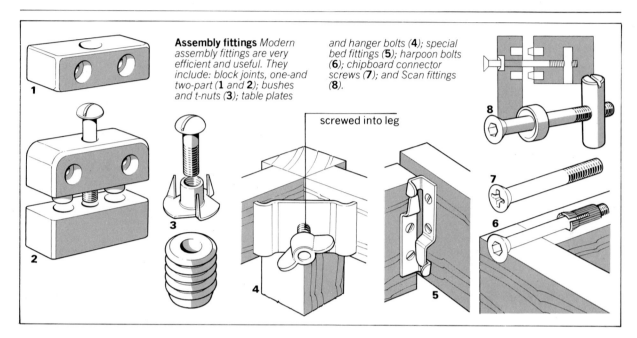

Assembly fittings *Modern assembly fittings are very efficient and useful. They include: block joints, one-and two-part (1 and 2); bushes and t-nuts (3); table plates and hanger bolts (4); special bed fittings (5); harpoon bolts (6); chipboard connector screws (7); and Scan fittings (8).*

screwed into leg

thick, blunt-ended screw with a shallow thread and a recessed head, designed for insertion in the edges of a board — again in a pre-drilled hole.

Finally, the harpoon bolt is like a countersunk screw with the end sawn off, and its own plug already fitted over the end. You drill a hole, knock in the screw and plug, and tighten up to expand the plug — which locks the fixing in place (although it can be unscrewed at any time). On this particular item, the recess or 'socket' in the head is made for a hexagonal-sectioned Allen key.

Assembly fittings

There are other ways of fastening pieces together than the direct use of screws, nails and closely related fixings. Most are stronger and impart more rigidity.

The crudest of the fittings in question are metal plates — rectangular, L-shaped, T-shaped and triangular — with holes drilled in them for screws. They can work well, but are not usually associated with fine cabinet-work. More important are special plates for fixing table-tops to the rails between the legs; these incorporate slots (elongated holes) so that the screws driven through them into the top do not restrict any movement induced by changes in humidity. (A 'button' is a similar device made of wood.)

The hanger bolt is a headless screw with a wood thread at one end and a machine (engineering) thread at the other, used with a special plate to effect the tricky jointing of two rails to one leg.

Block joints are plastic blocks with holes in them; they fit into the angles between pieces (usually panels) and are screwed both ways. More sophisticated variants are made in two parts, fixed together on assembly with a screw or by turning a locking cam.

The latter introduce the world of knock-down (KD) fittings — that is, fixings which allow easy dismantling. Apart from special ones made for beds, which merely work by gravity, other KD fittings return closely to the screw principle. One is a plastic or metal 'bush' — a plug threaded on the inside to receive a blunt-ended machine screw. A T-nut is a bush with a pronged flange that digs into the adjacent surface as the screw is tightened, providing clamping pressure.

And the Scan fitting goes further still. It consists of a machine screw, complete with collar, and a 'cross-dowel'. This is a short cylindrical bar with a threaded hole across its middle to receive the screw. After appropriate holes have been drilled in each component, the scan fitting allows (like the T-nut) the rigid KD assembly of frames rather than just panel structures.

Sideboard

- *Achieving stability*
- *Joints for panels*
- *Laminating flat work*
- *Gluing up*
- *Box construction*

This sideboard is a fairly substantial piece, but it exemplifies very nicely the simple procedures which modern materials and techniques make possjble.

Features
The main constraint upon a sideboard is that its top should be at a convenient height for a standing person. This is generally reckoned to be about 35 7/16in (900mm) or perhaps a little less (the same standard is used for kitchen worktops). Also needed are as large a surface as possible for laying out cutlery, crockery and so on; storage space, including drawers deep enough to be useful; and preferably some toe space for standing in front.

The Chinese or Japanese overtones in this design are introduced principally by the predominant color, by the inward turn at the foot of each side panel, and by the upward flare in the 'roof' of the small upper unit. Another hint is provided by the appearance of framing round the two outer drawers. Achieved by exposing the front edges of horizontal and vertical panels (and, conversely, by making the middle drawer-front overlap the panel so no edge is apparent), this echoes the squarish brackets often found next to the tops of legs on tables of the Far East.

The molding (known as a quadrant, cove or quarter-round) along many of the edges also introduces visual interest, in particular creating shadows which would not otherwise occur.

With the sole exception of the drawer bases, the cabinet is made wholly of MDF. Related to this choice is the decision to spray pigmented lacquer throughout.

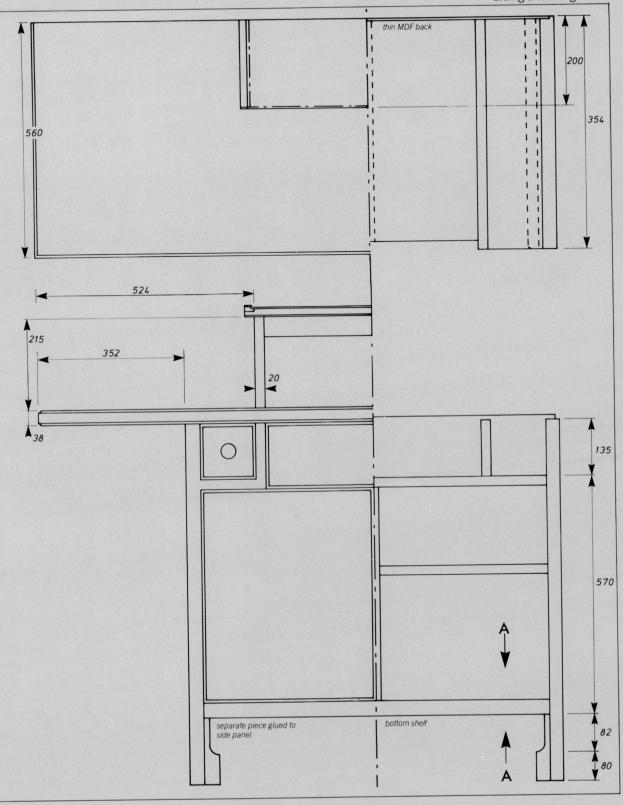

thin MDF back

200

354

560

524

215

352

20

38

135

570

A

separate piece glued to side panel

bottom shelf

82

80

A

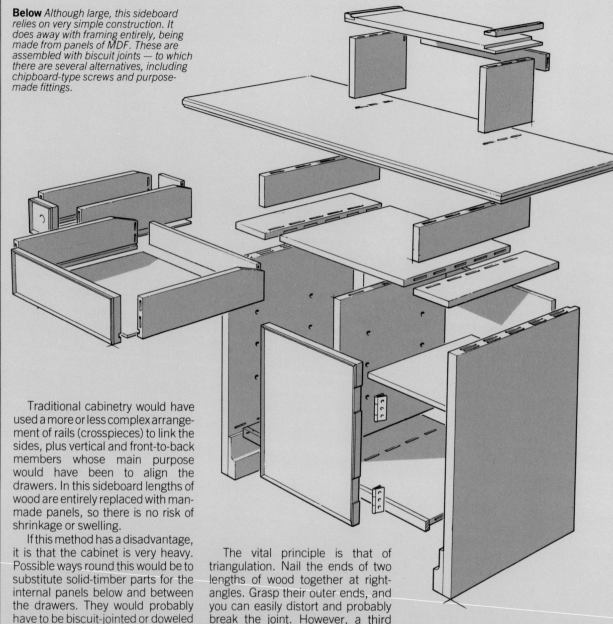

Below *Although large, this sideboard relies on very simple construction. It does away with framing entirely, being made from panels of MDF. These are assembled with biscuit joints — to which there are several alternatives, including chipboard-type screws and purpose-made fittings.*

Traditional cabinetry would have used a more or less complex arrangement of rails (crosspieces) to link the sides, plus vertical and front-to-back members whose main purpose would have been to align the drawers. In this sideboard lengths of wood are entirely replaced with man-made panels, so there is no risk of shrinkage or swelling.

If this method has a disadvantage, it is that the cabinet is very heavy. Possible ways round this would be to substitute solid-timber parts for the internal panels below and between the drawers. They would probably have to be biscuit-jointed or doweled to the sides and top.

Stability
Adequate strength and stability are essential to all good furniture: so basic, in fact, that they are easy to forget. Pieces which are outwardly similar may perform differently in these respects because their designers have taken different approaches to important details.

The vital principle is that of triangulation. Nail the ends of two lengths of wood together at right-angles. Grasp their outer ends, and you can easily distort and probably break the joint. However, a third piece fastened between those outer ends creates a triangle which will be, relatively, far harder to deform.

Triangulation is basic to almost any rigid wooden construction — but it is usually hidden. A four-sided box, for example, is quite easily persuaded to form a diamond shape, whereas adding a fifth side makes it far stiffer. The extra panel creates, in effect, an infinite number of triangles

which include the adjacent sides. The larger the triangles, the more they can resist leverage.

The principle operates even between two pieces: the larger the meeting surfaces parallel to or facing the direction in which any leverage is applied, the larger the 'triangles' in the joint. This is why 'shoulders' often add to the rigidity of joints: they provide additional meeting surfaces in

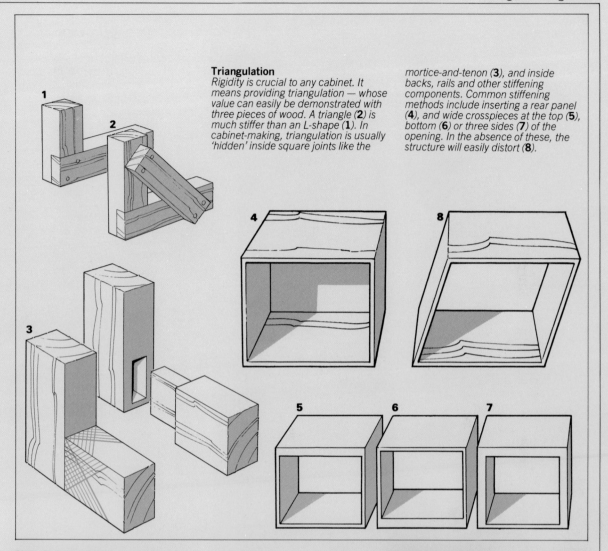

Triangulation

Rigidity is crucial to any cabinet. It means providing triangulation — whose value can easily be demonstrated with three pieces of wood. A triangle (**2**) is much stiffer than an L-shape (**1**). In cabinet-making, triangulation is usually 'hidden' inside square joints like the mortice-and-tenon (**3**), and inside backs, rails and other stiffening components. Common stiffening methods include inserting a rear panel (**4**), and wide crosspieces at the top (**5**), bottom (**6**) or three sides (**7**) of the opening. In the absence of these, the structure will easily distort (**8**).

Right The portable circular saw is often the easiest tool for cutting a large board into usable sections. There are two principal ways of guiding it: to hook its attached 'fence' over the edge of the board, or (as here) to run its sole plate along a straight-edged piece which has been clamped to the work in an appropriate position.

*The biscuit jointer is especially useful if you do a lot of work with panels. Here the base panel is recessed along a marked line (**1**) so the divider panel can be jointed on to it. The tool is run along a home-made chipboard 'square' (**2**).*

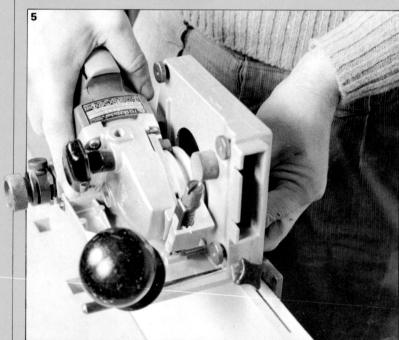

*The recess center lines are transferred to the square (its edge taped for clarity) and thence to the bottom of the divider panel (**3** and **4**) (the block of wood gives the divider's inset, equal to the door thickness). Recesses are cut with the machine again (**5**).*

one of the directions required for stiffness. Large empty areas in a structure, for example door openings, naturally counteract this principle, so it is a good idea to border them with stiff joints where possible. Similarly, one very stiff panel in a box helps to make the entire structure more rigid.

The strength of any glued joint depends mainly on the area of the glued surfaces in relation to the sizes of the components. However, all this assumes that the joints themselves are close-fitting and properly glued. If not, their design will be wasted.

Any likely distortion in this particular cabinet would be in elevation rather than on plan. In other words, it is more likely to creep into a diamond shape seen from in front than seen from above. It gains its considerable stability from its weight and from the sheer number of panel joints — rather than from the inherent stiffness of the joints themselves, because many of the panels are fairly thin. Exceptions are the joints between worktop and sides; also, the ends of the MDF 'rails' which run edge-on along the front of the bottom panel and inside the upper unit offer quite a lot of bearing surface against the sides, in the direction in which it is needed.

A final factor is the addition of a back. This — the fifth panel — always makes an enormous difference to the rigidity of a cabinet.

Panel joints
The inherent strength of the joints used in this sideboard is about as high as it can be, for they are made by the very effective biscuit method. However, the alternatives make a study in themselves.

Joints in general divide into those suitable for panels (like those used here) and those suitable for lengths of timber (framing joints). A few, including the biscuit joint, have applications in both spheres. The choice of an individual joint for a particular purpose is, of course, basic to the whole procedure of designing in wood and boards. Relevant factors are strength; the exact nature of the material used, including the

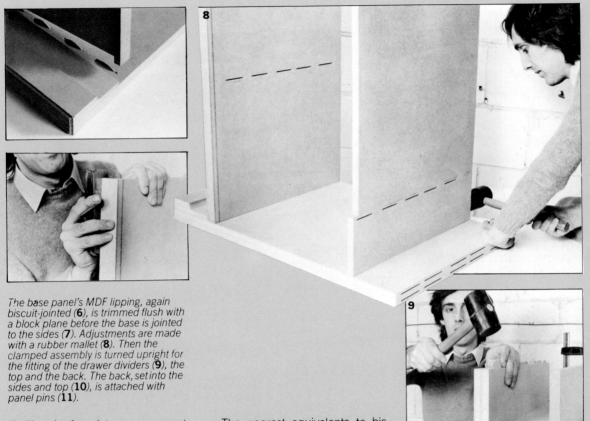

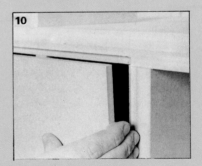

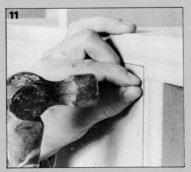

The base panel's MDF lipping, again biscuit-jointed (6), is trimmed flush with a block plane before the base is jointed to the sides (7). Adjustments are made with a rubber mallet (8). Then the clamped assembly is turned upright for the fitting of the drawer dividers (9), the top and the back. The back, set into the sides and top (10), is attached with panel pins (11).

likelihood of moisture movement; tools and machines available; the sizes of the components and their relationship to each other (is it an L-joint, a T-joint, an X-joint or even something else); and, in many cases, appearance. Some joints are hidden, but some are not, and it is quite posssible to make a feature of them.

The first possibilities in this case, as with most panel constructions, are chipboard-type screws, and assembly fittings — both of which can make remarkably strong joints. Screw-heads generally need covering; this can be done by plugging with timber, by using one or other type of plastic top, or by filling. Filling would work well here if carefully done, because the finish is opaque.

Sometimes a length of wood glued and screwed into the internal angle of a joint provides either reinforcement or the primary fixing. This cannot, however, be regarded as a neat solution.

The nearest equivalents to biscuits are dowels: short lengths of wooden rod, glued and driven halfway into each component. They are either bought ready-made from beech in various diameters, or cut from longer pieces; they should have chamfered ends for ease of insertion, and at least one flute cut along the length to allow glue to flow. They are quite effective; but it is notoriously difficult to align the holes properly, even with the help of the various gadgets available for the purpose. An established technique is to drive a pin some way into the center of each hole in one piece, cut its head off, position the second piece so that the protruding pins mark the hole centers there too, and pull them out before drilling. (Dowels are never normally used singly.)

Often a straightforward way of jointing boards is to cut a groove or rabbet in one piece, and glue the second piece into that — frequently with the aid of a tongue which has been

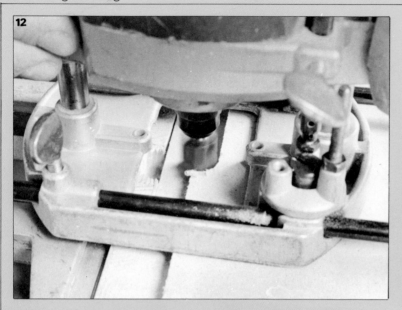

The top of the small upper unit is rabbeted at each end with the router (11); the rabbet is cleaned up with a suitable plane (12). A cove (or quadrant) molding is then worked on another piece (13), which is trimmed off and glued into the rabbet as a decorative feature (14). Finally, it is trimmed flush with the front and ends of the top panel. A cove molding is worked on most of the panel's edges — and also on the doors, drawer-fronts, sides and top. This helps to relieve the uniform appearance of the board material.

cut in it. A 'barefaced' tongue is formed by cutting a rabbet in one side only. A 'loose tongue' or spline is glued into twin grooves, one in each piece, thereby linking them. For joints in man-made boards it can be made either of plywood, or of solid timber with the grain running across it for strength.

Grooving and rabbeting are usually done with a router, circular saw, or a shaper. With a circular saw, you will probably need to make more than one parallel cut, each time adjusting either the saw's integral fence or the straight-edge along which you have been running. Tonguing requires a router or shaper.

On this sideboard, the side and top edges of the back panel are pinned into rabbets. The rabbet for the top edge runs along the rear edge of the worktop — but not all the way along: it is stopped at both ends. To make a stopped rabbet or groove with a router, position stop blocks on the workpiece to prevent the tool going further than you want it to. This particular panel is really so heavy and unwieldy that a router is the only practical answer.

Grooves, especially, must often be stopped to prevent them peeping out where they should be hidden — e.g. by a joint. The drawer-fronts on this piece provide an example.

The other common method of adding a back is to groove it in. It can also be simply pinned to the rear edges of the cabinet — inset about ⅛in (3mm) from the sides, so it cannot readily be seen unless you are actually looking for it.

Laminating panels
Because the thickness of MDF required for the top — both for looks and stiffness — was not available, it was made up by sticking thinner pieces together. The same was done at the lower ends of the side panels and the ends of the 'roof'.

Building up components in layers is called laminating. Sticking down plastic laminates (themselves layered) is only one application of the technique. Another use is in the making of curved shapes. Common to all laminating is the need to spread the glue evenly (preferably with a rubber roller) — and to apply pressure over the entire glued area while it sets, except when using contact adhesive, which grips instantly. For large, flat pieces such as those for the worktop, heavy crosswise battens cramped at either side will do the job. Putting a very slight convex curve on their lower edges will ensure that no area escapes the pressure. The cramps should be tightened from the middle batten outwards, to ensure that no excess glue is trapped. The same procedure is adopted for caul veneering.

Gluing up
This project demonstrates one of the most important procedures in furniture-making: gluing and assembly. This often has to take place in a number of separate steps; it depends on the structure of the piece.

Trouble-free assembly begins at the design stage, when you must ensure that you will in fact be able to put the item together at all. It is all too easy to make a mistake during planning so that one step in assembly makes the next one impossible.

If that is taken care of, the first essential is to check that all the parts fit properly, by assembling them 'dry' (without glue). Once you are quite satisfied about that, clear a level surface (the floor if need be) and lay out your clamps — having adjusted them to the correct openings. Provide yourself with a clean rag and some clean water. Only then should you mix (if necessary) and apply the glue. A brush is usually the best instrument for this, and the maxim is: not too little (or the joint will be 'starved') and not too much (or you will waste and have to wipe up a lot of excess glue which has been squeezed out of the joint).

Get the clamps on quickly, for the glue will already be 'going off'. Do not forget 'softening' blocks of wood between their jaws (if any) and the workpiece. Often you can use hefty battens as softening to spread the force of the clamps and thus broaden their effectiveness — for the

problem is always to achieve even pressure. See that they are not neglecting any particular area, and tighten them well — but not so fiercely that you squeeze all the glue out. And remember that clamps are very powerful. They can easily distort and break your work if you do not use them with care.

Then check scrupulously for squareness and accuracy in all directions. The best method of seeing whether a square or rectangle has 90° corners is not to use a square, but to measure the diagonals to check whether they are equal. And the best way of doing that is to use, not a tape measure, but a stick with a nail through one end so you can locate it in the far corner, 'ticking off' the diagonal distance on the near end of the stick with a pencil.

The sides of the upper unit are biscuit-jointed to the main top of the sideboard, and the upper unit's top is biscuit-jointed to its sides (16). Then an MDF 'rail' is added at the back to increase its rigidity (17).

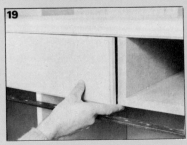

Before the drawers are assembled, their sides and fronts are tried in the cabinet to check for fit (18 and 19). The doors are tried likewise before being butt-hinged on (20). Note that clamps still hold the piece together during this dry-assembly stage.

FINISHING

A really bad job can never be wholly retrieved by its finish. However, bad finishing can certainly ruin a good piece of work, and there is no denying that surface colors and qualities contribute hugely to the impact of furniture in general.

Finishes demand close and discerning attention. Understanding how the various effects are achieved, and with what materials, can involve a long quest, because wood finishing can be practised at many levels. An enormous number of methods have been developed for changing the appearance of timber — either enhancing or disguising it. Acceptable results do come from readily available materials and simple procedures; but you are unlikely to achieve real distinction without both care and initiative.

The reasons for applying finishes stem from the very texture of wood, which soon allows foreign matter to pass below its surface. Most timbers are easily marked and discolored in various ways; they pick up dirt readily. Finishes offer protection. The degree to which they do so, and the enemies which they are able to repel, vary enormously.

Secondly, the color of many species — especially the darker ones — is much enhanced by even a clear and almost colorless finish (no finish is completely without color). So, in most cases, is the texture.

SANDING

It is unoriginal but quite true to say that a finish is only as good as the surface to which it is applied. The abrasives used in cabinet-making are, in effect, specialized tools for bringing exposed surfaces to the right texture. They are used not only before finishing treatments are applied, but also between coats and even afterwards. All work by scratching the surface; in almost every case, the scratches are made by small sharp-edged particles of 'grit'. Sand is no longer used for the purpose, but 'sanding' is still the popular term for the process.

Coarse sanding will roughen smooth surfaces, but the furniture-maker is generally concerned with smoothing rough ones. The technique is to proceed from relatively coarse grades to finer ones, thus gaining maximum efficiency at each stage. In preparing bare wood to receive its finish, even the clean action of a sharp cutting tool will rarely leave a smoother texture than the best and finest-grade sandpaper — and all but the very glossiest surfaces can be brought to an even deeper shine with very fine abrasives, used on top of the finishes already applied.

Materials

Abrasives can be classified by type of grit, by grade, by the form in which they come, and even by method of use.

The cheapest grit is crushed glass, but it wears smooth so quickly that more expensive abrasives generally provide better value. Glasspaper is not regarded as a craftsman's material — with the exception of the ultra-fine grades known as flour paper, which are often used to rub down finishes (especially french polish) because of their relatively gentle action.

Garnet paper, coated with orange grit from a natural semi-precious mineral, is a favorite for hand-sanding. It stays sharp a satisfyingly long time. With some grades of garnet, there is a choice between thick and thin paper (the latter for very fine work).

Aluminum oxide, an artificial grit, is harder still. Although available on the standard 11 x 9in (275 x 225mm) paper sheets for hand work, it is more commonly found on disks, belts and special rectangular sheets, all of which are made for fitting to power tools. In fact, it is the standard abrasive for power sanding. Belts are often of cloth rather than paper, and disks may be of special fiber. Colors include bright yellow, orange, brown, green and dark red. Some papers and cloths are resin-bonded, the grit being stuck to the backing with a hard plastic adhesive rather than the animal glue commonly used for glass and garnet. This provides a remarkably tough and homogeneous, if less flexible, surface.

Silicon carbide, the hardest grit of all, is generally black. It is most often resin-bonded to a paper backing. 'Wet-and-dry paper', as the result is called, can be used not only for ordinary sanding, but also with a little water, soap and water, white spirit or light oil for smoothing down finishing coats — by far its commonest use in furniture-making.

There is another type of silicon carbide paper which comes ready-coated with a white lubricant. Many people favor its particular combination of

*The palm sander (**below**) is a lightweight type of orbital sander. The belt sander (**left**) works fast and effectively, needing commensurate care.*

both hardness and smoothness of operation.

Glasspaper is usually graded, from coarsest to finest, as 3, 2½, S2 (for strong 2), M2 (for medium 2), F2 (for fine 2), 1½, 1, 0, and 00 or 2/0. Some garnet paper manufacturers also use this system, under which the paper comes in grades 1½, 1, ½, 0, 00 or 2/0, 000 or 3/0, 0000 or 4/0, 00000 or 5/0, 000000 or 6/0, 0000000 or 7/0, and 000000000 or 9/0 (perplexingly enough, these do not correspond to the equivalent grades for glasspaper).

However, both papers are also graded under the modern system used for aluminum oxide and silicon carbide. This allots to each grit size a number — the number of holes per square inch of the mesh through which that particular grit will pass. Coarser grits require larger and therefore fewer holes, so they bear the smallest numbers. Typically available are 30, 36, 40, 50, 60, 80, 100, 120, 150, 180, 220, 240, 320, 360, 400, 500 and 600 grits. The highest is an ultra-fine 1200 grit — no more than an abrasive powder.

The choice of abrasive and grade for a particular job depends very much on personal taste. Try 80 or 100 grit garnet paper for a first sanding by hand, followed by 120 and perhaps 240 for finishing. With a sanding machine, 80 for initial sanding, followed by 100 and 120, is about right; the abrasive is usually aluminum oxide.

240 grit silicon carbide paper is good for 'cutting down' or 'flatting' finishing coats ready for subsequent ones, as is steel wool (wire wool), which consists of bundled steel strands. The only grades normally used in woodwork are 00, 000 and 0000 (2/0, 3/0 and 4/0 respectively).

Fine steel wool is also used for the final dulling of gloss surfaces to produce a satin or matt effect. Other possiblities include brushing on pumice powder or rottenstone (another powder). Conversely, you can apply special burnishing creams and 'cutting compounds' for an even higher gloss. Brass and silver polishes may come in useful, too.

Techniques and machines

A rubber, cork or felt-faced block is essential for sanding flat surfaces by hand. It helps to distribute pressure and thus to avoid uneven results. Tear off a neat rectangle of sandpaper (a sixth or a quarter of a standard sheet) and wrap it tightly round the block. This will save sandpaper and make for precise work; likewise, curved surfaces and fine flat details require a small sheet, folded in half only and held delicately in the fingers.

It is essential to retain a positive but light touch — and to check constantly that you are not rounding over a corner that is meant to be sharp, sanding through a veneer (surprisingly easy to do), or damaging some other detail. The rule is to sand along the grain, except where that is impossible because pieces with different grain directions meet, in which case you must pick extremely fine paper and work in a circular or elliptical motion.

Sanding machines offer alternatives. The simplest, a flexible rubber disk fitted on a spindle or 'arbor' into a drill chuck, and faced with a separate disk of abrasive, has its uses — but only for certain contoured work, not for flat surfaces.

Much more useful are portable belt and orbital sanders. The former bring up a surface fast (they must be kept constantly on the move to avoid creating instant unevenness), but the latter are better for finer work since they have a lighter and omni-directional action. Both are available in sundry patterns, including some with variable speeds, and a dust bag is now standard.

Fixed sanding machines include the linisher, a belt sander whose exposed surface faces sideways or upwards; the fixed rigid disk sander with its vertical surface; and the bobbin sander, whose spindle moves up and down as it turns. These are seldom found outside trade workshops, but bench-top versions of the first two are available. The fixed disk sander stands apart, because its configuration makes it of little use for finishing, the usual job of a sanding machine; on the other hand, it is very handy for bringing components to exact shape and size, in which role it can sometimes replace saws, planes and the like. A tilting table and adjustable fence increase its versatility.

Above The cabinet scraper, properly sharpened, is most useful for taking off fine shavings. It will smooth awkward areas where grain directions vary and sandpaper will not work properly.

Preparation for finishing

If you want the best for your furniture, take extreme care when sanding, using a cabinet scraper first where possible. Finishes often magnify bumps and hollows.

Glue is another problem. Even if you carefully wipe up any excess, as you should, a certain amount often remains to lie invisibly on the surface and prevent finishes penetrating properly, with pale patches as the result. Scraping is a better remedy generally for getting rid of such patches than sanding.

After sanding, and immediately before finishing, the surface should be thoroughly brushed clear of dust, and preferably wiped with a cloth soaked in a little white spirit to get it really clean. The spirit will darken the wood temporarily until it evaporates.

Since most finishes cannot be handled until dry, they immobilize the work for a while: ensure that your space and time allow for this. A complete 'finishing schedule' may require several days. Moreover, different parts — especially if finished in different ways — may need to be dealt with before assembly, risking consequent hold-ups until they are all ready.

CHOOSING A FINISH

Many different factors are involved in the choice of a finish. On the one hand are the characteristics of the finish itself — its color; its degree of translucence or opacity; its resistance to knocks, scratches, heat, dirt, water and chemicals (such as alcohol); its method of application; its drying time; its texture; and the ease or difficulty with which it can be repaired in the event of damage. On the other hand are the color, texture and (if applicable) figure of the timbers and boards used, including veneers; the treatment the item will receive in use; and a great many subtle considerations of taste.

The average finish involves several applications, often of different materials. These materials may not be compatible (even if they come from the same manufacturer, which is always a sensible pre-condition). Adverse reactions between layers are far from uncommon, and they may sometimes mean starting again from the beginning. Traditional finishing, moreover, can involve specialized hand work with home-made recipes.

Even professionals are not all aware of the full range and possibilities of finishes. Many use only certain finishing schedules which they know from experience is reliable. The beginner should experiment on matching offcuts before taking any firm decisions.

Bleach and stain

Bleach and stain are two materials that can be used if you do not want to conceal the figure of timber or veneers.

The only way of making wood lighter in color is to use bleach. Wood bleach consists of two liquids, applied separately. It works dramatically on some timbers, and has little effect on others.

If you want to darken a timber, or to change its tone without making it lighter, there are two alternatives. One is to apply a material that will color the wood itself, followed by translucent oil, wax, french polish, varnish or lacquer. The other is to apply oil, wax, french polish, varnish or lacquer which is already tinted with the color you want.

Although the second method is faster, because it involves only one operation, the first method is generally preferable since the color integrates with the wood rather than lying on top of it and clouding the coating. Therefore it also remains in place even if the coating gets chipped.

True stains (as opposed to 'wood colours') contain a dye in a solvent. Common solvents are water, alcohol and naphtha. The stains most widely available are ready-mixed; alcohol and water stains are both available either ready-mixed or as powdered aniline dyes for mixing with the solvent concerned. The latter come in a far greater range of colors than ready-mixed types.

Water stains, unlike others, 'raise the grain' slightly: the moisture swells and thus roughens it. This effect can be avoided by first dampening the surface and (when dry) sanding it smooth. A further dampening before the stain is applied helps to spread it evenly.

All stains should be applied fast and in sweeping strokes: because they penetrate, it is easy to get a blotchy result. Keep a 'wet edge'— in other words, do not let an area of stain dry before you stain the area next to it, otherwise there will be overlaps which remain darker.

Some stains (though not water stains) have a strong tendency to 'bleed': the dye comes out of them even when they have dried, and affects subsequent treatments — which thus contain uneven streaks of dye. Even wiping the dry stain with a rag first does little to avert this problem. A thin 'sealing' coat of 'white' french polish, or some other form of shellac, after staining is one answer, because only alcohol- (spirit-) based stains will bleed into it — the point being that, if the solvent in the finish is different from that in the stain, it is likely to cause less trouble.

It is worth mentioning one stain that works by chemical reaction rather than direct coloration — bichromate of potash, which is yellow yet turns mahogany a rich red-brown.

Stains of the same type can be mixed; others cannot. Water stains can of course be thinned with water, alcohol stains with methylated spirit, and most others with turpentine. You can apply stain with either a brush or a clean rag.

Stoppings and grain fillers

Texture demands just as much attention as color. If the timber is close-grained, you can do little to change that even if you want to. But with open-grained woods and those with a medium grain, there is a choice of treatment. Either they can be left alone or the grain can be filled to give a close, fine texture. This will make a big difference to the final effect. A filled surface also means fewer finishing coats, because they have less tendency to soak in.

Grain filler is a stiff paste, which may need thinning (probably with turpentine) to give it the right consistency for easy application. It can be applied after staining; but it has its own color, and can also be mixed with stain. You can put it on with a brush or more usually a rag — working across the grain so that the filler has a better chance of clogging the surface properly. The excess is wiped off along the grain, and the remainder left to harden. The surface should then be lightly sanded for perfect smoothness. Speed and care are needed in application, especially with strongly colored fillers, to avoid blotchiness.

Unlike grain fillers, stoppings (stoppers or wood fillers) are for filling holes, dents and other blemishes — such as torn grain, and unintentional gaps in joints. They also sometimes provide an acceptable cover for nailheads which have been punched below the surface.

Traditional stoppings are stiff pastes. A recent introduction is a polyester filler, in paired tubes whose contents must be mixed before use. Other stoppings come as lumps of wax, which must be flaked before being pressed into the hole. Fourthly, there are shellac sticks. Shellac is a processed insect secretion; in stick form it is solid and very hard, and must be melted into the hole with a flame and shaved flush once it has set.

Most of these are available in various colors, but traditional paste stoppings, in particular, always seem to end up a different shade from the surrounding wood. They cannot be mixed with stain as some manufacturers claim, and the only way they can be stained after application is with artist's watercolors (since the pastes themselves are water-based). Polyester filler takes stain reasonably well. Wax fillers must be sealed with shellac if subsequent finishes are to adhere.

If the ultimate finish is to be opaque lacquer or paint, the colors of grain fillers and stoppings do not matter. The cheap and effective answer here is the DIY decorator's friend — ordinary white or pale grey cellulose filler, ready mixed or in a powder. Because the water in the mix will rust metal, and the rust may well show through the finish, screws, nails and the like should always be dabbed with paint, lacquer, french polish or varnish before filling (but not with a water-based finish such as emulsion paint).

Useful applicators for these materials are decorator's filling knives (more flexible than decorator's scrapers, although they look the same) and artist's palette knives.

Oil

It is possible to finish wood with linseed oil. At least 12 applications are needed; each should be rubbed in well, then the surplus wiped off after a while and the wood buffed with a soft cloth.

More up-to-date oils give the same gentle luster, are used in the same way, and have the same advantages — namely that dust does not become embedded in them, and the finish can easily be repaired invisibly if damaged. As a bonus, they need far fewer applications.

Popular types are Danish oil, teak oil (suitable for other woods too), tung oil and various mixtures. Some contain polyurethane and other substances to provide more protection. There is no reason why you should not try your own experiments in mixing oil with varnish and lacquer.

Oil is valued for its 'natural' appearance, especially when it has no color added. It allows the wood to speak for itself, because — like wax — it does not form a film on top. All other finishes do.

Wax

Applying wax is a matter of rubbing it in well and evenly with a soft rag (ensuring no lumps are left), leaving it for a while to harden, and buffing it vigorously with a soft cloth until your fingers leave no mark on the surface when pressed.

Wax can, however, be used in two ways: as a finish in its own right, and as a final treatment on top of french polish, varnish or lacquer. Even in the former case, usual practice is to apply one or two thin coats of french polish as a sealer first. This will help you to build up a sheen in the wax more quickly.

Wax is often applied with fine steel wool instead of a rag: where it goes on top of a complete gloss or semi-gloss finish, this method has the effect of dulling the shine; the result is a 'satin' texture.

While there is a vast range of waxes, plain and colored, used individually and in mixtures, the chief ones are beeswax, carnauba wax and paraffin wax. The classic recipe is to dissolve 1 lb (2.2kg) of beeswax in ½pt (300ml) or so of natural turpentine in a double boiler — but there are many alternatives for you to try. Again, durability is not the strong point of wax; heat, in particular, will usually mark it instantly. However, as with oil, ease of repair may be considered to make up for this.

Shellac and french polish

Professionals often use the word 'polish' synonymously with 'finish'. For the newcomer, 'polish' is probably best kept to denote everyday maintenance — what you do with a yellow duster after furniture has left the workshop or factory. There is, however, one exception: french polish.

French polish is not what is normally understood by the word 'polish' either: it is a sticky coating, made from shellac dissolved in alcohol, which forms a hard film as it dries. More accurately, perhaps, it is a type of varnish; but that term is reserved for translucent finishes applied solely by brush, while any coating meant for spraying is called a 'lacquer'. Technically, a lacquer is thinner than a varnish — it has a 'solid content' of less than 40 percent.

The term lacquer is, of course, also given to the hand-applied, highly decorative and deeply colored gloss finishes invented in the Far East. But these are a very specialized matter.

A paint is really an opaque varnish or lacquer (one which has been 'pigmented' with color). Indeed, some tinned paints are sold as lacquers. A tinted lacquer or varnish is one which, though color has been added, remains translucent.

French polish is the standard treatment for most types of antique furniture. There is no denying that it is old-fashioned in its laborious method of application. However, it does produce a very attractive finish.

Traditional french polishing relies on subtle skills of hand and eye which can only be learned by practicing. Application is by a 'rubber': a piece of cotton wadding, soaked in polish, with cotton cloth wrapped around it in a very particular way. The polish is, in effect, squeezed over the surface. Numerous very thin coats are applied, and each stage of the procedure has a name — 'coating in', 'bodying up', 'stiffing out' and 'spiriting out'. Linseed oil is used as a lubricant, and alcohol as a thinner.

As with other film-forming finishes, the first coat is a sealer. This may be a special 'sanding sealer' — whether of shellac or other materials — rather than ordinary french polish. Some sanding sealers provide a finish in their own right.

The first coat may be applied with a brush, since it will be lightly sanded down with flour paper, fine garnet paper or fine ready-lubricated silicon carbide paper — as indeed can subsequent coats where necessary. This rubbing-down ('flatting' or 'cutting back') is standard on varnishes and lacquers too: it is also known as 'de-nibbing' because one of its purposes is to remove the 'nibs' of dust which will almost inevitably have settled. It leaves an uneven, chalky surface which the next coat will correct.

Those who see no point in learning the full traditional procedure for french polishing can adopt a good substitute method, especially for open-grained surfaces — namely, brushing on all the coats instead of just the first one. Since most shellac preparations dry fairly fast, this tends to

Hall Table

Laminating *Laminating can be invaluable in getting round the natural restrictions of wood grain. You can use layers of veneer (1) or very thin plywood (2). Three methods are shown at right: pinning to a former (3), clamping with a shaped block (4), and clamping with a steel strap (5).*

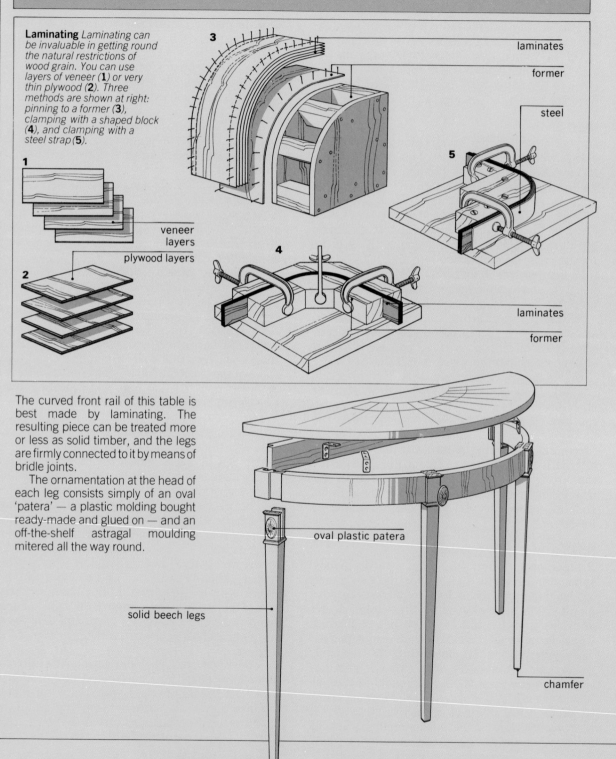

veneer layers

plywood layers

laminates

former

steel

laminates

former

The curved front rail of this table is best made by laminating. The resulting piece can be treated more or less as solid timber, and the legs are firmly connected to it by means of bridle joints.

The ornamentation at the head of each leg consists simply of an oval 'patera' — a plastic molding bought ready-made and glued on — and an off-the-shelf astragal moulding mitered all the way round.

oval plastic patera

solid beech legs

chamfer

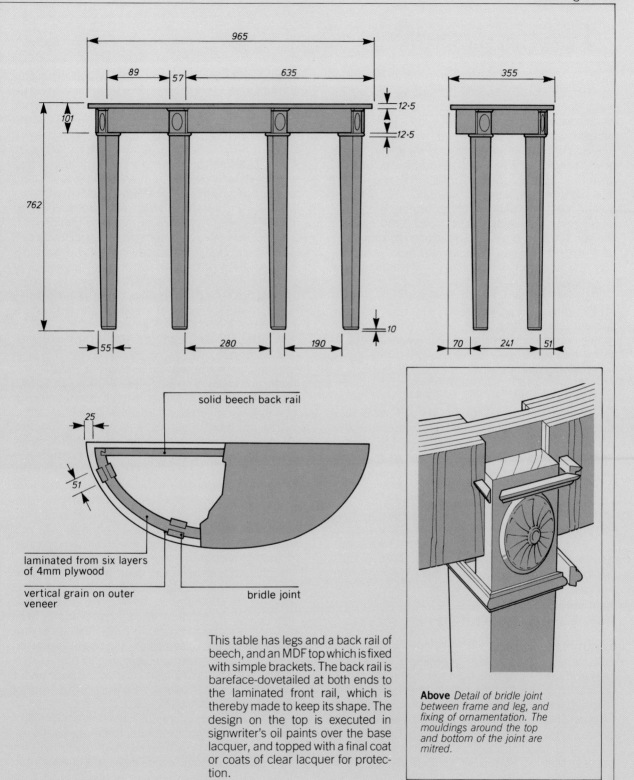

965

89 57 635

12·5

101

12·5

355

762

55 280 190 10

70 241 51

25

solid beech back rail

51

laminated from six layers
of 4mm plywood

vertical grain on outer
veneer

bridle joint

This table has legs and a back rail of
beech, and an MDF top which is fixed
with simple brackets. The back rail is
bareface-dovetailed at both ends to
the laminated front rail, which is
thereby made to keep its shape. The
design on the top is executed in
signwriter's oil paints over the base
lacquer, and topped with a final coat
or coats of clear lacquer for protection.

Above *Detail of bridle joint
between frame and leg, and
fixing of ornamentation. The
mouldings around the top
and bottom of the joint are
mitred.*

produce a rather ridged and uneven surface; the answer is especially thorough rubbing-down with sandpaper or steel wool at each stage to level it off — unless you buy a special brush polish, formulated for slower drying.

French polish comes in at least six standard colors: 'white' (very pale), 'pale' (amber), 'button' (orange), 'garnet' (dark brown), red and black. The last two have spirit stain added. 'French polish' itself is a medium golden-brown. Whatever shade you use, you can always add extra color to the surface between coats in the form of stain mixed with a little polish. This is done after the sealing coat, because that will already have changed the color somewhat.

Polishes also vary in clarity — that is, in degree of cloudiness. The clearest, which have been bleached, are called 'transparent'. Some modern polishes include substances such as melamine to give them some of the hardness and durability of synthetic lacquers.

Varnishes

Several traditional varnishes are still available, but they have yielded by far the greater share of the market to modern types — notably polyurethane. This is faster-drying but only a little more resistant to damage than they are. Polyurethane lacquers are also available.

The initial sealing coat of a polyurethane varnish is normally thinned by about one part in three of turpentine. Traditional varnishes, like shellac, dry by evaporation of their solvents (the ingredients which have been keeping them liquid). Most polyurethane varnishes dry partly this way and partly by chemical reaction between the remaining substances. In at least one case, reaction depends on the moisture in the atmosphere.

Lacquers

Lacquers contain certain substances — notably polyurethane, nitrocellulose and melamine — which form more or less hard and tough films. Though the initial drying period of a lacquer may be anything from a few minutes to six or eight hours, full setting ('curing') takes a matter of days.

Lacquers are available tinted, pigmented and in several textures. Because of their complex formulations, you do need to make sure successive coats are compatible.

Nitrocellulose lacquer is the fastest-drying of all, which means that dust has little time to settle and spoil the finish. Moreover, it shares with shellac (also available in lacquer form) the quality of 'reversibility': it can be dissolved with its own solvents — unlike even more modern lacquers, which can only be thinned while still liquid, and which set irreversibly into a finish that nothing short of paint-stripper or a blowlamp will remove.

Each successive coat of nitrocellulose, therefore, slightly dissolves and thus blends with the previous one, even though that is already dry (as it should be). And, in addition to the usual light sanding between coats with flour paper, fine garnet paper, or perhaps silicon carbide paper, you can 'pull over' the final coat with a special mixture consisting largely of solvents: this will soften it and even it out to a high gloss.

A nitrocellulose sanding sealer is the usual base coat. Normally, of course, nitrocellulose's drying time makes it impossible to apply by brush; but again, you can buy special nitrocellulose 'brushing lacquers'. Some varieties can even be applied with a rubber like that used for french polishing.

Pre-catalyzed ('pre-cat') lacquer includes a substance such as melamine which hardens by reaction. The catalyst for this reaction is already present in the lacquer and takes effect as the solvents evaporate from the surface after application. Nitrocellulose is added for faster drying (just as catalyzed ingredients are often added to nitrocellulose to improve its durability); it brings with it the reversibility that means the lacquer can be pulled over.

Acid-catalyzed (AC) lacquer dries by the same process, but the catalyst is added just before spraying. In other words, the lacquer comes in two 'packs' rather than just one. It is particularly hard and thus well suited to table-tops. Though meant for spraying, catalysed lacquers of both types can be thinned for brushing — and at least one AC lacquer is specially packaged for this purpose under the label 'plastic coating'. Polyurethane lacquer may be either one or two-pack.

It is sometimes recommended that each coat of a pre-cat, AC or polyurethane finish should be applied before the previous one is quite dry, to give better adhesion and so a more homogeneous film. Because of their hardness, these finishes are best sanded between coats with silicon carbide rather than any other abrasive (the resulting slurry, especially if it contains oil, should be removed before continuing). For a high gloss, rub on burnishing cream with a very soft pad — ideally of felt or lambswool — but only after the lacquer or varnish has cured fully: consult the supplier.

Paint

Enhancing the natural appearance of solid timber and veneers is only one approach to finishing. Featureless plywood and ordinary timbers may suggest other treatments; hardboard, MDF and chipboard require them.

Paint and opaque lacquer are two possibilities. The great range of ornamental finishes developed over the ages — such as stenciling, marbling, graining and scores of others — hold out inspiring opportunities and are currently in vogue. In fact, much more paint was used to decorate the furniture of the past than many people think.

Ordinary house paint will work as well on furniture as anywhere else. On the whole a tougher finish is offered by those paints which require turpentine for brush cleaning, but water-based emulsions are improving rapidly in this respect. Matt, eggshell and gloss textures are all available, and you can vary these by rubbing them down and using clear varnish or lacquer on top.

FINISHING TECHNIQUES

There are three main methods of applying finishes — by rag, brush and spray.

Although french polishers are very particular about their rags, clean cotton should suffice for most purposes where a rag is suitable. It must not shed fluff or loose threads.

Brushes come in enough varieties to fill a small catalog. The 'polisher's mop' is a soft, bulbous, full-bristled brush, usually of bear-, goat- or squirrel-hair, which is very pleasant to use. Fine artist's brushes are indispensable for touching in small areas. Good decorator's paintbrushes are used for painting and varnishing.

All brushes must be maintained with loving care. After each use, clean them in the appropriate solvents (often turpentine, but sometimes alcohol or special lacquer thinners). Usually you will need to repeat the procedure at least twice, until little or none of the finish remains to color the solvent. Then make sure the brush dries to its correct

shape, if necessary by wrapping it in cloth or absorbent paper (leaving it standing in solvent usually results in permanent or semi-permanent distortion). Such apparent chores, like all maintenance, bestow their own reward in tools and equipment which are always ready for use.

Spraying is yet another field of study. One possibility is to buy aerosol cans. These generally contain cellulose or polyurethane lacquer, and car accessory shops are good places to look for them. They are, however, extremely expensive.

Sprayguns themselves are still not much used outside the trade, but without question they can very quickly provide a really excellent finish, smoother than any you could brush on. There are two types. Some require air from a separate compressor or pump; airless guns do not. The latter are versatile, and cost about the same as a good router or circular saw.

There are a few rules for spraying. Firstly, follow the instructions from the maufacturers of both gun and lacquer — especially with regard to safety, for lacquers can be toxic and are usually a fire hazard. Secondly, be sure to clean the gun thoroughly with the appropriate thinners after use, just like a brush. Thirdly, always spray about 6-10in (150-250mm) from the surface — and keep the distance constant; working closer may cause rippling, and working further away may result in wastage and lack of precision. Fourthly, overlap strokes so no patches are missed.

Finishing boards

Even if you decide on an opaque finish, board materials make their own demands.

An exception is hardboard, with its extremely hard, smooth surface. But the edges of plywood will need, at the very least, thorough sanding; and if for some reason you are exposing the edges of blockboard or chipboard, they will need filling too. Chipboard, in fact, is so ragged that even this is not always enough — though car-body filler may be equal to the task. A special filler is made for MDF edges.

Chipboard faces are not usually considered smooth enough for painting unless they have been factory-filled. However, with chipboard, MDF and indeed hardboard there is always the possibility of applying a clear finish to expose the random-grained surface.

Chair

- *Laminating curves*
- *Designing chairs*
- *Types of chair*
- *Avoiding short grain*
- *Using a router*

A good rule when making a set of chairs is to build at least one mock-up or prototype. So many complex features need to be considered that you are not very likely to get them all right first time.

Chairs are special. Firstly, the convenience and comfort of users impose perhaps more stringent demands on a chair than on most other items. The seat must be the right height from the ground, the right depth from front to back, and the right width. It usually slopes backwards, and often curves from side to side. Any arms must be at a comfortable height. The back must offer support where needed without being obtrusive. These are only the main considerations — and the problem with all of them is, of course, that bodies are very different.

Office chairs, often the products of much research on these matters, offer useful pointers; but there is no substitute for careful assessment of personal likes and dislikes.

In addition, chairs come in for heavy use because they are portable and relatively light. People stand on them and tip them back. To accommodate these uses, chairs need to be strong and rigid.

Convenience and overall appearance, however, often demand that chair designs incorporate all sorts of curves and tapers in three dimensions. It is relatively rare for components to meet at 90°, and compound angles are common.

This adds up to an interesting exercise; and a quick look around any big furniture store — let alone a modern furniture gallery — will show what a wide variety of tactics have been used in approaching it.

Features

This chair does not look particularly unusual. However, it solves (or attempts to solve) the traditional problems in some new ways.

Classic chairs come in two broad types. The Windsor (or chair-maker's) chair in its simplest form has round-section spindles for its legs and framing, and a solid seat into which back members and legs all fit in round holes. In the cabinet-maker's chair, the seat is an open frame ready to accept cane, rushes or upholstery; the front legs are

jointed into it — as are the back uprights or backstands.

Both types are traditionally held together with mortices and tenons. In the Windsor chair these terms are used loosely because the mortices (sloping if necessary) are round. Wedges are usually driven into the endgrain of the spindles where it is exposed through the seat. Cabinet-maker's chairs often require either an angled tenon or an angled mortice to join pieces at other than 90°. Dowels are nowadays in common use for chairmaking as well.

Basic designs

*Two classic chair patterns still flourish today after centuries of use, and despite a great many modern rivals. They are the Windsor chair (**Far left**) and the cabinet-maker's chair (**left**). The Windsor format was evolved by full-time chair-makers. Its central feature is its seat, which receives all the other main components. Usually these are cylindrical and fit into drilled holes, where they are often wedged. The cabinet-maker's chair, on the other hand, employs a series of conventional framing joints — typically mortices-and-tenons, though dowels often replace these. Strong, well-made joints are especially important in chairs, and varied angles often add to the constructional challenge.*

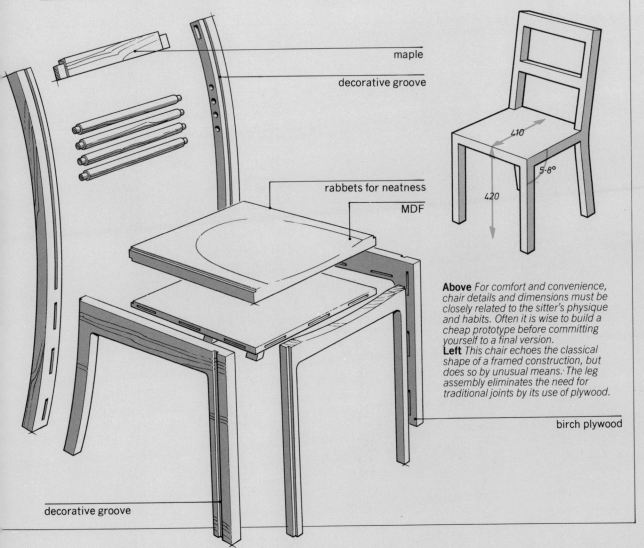

maple

decorative groove

rabbets for neatness

MDF

410

5-8°

420

decorative groove

birch plywood

Above *For comfort and convenience, chair details and dimensions must be closely related to the sitter's physique and habits. Often it is wise to build a cheap prototype before committing yourself to a final version.*
Left *This chair echoes the classical shape of a framed construction, but does so by unusual means. The leg assembly eliminates the need for traditional joints by its use of plywood.*

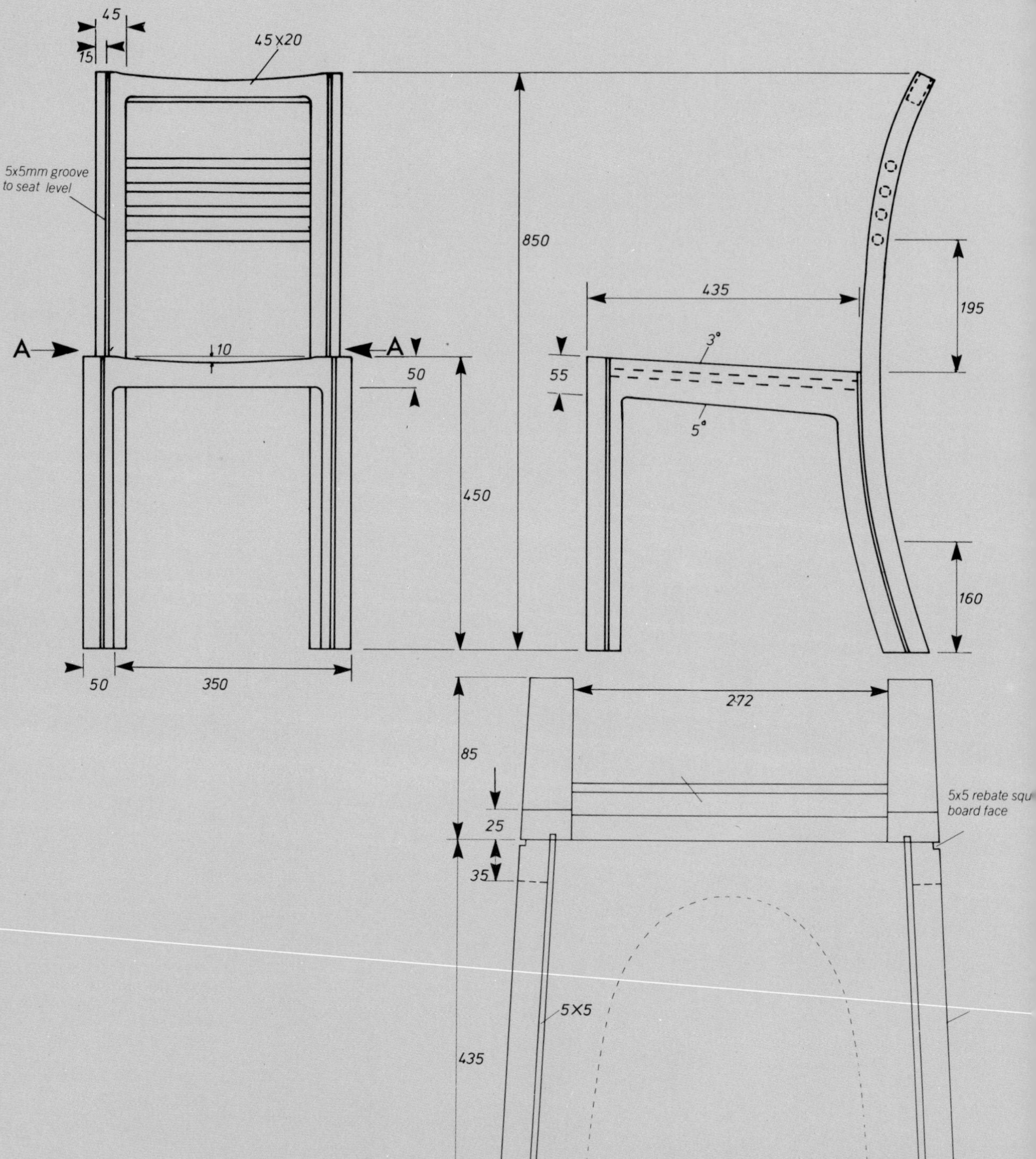

45

45 x 20

15

5x5mm groove
to seat level

A →

← A ▼

↓10

50

850

850

435

3°

55

5°

195

450

160

A ▼

50

350

272

85

25

35

5×5 rebate squ
board face

435

5×5

5x5 rebate in seat

SECTIONAL PLAN AA

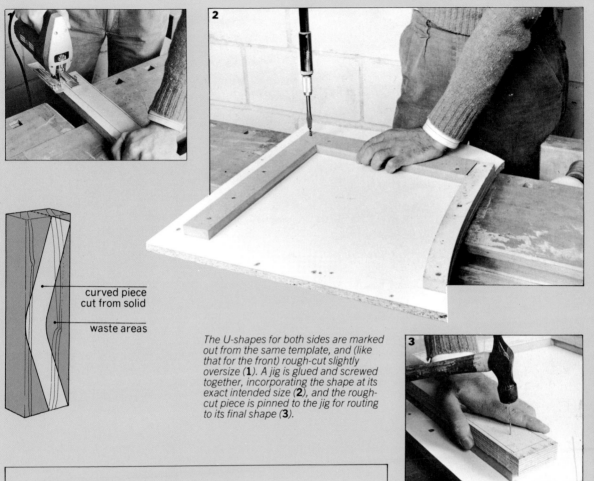

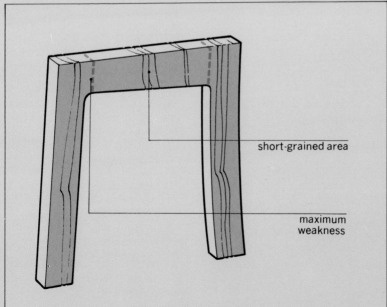

*The U-shapes for both sides are marked out from the same template, and (like that for the front) rough-cut slightly oversize (**1**). A jig is glued and screwed together, incorporating the shape at its exact intended size (**2**), and the rough-cut piece is pinned to the jig for routing to its final shape (**3**).*

curved piece cut from solid

waste areas

short-grained area

maximum weakness

Left *If the piece were cut from a wide board of solid timber instead of from plywood, it would be extremely weak in the short-grained parts. It would break under the least stress, probably in the corners. Traditionally, of course, this problem is overcome by providing a rail to link the two legs, so that each part of the shape makes maximum use of the strength in the long grain.*

The router is fitted with a straight cutter, which has a guide bearing of the same diameter (bearings of different diameters are also available) (4). The piece is trimmed flush with the shape on the jig by first running the bearing against that; the cut is completed in two 'passes', during the second of which the bearing is run against the piece itself (5). Finally, a special home-made curved fence is fitted to allow the machine to follow the curve of the workpiece as a small rabbet is cut to neaten the join between panels (6).

This chair is very much based on the second type, but the three-way jointing of legs and seat frame is avoided by shaping the front and sides from plywood and biscuit-jointing the pieces together. The configuration of the rear uprights and their linking rails (all of maple) is familiar enough, but they are attached to the rest of the chair with biscuit joints again.

In other words, the chair is built rather like a modern cabinet. In this way, one special property of plywood is exploited — the fact that it is equally strong in length and width. Though such U-shaped pieces could be steam-bent in certain species, they could not possibly be cut from solid timber because either the horizontals or the verticals would be extremely short-grained and therefore weak. Moreover, the relative thinness of the plywood is counteracted by the corner joints which run the entire length of each front leg.

Shaping these components is best done with a jigsaw or bandsaw, but they will need trimming afterwards. Here a router was used for that. A template is vital not only for initial marking but also subsequently as a guide for the router cutter. It may need to be larger or smaller than the component will be, depending on the precise shape and operation of the cutter. Jigs and templates can be used again and again, making repeat production relatively easy.

Curved backstands are very common. Splaying the back legs increases stability, curving the upper part usually increases comfort, and both usually enhance the chair's appearance. Backstands are sometimes set at an angle (on plan), but these ones stand square to the front. Square inner faces make it easy to add connecting rails and to cramp up afterwards, but the outer edges are bevelled to continue the front-to-back taper of the seat. This is done by hand, because the bevel must follow the curve — a very ticklish problem in machining; the same applies to the rear edges of the plywood sides.

A curved piece cut from the solid (unless for steam-bending) obviously requires a board wide enough or thick enough, or both, to accommodate the whole shape. But there is a fascinating and elegant alternative method, namely laminating.

Laminating curves
A laminated structure is simply one built up in layers. Plywood is a good example: laminating your own components means, in effect, producing purpose-made plywood. As a rule, the individual layers are either 'constructional veneers' — special ven-

The ordinary straight fence is used for cutting the narrow decorative groove along the length of the backstands — after they have been sawn and planed to shape, and the recesses cut for the biscuits (**7**). (The mortices for the back rails are marked first of all.)

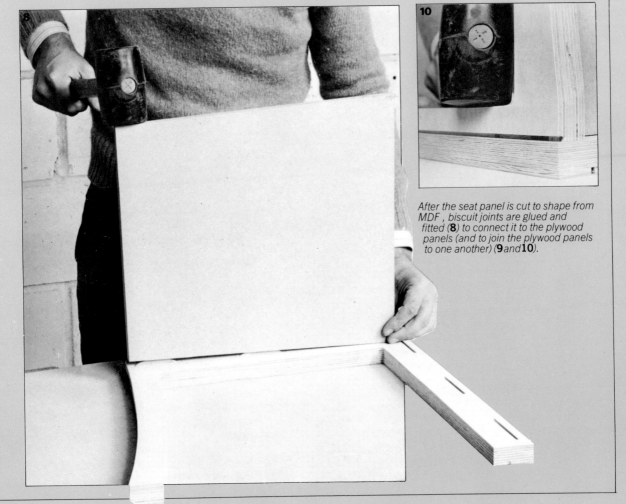

After the seat panel is cut to shape from MDF , biscuit joints are glued and fitted (**8**) to connect it to the plywood panels (and to join the plywood panels to one another) (**9** and **10**).

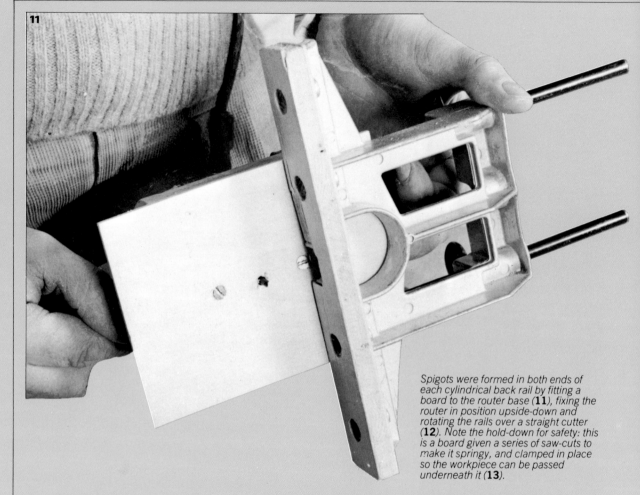

11

*Spigots were formed in both ends of each cylindrical back rail by fitting a board to the router base (**11**), fixing the router in position upside-down and rotating the rails over a straight cutter (**12**). Note the hold-down for safety: this is a board given a series of saw-cuts to make it springy, and clamped in place so the workpiece can be passed underneath it (**13**).*

eers up to ⅛in (3mm) thick, available from veneer merchants — or even 1.5mm thick plywood (sometimes called bending plywood). In the case of veneers, all the grain should run lengthwise along the component for maximum strength. With plywood, the grain of the outer veneers in each layer should run across, to make bending easier.

In essence, the technique is a matter of commonsense. You make up some kind of former to the shape you want, stoutly built and often fixed to a base board; plenty of glue and screws are usually the answer here. You cut the laminates oversize, glue them all with UF glue (the only commonly available type which can be relied on to stay rigid), and clamp them to the former in a bundle. You will probably need quite a few C-clamps to hold them snugly in place while the glue sets — plus shaped wooden blocks, and maybe a 'strap' of thin plywood or flexible steel, to spread the pressure evenly along external curves. An alternative may be to 'clamp' by hammering in nails or pins, making sure these are driven through sections which will later be trimmed off.

Waxing the former beforehand will aid release. Afterwards, all you need to do is to trim the piece like any plywood.

This technique is worth getting to know. Laminating answers in a highly effective manner the old question of how to make up curved components which are uniformly strong and resilient throughout.

12

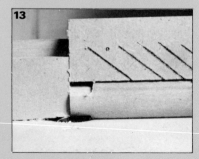

13

The rear frame (consisting of backstands and rails) is glued up (**14**) and held fast with a band clamp (**15**). Then the biscuit joints down the rear legs are put together (**16**), and the whole chair is clamped likewise.

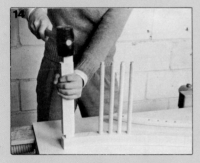

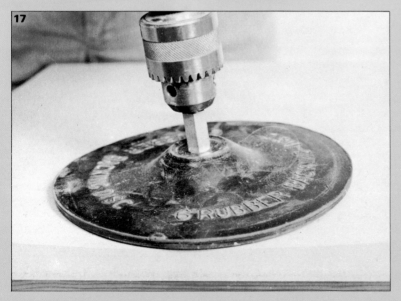

A disk sander (**17**) is used to make anatomically shaped hollows in the separate drop-in MDF seat panel (again rabbeted on two edges for a neater join) (**18**).

FITTINGS

For almost every project the furniture-maker needs to draw, in some way or another, from a vast number of fittings — which are as important in their own way as the raw materials.

A sound knowledge of what is available not only saves fruitless searching; it also enables you to take fittings into account from the outset. They can often be crucial to a design, both in usefulness and appearance. This is where a good catalog — or, much better, browsing around well-stocked showrooms — can be of immense help.

Hinges

Hinges often play a central role in the construction of a piece. Whereas you can often choose, say, a particular style of handle at the last minute, it is unwise to go ahead with a project that needs hinges unless you have a clear idea of which ones to use.

Hingeing methods take a bit of disentangling, and terminology can make this difficult. The best way of bypassing the problems is to pick up a hinge and play with it to see how it works. You need to visualize clearly where the door (or flap) will be when closed, where it will be when open, and how it travels between the two positions. Other considerations will be strength, appearance and ease of fitting. Before buying a hinge, never neglect to check that you know exactly how it works.

Hinges divide into two groups: those that open and close on a single axis, and those that have a more complex action. At the head of the first group are the familiar butt hinges (often known simply as 'butts'), each of whose two 'leaves' screws to one component. They come in a wide range of sizes and qualities, and in several materials — the most popular for cabinet work being brass. Some have decorative knobs (finials) at both ends of the central axis or 'knuckle'. As a rule, the knuckle is the only part visible when the door is closed, but some variants have ornamentally shaped leaves for screwing to exposed faces. Some butt hinges are designed so that one half can be lifted off the other, enabling a door to be removed without unscrewing.

A piano hinge is an enormously long, narrow butt hinge (named, of course, for its role in attaching piano lids); you can cut it with a hacksaw to the required length. Other types are made especially for hingeing table flaps (leaves) and 'fall-flaps' (as on desks).

Flush hinges are similar to butt hinges except that one leaf is cut away to allow the other to sit inside it when closed, thereby reducing the total thickness. Most, however, are only for light uses.

Some hinges of this general type are cranked. That is, one leaf includes a 90° bend, the effect of which is to throw the axis clear of the cabinet.

There are also hinges which pivot on a single point, yet have no knuckle because the leaves slide across each other. The most traditional of these is the center hinge, a neat device consisting of a pair of plates of which one is screwed to the upper or lower edge (in the case of a door) and one to the cabinet. The effect is the same as pivoting the door on a wood or metal rod or rods: an elementary hingeing principle itself can sometimes provide an elegant solution. Necked center hinges throw the axis to one side.

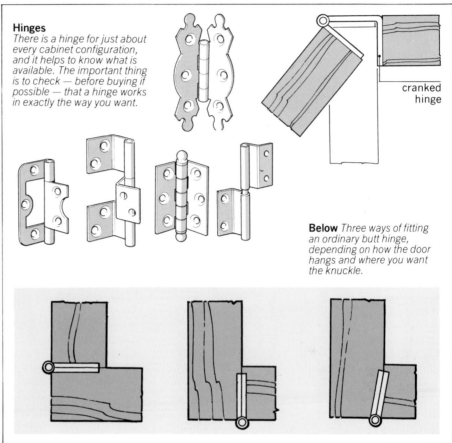

Hinges
There is a hinge for just about every cabinet configuration, and it helps to know what is available. The important thing is to check — before buying if possible — that a hinge works in exactly the way you want.

cranked hinge

Below *Three ways of fitting an ordinary butt hinge, depending on how the door hangs and where you want the knuckle.*

Fitting these types of hinge requires extremely accurate work, usually with a marking gauge, fine saw and chisel. Recesses must be made in both components to the right depth, width and length. There must be a gap between door and frame, but it must not be too large. Usually these recesses are constant in depth, but for butt hinges they are sometimes tapered to angle the hinge one way or the other. It all depends where you want the knuckle: sometimes it must clear a beading.

'Pivot' hinges work on the same general principle as center hinges but are more obtrusive: they often require a slit to be cut in the upright edge of the door to accommodate them. They are either cranked or double-cranked (the latter means that both halves are cranked). They are not made in brass and are not really meant for what the old books call 'high-class work'.

With a barrel hinge, one half screws into the door, the other into the cabinet: a pin holds them together. The door can be lifted off.

Hinges with a more complex action come in four types: cylinder, Soss, Sepa and 'concealed'. All have ingenious geometry, and include a number of separate pivots.

In fact, the first three types are concealed far more effectively than so-called 'concealed' hinges, because they are entirely hidden — even from inside — when the door is closed; this is achieved by recessing them completely into the meeting edges. Cylinder hinges fit straight into drilled holes; Soss hinges require additional elongated recesses for their face-plates, and Sepa hinges require shallow rectangular mortices.

'Concealed' hinges occupy a territory all their own, for they are industry's answer to installing ('hanging') doors on mass-produced modern cabinets — especially for kitchens. They consist of two parts: the hinge itself, which almost always fits into a shallow circular recess (usually 35mm in diameter) drilled in the rear face of the door; and a separate mounting plate. The plate is screwed to the side of the cabinet, and the hinge is screwed to the plate. For the trade, this arrangement solves two problems. It replaces the butt hinge's traditional pair of rectangular recesses, not ideal for machine work, with a single drilled hole, and the plate fixing allows quick and easy adjustment.

'Concealed' hinges are also designed with a third fundamental aim, which arises out of cabinet construction. Generally speaking, doors must either be lay-on (overlapping the surround) or inset. Lay-on doors are standard in kitchens, and kitchen cabinets are usually lined up side-by-side Butt-hingeing them would make them impossible to open, because each cabinet is tight up against its neighbour. The geometry of a concealed hinge, however, ensures that the door opens at least to 90° within the cabinet's overall width.

Traditional center, cranked and pivot hinges do the same job — by changing the position of the axis — but lack the concealed hinge's ease of installation. Ease, that is, in industrial terms. For the home cabinet-maker it may be no improvement on older solutions. Apart from questions of appearance (it looks very modern), it is no use for inset doors. Moreover, it requires an end mill cutter. This will not work in a power drill used freehand, because it will dance about all over the place. Either you need a drill stand — or something even more sophisticated — or you need to drill one hole through a piece of wood or board as best you can, then pin that temporarily in each required hinge position as a guide.

Lastly, the thicknesses of the pieces concerned, and the amount of overlap, dictate whether you can use a concealed hinge at all, and, if so, which pattern (there are a great many). Unless you take all these factors into account, you may be in for a frustrating time. But the same principle applies to all hinges. Before choosing, make sure you will be able to fasten them properly to the cabinet and to the door or flap; make sure the door is the right thickness; and make sure it will open freely.

Hanging a door usually involves making sure it fits exactly into the opening (or, in the case of a lay-on door, over the opening); fixing the hinges to it, recessed as necessary; 'offering it up' so you can mark the appropriate positions on the cabinet; and making the fixing in the cabinet.

It can sometimes be difficult to discover just why a door does not hang properly. It may tend to swing open or closed of its own accord. Remember that possible adjustments lie in three directions: backwards and forwards, up and down, and in and out (i.e. from side to side as you face the cabinet), With concealed hinges, the mounting arrangement means that these can all be made — at least in theory — with a screwdriver. With those traditional hinges which are fixed by screws, it is wise to put only one screw in each leaf until all appears well. Meanwhile, you will probably need a suitable piece of scrap material on which to chock the door up to the right height.

Catches

Many concealed hinges remove the need for catches because they incorporate a spring which keeps the door closed anyway. With others, a catch is usually essential. It can often serve, in addition, as a doorstop, to prevent the door closing too far — which will otherwise have to be provided in the cabinet configuration itself.

Magnetic catches come in varieties which screw on, and varieties which press into drilled holes. A metal plate goes on the back of the door. The sprung ball catch is very neat, for it also presses into a hole — this time in the door edge. Various other patterns incorporate sprung rollers and tongues of one kind and another.

There is also a special type of sprung latch which does away with the need not only for a doorstop, but also for a handle or knob, because it springs open and snaps closed with alternate pressures.

Stays

Stays prevent lift-up flaps from slamming shut, fall flaps from crashing to the ground, and lids and doors from opening too far. They are therefore invaluable in certain circumstances. Types are available for all these uses and quite a few more. Like hinges, they are best examined closely before buying. Their positioning in the cabinet will need a bit of thought.

Certain stays for lift-up flaps double as hinges.

Locks

Cabinet locks are sometimes very sophisticated indeed — allowing, for example, the securing of several drawers at once with a single key. For most purposes, however, they need not be all that strong or complex, their aim being to deter.

There are three traditional types. The straight lock is screwed to the rear face of the door. The cut-in lock is recessed into that face and the edge. The mortice lock is recessed wholly into the edge (an operation requiring some skill if it is to go in square and its face-plate is to lie flush).

Other locks are made for insertion into circular holes, for drawers, for lids, for flaps, and for sliding doors — especially glass ones.

Hanging fittings

Cabinets are often hung on walls. There are a number of ways in which this can be done.

The first consideration is, of course, how the cabinet is made. As the back panel is often of thin plywood or hardboard, screwing through this would be far from secure. Most hanging arrangements require either a stiff back, or another suitable piece to (or through) which fixings can be made.

The worst way of hanging a cabinet is to screw it directly to the wall. Even assuming that wall plugs and the like are used where necessary, you will still have to hold the cabinet in position while marking and fixing; this may be very awkward. In addition, even slight inaccuracies in drilling may create appreciable misalignment which can be corrected only with great difficulty.

A better solution is to use a fixing in two halves, which attaches independently to the wall and cabinet before hanging. One method is to incorporate, along the top of the cabinet, a length of timber whose lower edge is beveled (its wider side to the rear). This matches up with a beveled piece, screwed to the wall, whose wider side faces out.

Among factory-made fittings are flush mounts and taper connectors, each consisting of two separate halves which slide together. The kitchen industry has also given rise to the development of a group of ingenious hanging fittings, each consisting of a cabinet-mounted component and a hook of some sort which goes in the wall. These offer the great bonus of allowing screw adjustment after hanging to get the cabinet perfectly level.

Shelf fittings

Shelves are almost universal components of storage furniture. Often they are integral to the piece, being jointed in as structural members. At other times they are independent. There are scores of ways of supporting them, and a few of these use special fittings. Such fittings generally take the form of plastic or metal pegs or blocks — screwed, nailed or pushed into the cabinet's sides; but 'bookshelf strip', slotted to accept lugs in the shelf ends, runs continuously in shallow vertical grooves, allowing adjustment of shelf positions.

Drawer fittings

There are many excellent ways of fitting drawers without the aid of any special hardware at all. However, modern drawer accessories and plastic drawers offer extraordinarily smooth running, for a much smaller investment in accuracy. That makes them well worth knowing about, especially for projects such as kitchen and bathroom fittings where modern gadgetry is not out of place.

Like concealed hinges and KD fittings, drawer runners are products of a thriving industry. They are available in plastic and metal, for many different drawer weights and arrangements. Most are for 'side-hanging', but patterns are available which support the drawer from underneath and even from above.

Complete plastic drawers with their own runners are also on the market. Some come as one-piece moldings, others clip together as kits. The latter are supplied as sets of sides, backs and fronts, plus linking components for the corners. Adding a different front is a possibility, and you will need your own base. In some kits, the lengths are cut to exact size at the factory to order; others can be cut by the buyer.

Other fittings

Choosing other fittings such as knobs and handles is simply a matter of taste; fitting them is rarely at all difficult. Castors and feet are only occasional necessities. Some items are purely for decoration, for example the brass 'military' reinforcement plates which nowadays serve little or no practical purpose.

With all of these, the only advice a sensible person needs is to go to a good supplier, see what is in stock, and take advice when necessary.

THE CARE OF TOOLS

Tools are extensions of your hands and eyes. It should be automatic to keep them as keen and efficient as they can possibly be. Neglect them, and you stand in your own way.

General maintenance

Basic procedures are a matter of common sense. For convenience as well as for safe keeping, tools should be stored in shelves or racks that provide plenty of room, or hung neatly from pegs or hooks where appropriate.

Rust is always a potential problem, especially if tools have to be kept in a damp atmosphere, but lightly wiping them with oil or graphite grease should keep it at bay. This is best done after use, when tools should be cleaned of dust, shavings and the like (which, apart from anything else, can harbor moisture). Make a habit of replacing chisel and saw-blade guards; usually of plastic, these can readily be bought if they do not come with the tool.

Sharpening chisels and plane irons

Sharpening calls for a little study, and, while such research may seem to carry one away from woodwork, it all has a very direct bearing on the results you produce. Once learned, sharpening can be satisfying. That is just as well, because it needs doing more or less every day you work.

For many woodworkers, sharpening really means sharpening chisels and plane irons, since they are among the commonest and most heavily used edge tools. Many sharpening operations can be done by either hand or machine.

Before a chisel or plane iron leaves the factory, its tip is beveled on a grinder. This 'ground bevel' makes a comparatively rough edge which is not sharp enough to work with. It needs 'honing' to greater keenness first — an operation which is almost always left to the buyer.

Honing is usually done at an angle 5° steeper than that of grinding: this produces a separate 'honing bevel' on the tip. Chisels, like irons for bench and rebate planes and spokeshaves, are ground at 25° and honed at 30°; low-angle block planes are ground at 35° and honed at 40°.

However, this is only a matter of convenience. Adding a second bevel, steeper and therefore shorter, is quicker than honing the entire ground bevel. But the latter procedure is a perfectly good alternative, and it has certain advantages: the

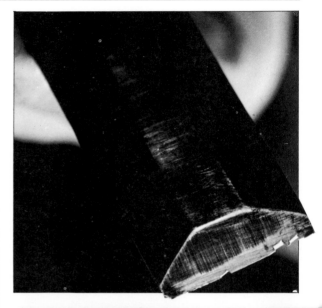

If a damaged edge (**left**) means that re-grinding is necessary, you can start by squaring it off (**below**). Then it must be ground at the correct bevel (**right**); on a high-speed grinder especially, be careful to use light, even strokes so that the steel does not overheat.

Honing follows grinding (**left**). This is usually done by hand, and either at the same angle or a slightly steeper one. The initial result is a burr or wire edge (**above**) on the back of the tip. Only when this is created can you proceed to the next step.

point is sharper because the angle is lower — and there can be no uncertainty about the correct angle, because you work at the angle that is already there.

Hand-sharpening

For honing by hand, the simplest appliance is what might be called a sharpening pad: a piece of abrasive paper or cloth glued firmly to a piece of board. The sheet need not be more than 9 x 3in (225 x 75mm) at most. A suitable abrasive is either resin-bonded aluminum oxide or silicon carbide, graded about 120 grit or higher. As a universal rule, finer grits produce keener edges and smoother (on metal, brighter) surfaces than coarse ones, but take longer to do their work.

The tool is placed bevel-downwards on the pad, with the ground bevel either horizontal or 5° above the horizontal, and rubbed firmly to and fro. There is a knack to this, since the angle must be kept constant to avoid rounding the bevel, and pressure kept even to avoid a skewed edge.

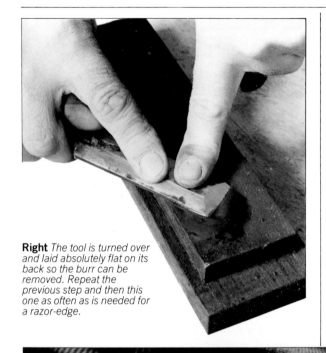

Right *The tool is turned over and laid absolutely flat on its back so the burr can be removed. Repeat the previous step and then this one as often as is needed for a razor-edge.*

*A few strokes on a leather 'strop' are an optional extra to complete the job (**left**). A really sharp tool should slice through almost any grain if properly handled (**below**).*

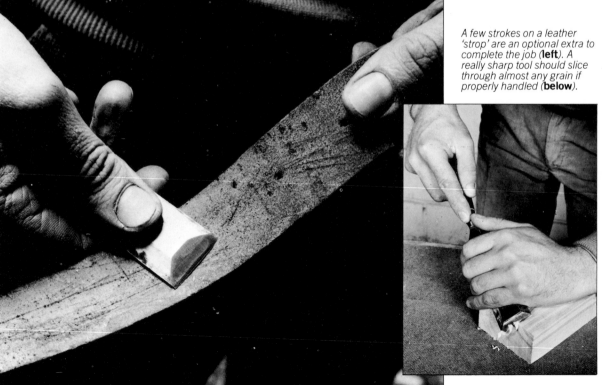

You will need to work from the shoulder and torso, keeping the wrist steady. Small, wheeled gadgets called honing guides, into which you clamp the blade, remove these problems.

After a while the metal will burr over on to the flat back of the blade, forming a 'wire edge': check for this by feeling with your thumb. The next step is the remove the burr by placing the blade absolutely (and that means absolutely) flat on its back on the pad, and rubbing to and fro again. If this makes the wire edge reappear on the beveled side, repeat the procedure on the front and back again until it has gone. The result should be a razor-sharp edge. In fact, if not positively dangerous, it is still blunt and will repay further work.

The nearest alternatives to the sharpening pad are 'stones' — blocks of abrasive, artificial or natural. These are more common than pads and, in most cases, capable of finer results. All come in several grades. A lubricant must be applied to the surface during use so that waste particles of metal and abrasive flow away instead of clogging the stone and preventing effective cutting. The lubricant is sometimes water and sometimes oil (light machine oil will do, though there are alternatives).

Natural oilstones are commonly quarried in Arkansas, and are named after the state. Artificial oistones are of aluminum oxide or silicon carbide; widely available are 'combination stones', which have one coarse and one medium-grit side. Natural Welsh slate can be used with either oil or water. Some artificial waterstones are made of industrial diamond, and others (from Japan) of aluminum oxide. On the whole, waterstones work faster than oilstones; Arkansas stones are the slowest of all.

The cheapest of these are artificial oilstones. Arkansas, diamond and Japanese stones can be very expensive — but the finer grades can produce edges of a brilliance and sharpness normally associated only with surgical instruments.

A superfine finish may also be achieved, after 'stoning', with a piece of leather 'dressed' (spread) with an abrasive paste (cutting compound) or abrasive powder such as emery powder. This is often used for carving tools. Japanese stones, however, which run to no less than 6000 and 8000 grit, make this extra procedure unnecessary; so does 600 grit paper, whether used on a pad or with a belt grinder.

Machine-sharpening

All sharpening jobs can be done by machine. As usual, there are a number of options. The least sophisticated of these is a powered version of the sharpening pad, in the shape of a disk of abrasive paper (or cloth) glued to a disk of plywood the same size, and mounted in an ordinary drill — ideally by means of an arbor like those used with many ready-made attachments. Certain disks purpose-made for portable 'angle-grinders' may also be suitable, but check carefully. In either case, you hold the tool against the disk while it revolves. It should only be necessary to renew the bevel; the flat side is best left alone.

It is essential, first of all, to clamp the drill firmly in position for such work; you may need to buy or make a suitable holder. Second, you should hold the tool so the disk is always revolving away from it, or the tool may dig in. (It does not matter whether the disk is horizontal or on its side, but the former arrangement is more convenient except for sharpening twist bits.)

Thirdly, use the slowest available speed if the drill offers a choice. Even this arrangement will generate sparks and can overheat the steel if you are not careful, thus weakening it. The telltale sign is 'bluing' or discoloration. If that takes place, you must continue till you have ground away the affected part, and even then the metal may not be quite as good as it was.

This problem does not arise with the traditional whetstone or grindstone, electrical or even hand-operated, because it revolves more slowly. It is cut from natural stone, and generally lubricated via a water bath or drip.

Most modern trade workshops, however, rely on the high-speed or bench grinder — basically an electric motor with a spindle sticking out sideways, usually at either end. On each spindle is mounted a grinding wheel of artificial abrasive, tools being presented to its edge (never its face) for sharpening. In front is a tool rest, which makes it easier to achieve the correct bevel, and above that a transparent eye-shield. Bluing is an ever-present risk on this machine; to prevent it, a container of water should be kept nearby, so that tools can be dipped every few seconds to cool them. However, the machine does work fast.

Since high-speed grinding uses only the wheel's edge, it produces a bevel which is slightly curved ('hollow-ground'). This can be useful when you come to hone the tool afterwards, because you can then rest the bevel on its two extremities (ensuring a consistent angle), while the hollow remains untouched and thus speeds up the job by reducing friction.

A final possibility is the belt grinder, a type of linisher. It will provide an exceptionally good finish if fitted with a fine-grade belt.

Several machines combine more than one of these tools — coupling, for example, a bench grinder and a whetstone or belt grinder.

Regrinding

Sooner or later, you will find a tool's edge is in bad enough condition to require renewal of the original (ground) bevel before honing. Naturally, this demands a coarser and therefore faster-cutting abrasive because more steel needs removing. The coarse side of a combination stone will serve, but this — like an 80 or 100 grit sharpening pad — is a very slow alternative. A powered disk, again 80 or 100 grit, works a lot more quickly.

Grinding wheels need to be about 60 grit for this job, and finer for honing — the advantage of double-ended machines being that you can fit a different grade of wheel at each end and use one for each operation.

Maintaining sharpening equipment

Instruments for sharpening are no exception to the rule of regular maintenance. To start with, stones of all types — unless 'factory-sealed' — need soaking in the appropriate lubricant before you first use them. They are generally kept safe in boxes with lids, and hardwood blocks of the same height are often placed at either end so that their surfaces continue the surface of the stone. The idea is to enable each sharpening stroke to over-run, and thus more readily to cover the stone's full length — it being important to use the whole length and width so that the stone wears evenly and thus stays flat. A hollowed stone cannot produce a straight edge.

Stones that have become uneven must therefore be 're-surfaced' by rubbing them face-down on the appropriate abrasive. For artificial stones that is carborundum powder, with water, paraffin, or paraffin and oil as a lubricant — except for Japanese stones, which require 200 grit silicon carbide paper and water. Natural stones need silver sand and water, on a York stone or marble slab.

Grinding wheels 'glaze over' with use: the surface becomes too smooth to cut properly. This is remedied with a 'wheel dresser' — an instrument that takes various forms, all of which are held against the wheel as it turns.

Other sharpening jobs

Tools without straight edges demand their own sharpening techniques.

Twist bits can be tackled freehand on powered equipment, being rotated against the abrasive at the appropriate angle — a tricky procedure which calls for a close look at the tip configuration of a sharp bit before you start, and then preferably some practice. Alternatively, special honing guides are available for sharpening twist bits on the pad or stone. There are also powered devices like electric pencil-sharpeners.

Woodworking, auger and spade bits must be touched up entirely by hand, using a fine needle file or a slipstone — a small stone, natural or artificial, which is held in the hand. Slipstones come in several patterns; the most useful is probably the 'knife-edge' type, which is wedge-shaped. It is vital to sharpen only the insides of cutting edges and spurs — never the outsides, or a bit's diameter can be changed and its action impaired. Existing bevel angles must be preserved, too.

A drawknife is sharpened with a large slipstone. Out-cannel gouges may be treated like chisels, though they must of course be rotated. In-cannel gouges require a slipstone, or a round or half-round file. As with other tools which possess curved edges — radius spokeshaves, beading cutters for rough planes, and so on — you must be careful not to change the profile of the cut by changing the slope of the bevel.

HSS router cutters can be sharpened at home, but again you must know what you are doing. As with drill bits, the outside faces must be left alone, otherwise the cutter may be unbalanced and the overall diameter altered; in addition, the 'clearance angle' behind the edge may be reduced to the point where waste can no longer escape properly, so that the cut suffers. All you do, therefore, is just to run the insides of the flutes over a sharpening stone.

Right and **below** An auger, like any other drill bit, must be sharpened with great care if its diameter is not to be

It is worth pointing out that cutters and blades for power tools in general are definitely not 'fit and forget' items. If blunt, they will produce inferior results such as ragged surfaces. Even the shank of a router cutter, for example, should be kept smooth and clean to avoid imbalance which can affect both the cut and the motor.

TCT router cutters need specialist attention. Cutters for fixed machines such as shapers and jointers should be maintained strictly as instructed by their manufacturers. This too may entail regular expense.

In theory, saws of all kinds — except for hardpoint hand saws and TCT circular-saw blades — can be sharpened at home. However, you have to consider several separate features: the teeth's protrusion, their bevel, their sharpness, usually their set (sideways slope), and sometimes others. These must all be put to rights — and accurately, too. Equipment is available for this, and there is no reason why you should not learn to use it if you are keen. But, if you are devoting time to becoming skilled at woodwork itself, you may feel that a professional could take this labor off your hands, at least for the moment. When it comes to such tasks as straightening bent blades you have little choice but to call in outside help.

Incidentally, some people make a habit of reducing the set on fine back saws, such as dovetail saws, by lightly passing them over a stone, flat on their sides. This ensures a narrower kerf.

The cabinet scraper, as its name suggests, is sharpened differently from most other tools. First, its edge is filed square, straight and clean (unless it is brand-new). Second, the edge is smoothed on a fine stone or pad: the scraper must be kept dead upright. Third, it is rubbed on its face, like a chisel, to remove any burr. Fourth, the face is rubbed firmly with the back of a gouge, or with a special tool called a burnisher or ticketer — next to the edge, to harden the metal. Use spit as a lubricant. Lastly, the gouge or burnisher is drawn equally firmly along the edge itself — but not quite squarely, so as to produce a slight burr. It is this burr that does the cutting. When it loses its efficiency, it can be re-made — up to about three times before the procedure needs repeating from the beginning.

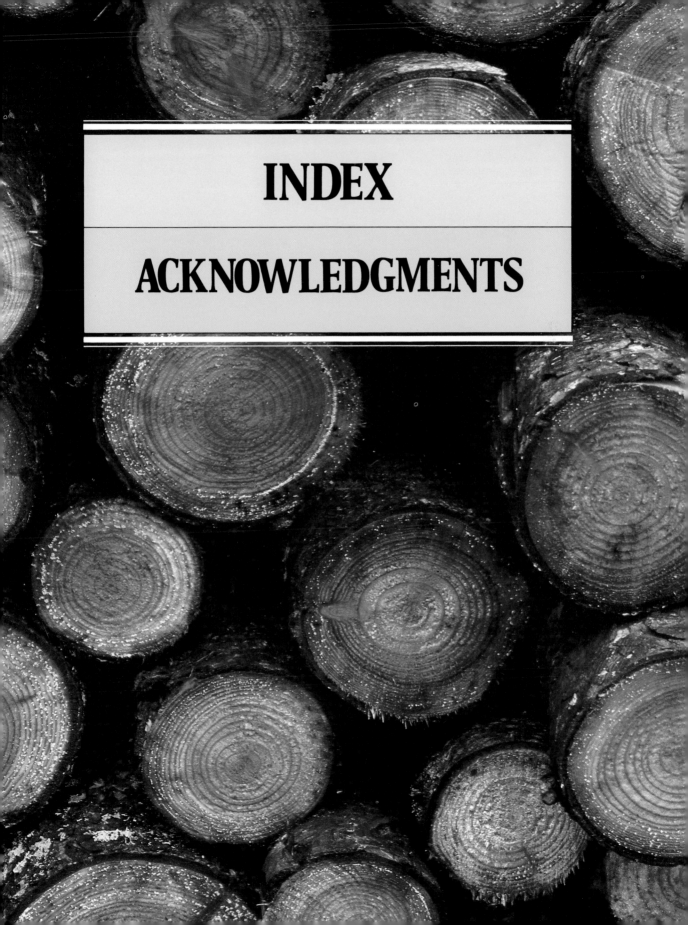

INDEX

ACKNOWLEDGMENTS

INDEX

Figures in *italics* indicate pages on which relevant illustrations or captions can be found. Keywords in SMALL CAPITALS refer to worked projects.

ACKNOWLEDGMENTS

The illustrations on the following pages have been reproduced by kind courtesy of the following:

2-3 David Jones: **6-7** Meyer International; **10** (r), **11** (a), (bl) The Bridgeman Art Library; **18-19** Michael Freeman; **21** Meyer International; **22** Mike Busselle, David Savage; **23** Michael Freeman; **25** David Savage; **26** Jakki Dehn; **27** Martin Grierson; **31** Mike Busselle; **32-3** Meyer International; **34** Bob Pulley; **35** Michael Reed; **38-9** Formica; **41** David Jones; **50-1, 54-5** Peter Milne; **59** Mike Busselle; **74, 85, 88, 89** (t) Record Tools.

All other photographs courtesy Quarto Publishing.

Key: (a) above; (b) below; (l) left; (r) right; (t) top